I Ain't
Studdin' Ya

I Ain't Studdin' Ya

My American Blues Story

Bobby Rush

with Herb Powell

hachette
BOOKS

New York

Hachette Books
Hachette Book Group
1290 Avenue of the Americas
New York, NY 10104
HachetteBooks.com
Twitter.com/HachetteBooks
Instagram.com/HachetteBooks

First Edition: June 2021

Published by Hachette Books, an imprint of Perseus Books, LLC, a subsidiary of Hachette Book Group, Inc. The Hachette Books name and logo is a trademark of the Hachette Book Group.

The Hachette Speakers Bureau provides a wide range of authors for speaking events.

To find out more, go to www.hachettespeakersbureau.com or call (866) 376-6591.

The publisher is not responsible for websites (or their content) that are not owned by the publisher.

Print book interior design by Jeff Williams

Library of Congress Cataloging-in-Publication Data has been applied for.

ISBNs: 978-0-306-87480-2 (hardcover); 978-0-306-87479-6 (ebook)

Printed in the United States of America

LSC-W

Printing 1, 2021

I reverently dedicate this book to
the memory of my deceased children,
Valerie, Donell, and Sherry.

Contents

Contents

——— PART 2 ———

Contents

Contents

—— PART 3 ——

Introduction

When you're in your mid-eighties like me, you know you're way past the first song of the show. You're actually walking back to the stage for one more encore. The bus is outside the nightclub, warming up. It's ready to take you to the airport or to your hotel or to take you home for good. Or you may just drive another three hundred miles into the abyss of the night. So if I'm thinking about my daddy a lot, it just means I'm thinking about my longevity and how I got to be one of the last men standing of the original American music bluesmen.

Many people know my name: Bobby Rush. But way more do not. Oh, you've heard about the blues greats, B.B. King, Muddy Waters, Howlin' Wolf, Elmore James, and others. And you should have, because these men gave us one of the greatest art forms in the history of humanity. These greats were my teachers, peers, and, most of all, friends.

But I've been lying to ya.

Some say I was born in 1940; I'll take that. Some say I was born in 1934, and I'll take that, too. But they also say I was born in 1937. And I'll bet you I'm the only person in the history of show business that made themself to be older—not younger—than they really are. I started lying about my age when I was twelve, becoming fifteen overnight—and I ain't never looked back. If you can't give me a pass on that, then I ain't studdin' ya.

My daddy knew the Bible from front to back. I've recorded over four hundred songs and can remember at least two hundred and fifty of them—music and lyrics. I guess I inherited his superb memory. And I'm glad I did because now, as I sit down and try to tell you my story, I realize it's a blessing to remember to remember.

After B.B. King died, it closed the door on our almost-sixty-year friendship. Some said I was the next in line to carry the torch. I don't know if that's true, because B.B. and I traveled the same road, but we cruised on different wheels. And that's the beauty of life. But I am connected to him and so many others because their stories are surely connected to mine. I am, we are, a part of a very American story. I am a proud Black man. I am a proud bluesman. And I am a product of the American South.

But now I'm just one man with one story left—mine.

PART 1

PART I

Son

The sugarcane stalks were just starting to turn yellow in late September. I looked at the back of Daddy's hands as he massaged the stalk. The contrast of his boot-black skin against the greenish-yellow leaf looked like the stark colors that I only saw on the shelves of the general store. "Hm-mm, it's just about dry enough, Junior," Daddy said. It wouldn't be another week before me and three of my brothers were out there cutting down the stalks with long-blade machetes.

This wouldn't be my first time chopping sugarcane. But when your mind is young, you put together things bit by bit. So I knew what the result of all this chopping would be—and that was syrup. Sweet, dark, Louisiana syrup. During my childhood, soppin' up that syrup with Maw's hot homemade biscuits was heaven on earth—the highlight of my day. Still, as much as I knew there was a purpose in this harvesting, I just wanted to be near Daddy.

My daddy was some kinda man, I tell ya. At around six foot two, he looked as tall as a tree to me. Good-looking, fit as a fiddle, black as midnight, tough as a bulldog, and yet a peaceful man. His entire demeanor commanded attention. A true bookworm, he read everything. Every day. All day. And yet he had only a third-grade education. With a daddy like mine, I don't carry one single note of the dark blues of not having a father. So fully present in my life, he is a large man in my memory, spirit, and heart.

A quiet but a serious man, he was everything to me. Despite his reserved style, my earliest memory of him is when he'd grab me with his enormous hands, lift me up high to the ceiling, and set me down on his right knee. He'd then pop me up and down to the rhythm of his whistling. Man, could he toot. The tone of his whistle was pure as a flute, and his licks were as soulful as Junior Walker's saxophone. You could tell whatever song he was tootin' because his melody was so accurate. He probably could whistle better than anybody I ever heard in my entire musical life.

But something happened to me the day Daddy pulled out of his pocket a dull silver harmonica. Whisking it back and forth against the fabric of his blue bib overalls, he put the shined harp in his mouth and started to play. On his rock-solid knee, my mouth hung wide open. I was astonished. I could do nothing more than to stare deeply into his brown eyes and listen to the greasy yet melodic sound coming out of the harmonica. In my childhood mind, it sounded like somebody was crying, but they weren't sad. The slew of changing tones Daddy was producing with his mouth created pictures in my mind. One tone sounded like an old hound dog; another sounded like a train—it fascinated me. I watched how he gripped the harmonica. I watched how his cheeks quickly ballooned up with air—and just as quickly drew small as he blew out. The mystical mixture of him rhythmically popping me up and down on his knee while I listened to the music coming out of that harp—became my first groove.

My first groove. It's something when a groove hits you. You feel it in your bones. You feel in your hands. You feel in your butt. You feel it in your heart. It's primal. It's magnetic. It's pure. It's irresistible. Knowing that his sound captivated me, Daddy performed for me. And since he didn't joke or play around much, this was a special moment. His eyes lit up. He bopped his head slightly from side to side. Sensing my ever-increasing interest, he smiled. Still, this was not the moment that put me on the road to becoming a musician. But it was damn sure starting the car.

When you're from the Deep South, Black, and born right after the Depression, there's a language that comes with that. So when I say my daddy was an upright man, maybe only some old people from Louisiana or Mississippi would understand what I'm talking about. Yeah, my daddy was upright in the traditional sense—as in righteous and decent. It didn't hurt Daddy's reputation that he was also a preacher. With that, it connected him to a tradition that was as old as time, and it showed through his actions of kindness and counsel to others.

But he was upright in another way, too. In Louisiana, cutting a Black man down to size was sport for white men. Between walking around with a bowed head and all that "yes sir" and "no sir" shit, passiveness was a way of life for most Black men—but not my daddy. Now I ain't saying he was the Malcolm X of the 1930s and '40s, but he did not let that unspoken code of "you better not get outta line, boy" shrink his manhood. He was more man than most men—Black, white, or Creole. So upright also means that he had a spine like steel, and that raised his stature. Daddy was the only Black man I saw in my early years that white men would consistently reach out to shake his hand. That may seem like a simple thing, but in the Deep South it wasn't.

Daddy was as equal to the white man as a Black man could be. At least in my little world of Claiborne Parish in northern Louisiana.

|||||||||

I was born in a shotgun house in Carquit, Louisiana. Carquit, smack-dab between Haynesville and the county seat of Homer, was like a million other tiny towns in the rural South. It was just a road with a sign. My mother, Mattie, and my daddy, Emmett Ellis Sr., had ten children but raised eleven. My oldest sister, Margie May, had a baby in her early teens. Not uncommon with the times, my parents raised Christine as my sister. Most of us didn't know that she was a niece until Christine was in her teens, which is when she found out herself. There's a funny difference between the South and the North. For decades, when a teenage girl would get pregnant, the family would often send her to relatives in the South to have and raise the baby. But when you're in Louisiana, there ain't nowhere farther South for you to send anybody! But it is a testament to the character of Maw and Daddy that my sister/niece Christine was loved just as much as we all were.

After Margie May, Mary Lee popped up, then Acen Jewel (but everybody called him A. J.), Alvin, Lillie Pearl, me, Verdie Mae, Gerdie Bee, Andrew, and Larry. You may or may not believe this, but there was no fighting amongst my siblings—ever. Daddy forever said to us to "take care of your brothers and sisters," and that instruction was planted early and planted deep. So deep that fighting amongst ourselves seemed to be out of step with our very DNA—the life he wanted us to live.

My older brother Alvin took good care of me when I was very young. I rode on his back everywhere. As he is almost ninety today, sometimes I'll call him "Horsey" to take us back in time to our humble beginnings. Those ordinary beginnings changed when I was three or four. The white man that my family was sharecropping for, George Tinkernut, moved to the city. Tinkernut, who admired Daddy, gave us his house. Now we had three bedrooms, a kitchen, and a living room. And a big old barn. And mane, let me tell you something, we was living high on the hog. But don't get too happy. The house was still raggedy. You could still count the number of chickens you had by looking through the cracks in the walls!

These A-frame houses, a common fixture in the American South, had no indoor plumbing, so we had an outhouse—the regular kind. The fancy kind was when they had two holes cut out of the hardwood bench for emptying yourself. Using the Sears and Roebuck catalog for toilet paper, you had to make sure you hung the catalog back up on a nail. Because if you left it on the plank of wood, sometimes snakes would hide behind it. And if there was anything my sisters were scared of, it was snakes.

With the number of people we had in the house, we owned two slop jars—fancy-looking white enamel-coated steel buckets with a lid, for peeing in the middle of the night. If you had to do number two, you had to put the slop jar outside the front door as to not stink up the house. We cleaned it out first thing in the morning—returning it to its sparkling white shine. Our primitive shelter also had no closets. One of the old jokes about this kind of living was: "What do you need a closet for when you only got five, maybe six pieces of clothes?" But you still made do. In the corner of the room Daddy attached to the walls a homemade wood rod. Putting a sheet over that rod—you know what you got? A closet. And you hung your clothes on another wall-mounted stick. But Daddy did buy a beautiful chifforobe (wardrobe) out of the Sears and Roebuck catalog for Maw's nicer things. The chifforobe had a mirror attached to the door. Later, that would come in handy for me.

To most of the Black people around, we looked like Mr. Charlie. Daddy seemed to have it together more than most. Between his ability to read and write and his churchy counsel, the huge barn we had on Mr. Tinkernut's land served others, as Daddy let Black folks from miles around store their hay there. It seemed that I was always being reminded that people respected Daddy. Though looking back, I'm sure some may have envied him, too.

Hay Wire

Unless you've lived on a farm, you can't imagine how much hay we used. In the years before people started using twine to wrap hay bales, they used a very thin metal wire. And out of fear that we might need something later—something that right now may seem useless—we threw nothing away. Nothing. So along with worn-out metal tubs, glass bottles and jars, and a hundred other things, hay wire was everywhere. It was on the post of the mule lot, pigpen, wrapped around tree limbs, and at the side of the house—you could always find it.

I really can't tell you what made me start making instruments. But all I can say is when I saw some white, tall drink of water trying to play a tub bass out back at Mr. Beer's store, my mind got me to thinkin'. It was just an old number three tub turned upside down with a broomstick nailed to it. *Mmm,* I thought, *with all that wire hanging around, I know there got to be an old tub thrown away out at the edge of the woods.* Finding a broomstick and an old sugarcane syrup bucket, I got some nails. I tried to make one—it wasn't too successful. First, the cane bucket was rusted a bit, and I couldn't figure that I needed to nail the broomstick to something like a two-by-four piece of wood first, and then nail that to the tub.

Not too long after that I saw what I'd find out later was what they call a diddley bow, but to me it was just a one-string guitar. It was nailed to a wooden sign pole on the main drag in Homer. Sitting on the wagon waiting for Daddy, I saw some kid come up and play it a bit. I never left the wagon, but I could see well enough what it was. And that was it.

It couldn't have been two days later before I was hammering a nail to the side of our shabby gray house. I don't know why Maw didn't stop me. But my baby sister Gerdie watched with curiosity as I drove those two nails about a foot and a half apart. My brother Alvin helped me drive two more nails in the wall, and I laid a brick with a pop bottle up top. With the ever-abundant hay wire, I wrapped it around the top end of the nail and strung it over the curved part of a pop bottle. I pulled it gently but strongly down, down, down to the lower nail. Taking another pop bottle, I strung it over the curve in the bottle and wrapped that wire around the top of that nail with the determination of my daddy swinging an axe. I was only six. And I did it! Plucking it for the first time wasn't even about music; it was the thrill of me building something.

But the wire was thin and sometimes rusty. It just kept breaking. Then one day the brick hit me in the head, the pop bottles crashing to the ground, breaking in pieces. My older brothers and sister used to say about me that when I was very young, if I didn't get what I wanted at the moment I wanted it, I would fall apart. But I grew out of that quickly. You had to. There was nothing but a spirit of "do" in my house.

So I wasn't going to let those broken bottles beat me.

Maw went through a broom maybe three times a year. You gotta understand, with cracks between the wood slats of the kitchen floor, Maw would sweep the kitchen of crumbs and anything else, and the chickens under the house would eat everything up. I found an old broom that had been thrown out in the thicket of weeds. The wire that strapped the broom bristles to the handle was raggedy, so I carefully unraveled it. I also added some more nails to hold the pop bottles in place if the wire broke. But this time I put the brick at the bottom so it couldn't knock me in the head again! The broom wire was thicker. It had a more resonant tone—that's the ticket.

But soon that raggedy wire broke. I was very disappointed and almost crying, so I ran to Maw.

"Maw, I need a piece of broom wire."

"You wanna make that old guitar outside that wall, don't you, boy?"

"Yes, ma'am."

"Well, you can have dis old broom here when it wears out."

But it was a new broom! It would take months for that thing to start falling apart. I couldn't wait that long. That broom wire was key to my everything: enjoyment, music, attention—everything. When Maw was out with Daddy in the fields, I grabbed that broom. I stuck that broom in a bucket of water and got it very soggy. Then, quickly sneaking around to the edge of the woods, I went down and into the cow pen. I fed them cows that broom—and they, thinking it was grass, ate it like ice cream!

Just having gotten the broom shabby enough, I returned it to the back of the house. I waited for some days, and when Maw was out back I said, "Maw, can I have this broom?" She said, "Oh yeah, boy, you can have dis old broom—it's all tore up anyway." She didn't know that it was the new broom. I returned to making my one-string guitar. And soon I was back to pickin'.

I felt bad about lying to Maw. But I had to.

I had to get it going again. I continued to play with it. Learned how to change the pitch by running my left hand up and down the string while plucking at the same time. I took a flimsy piece of leather from Daddy's old belt and used it as a pick. As I learned to diddle, my brothers and sisters paid me a bit more attention. As I found different pitches on that one string, I made up little rhymes and sang them in that key. I moved my finger around to a lower or higher key and made up little things in each pitch. I didn't know it then, but I was learning how to compose (a little), how to sing in different keys (a little), and how to entertain my baby sister Gert (a little). And all those littles added up to something big. A great big hunger. It's hard to put into words when you're that young what it feels like to become obsessed. I guess it's the homemade stew of craving to be special and craving to create something.

I started to dream. I recall working in the cotton fields in the heat of the day, and instead of working I was just staring at the sun, getting cooked—lost in a daydream of playing music. Maw crossed into my row and hit me in the head with a tin cup and said, "Boy, don't you know you'll go blind fixin' on the sun? Keep your head down and pick that cotton."

Every chance I had, I played with the broom wire on the side of the house. I played that one string so intensely that I would get lost in it, dreaming I'm onstage in a long tailcoat, a tailcoat like the man had on Daddy's Prince Albert tobacco can. I'm lost in a fantasy set in motion by the twangy sound of the diddley bow. As dark clouds gathered and moist, humid winds blew, I wasn't paying any attention to it. Eventually buckets of water fell from the sky. As the heavy warm rain ran down my face, my spell was only broken by Maw's loud demand of, "Junior, you better git yo'self in dis house. You'll be sicker than death."

Give and Take

Pretty much only white folks had syrup mills. With the wagon loaded up with our cut sugarcane, we would head over yonder to Mr. George's syrup mill. This would be an all-day affair. First, they used a tractor motor–powered grinder to pulverize our sugarcane harvest into liquid. Then they boiled that cane into syrup. The complete process took about seven hours. This day we ended up with about eighty gallons of the purest cane syrup. Keep in mind, Mr. George didn't charge you for the cane grinding. What he did was take half of the syrup, and Daddy took the other half.

He'd sell his—and we go home and eat ours.

They call it the barter system—but in my young mind it was just the math of simple country living. And much of our survival depended on it. Anything you could not raise on your own land you traded for. Even at the general store. Maw would send me there with three chickens in a croker (burlap) sack. I'd loosely tie a piece of twine at the top—just taut enough as to not smother them, but loose enough that the chicken heads could stick awkwardly out of the top. With the three blinking, bug-eyed chicken heads poking out, I'd throw the sack on my back and walk the two miles to Mr. Deb's store.

"Mr. Deb, my maw wants a can of lard and three pounds of meal."

"Boy, how many chickens ya got?"

"Three."

"That should do it."

That was just the math of country living. But in the sharecropping life, there was way more subtraction than there was addition.

With white folks taking, and Black folks giving.

A big part of the sharecropping deceit was that all the plantation owners had these little stores. Within a twenty-five-mile radius around the Homer and Haynesville area, Mr. Beer, Mr. Deb, Mr. Harper, Mr. Oldham, and so many others had these little general stores. Black sharecroppers would buy from these stores, and around 80 percent of the time they would buy stuff on credit. Which was referred to as "fall term." In other words, you paid up when your fall crops came in. Problem was, the little profit you made from sharecropping went right back into the hands of the very plantation owners that you were sharecropping for. Not to mention that if they charged you two dollars for flour, they were probably getting it for a dollar. So you got screwed six ways from Sunday: the product markup, the credit ruse, combined with any profit you may squeeze out being sucked like a vacuum cleaner right back into the white folks' hands. So you were never free. Never had the opportunity to buy land. Never had the opportunity to have a dream.

Skin

But I would experience another kind of math in my young life. I never could add up racial differences when I was young. We lived in a Black world. Yes, white folks were around, and I knew they were white. But it was just white folks. Meaning that the interactions were not human. White folks in our world were like amplifiers on a stage. They had a sound; they were present but not alive like a guitar or drums. They were just there.

But the calculation of Daddy + Maw + us children would create some early confusion for me.

My maw was white. Born of a white man and a Cherokee woman, to the world she was white. She wasn't even "high-yellow." It was like an open secret that everyone knew, but no one ever talked about it. This only made it an even deeper, yet open, secret.

She would always say she was one-fourth white, but all her sisters and brothers looked whiter than white except for one. See my young mind's math problem? She was white visually—but she was damn sure Black to me. At five foot five with crystal blue eyes, she was strikingly beautiful. When she was young her hair was long and flowing blond; as she got older it turned a lovely auburn color. With a trim yet curvy figure, she was built like a brick shithouse. Everybody looked at Maw— women, men, boys, girls, Black, white, Creole, aged eight to eighty, blind, crippled, or crazy. She was stunning.

The following summer, after we moved into Mr. Tinkernut's house, a white ice-delivery man rode up to the fence of our home. It was so hot that day you could fry catfish on the ground. I couldn't have been older than five or six. My brother Alvin and I were shooting marbles within the white picket fenced-off yard. The dirt road to the house was fenced in, too—so you couldn't just drive up.

Beep, Beep Beep! the iceman's horn blurted out.

"Hey, boy, y'all niggers want some Goddamn ice?"

My brother and I didn't say a word. He hit the horn again in longer, more annoying beeps. *Beeeeep, Beeeeeeep Beeeeeeep!*

"Hey, boy, did you hear me! I said, y'all niggers want some ice?"

Just like a rocket, Maw briskly pushed the screen door wide open and hightailed it towards the truck. The iceman jumped out of his truck, cupped his hands to his mouth, and nervously shouted out: "Oh, oh, I'm so sorry, ma'am, I thought only niggers lived here now."

Maw stopped her march and placed her hands on her hips. She waved her arm in the air to Alvin—motioning him to open the gate. The iceman drove slowly in. I didn't hear what they said, but I saw the iceman take off his hat and quickly brush his oily hair back with his hand to make himself presentable. He clasped his dingy hat with both hands, holding it in front of him waist-high, as to show respect to Maw. They exchanged a few words, and the man brought the ice in the house. He humbly bowed his head, tipped his hat to Maw, got in his truck, and drove off. That iceman went from calling us niggers one second to bowing his head in front of Maw. *Mmm . . . that's interestin'*, I said to myself. I reckoned from this that white men behaved themselves around Maw.

By the same token, when I was seven or eight years old, Daddy, Maw, and I took the wagon over to somebody's big place in Homer to load up with bales of hay. Daddy walked into the barn. There was this tall and dingy-looking white man guiding his mule behind him with a frayed rope. I guess he saw Daddy and Maw earlier talking from afar, because as Maw and I waited on the flat wagon, he approached us.

"Mattie, what you doing with dat thar nigger?" he said.

"I'm a nigger too," Maw said.

"Oh, no-no-no, you is not no nigger."

"Yes, I am too. Ask Mr. Beer."

Mr. Beer ran one of those small plantation stores I spoke of earlier. So in my young mind, he was an authority figure. But why did Maw have to declare that she was a nigger? After all, I was her son, and I knew I was Black. And I was aware of her white appearance—but my young brain couldn't distinguish that she was anything different from what Daddy, I, and my brothers and sisters were.

Although I couldn't understand the attitudes or, really, can of worms towards Maw's white skin, I witnessed things that added even more confusion.

I remember like it was only yesterday: Maw and I were on the wagon going to a larger general store on the other side of Haynesville. I felt special that it was just her and me. With so many brothers and sisters, this kind of moment alone with Maw felt almost holy because it was so rare. Sitting close beside her, I could smell her hair mixed with the scent of bleach that was in her freshly washed white dress. As we got about thirty feet from the store, she said, "Now Emmett, you get in the back of the wagon." I didn't ask why—I didn't have to. I was six or so and had total trust in that whatever Maw told me to do was right, even though, looking back, it felt a wee bit odd.

"Now you stay right here, Emmett." With that, she gathered her satchel and hopped off the wagon. I had a bird's-eye view through the tall and wide plate-glass store window. I stared and stared. In the store were all men, two proprietors and two or three patrons. They were all smiles as my maw was looking at the shelves, seeing what was in stock. I realize now that Maw was playing up to them, and they all were having just a good ole time. And at the same time she was cunning, because on this day she seemed to get anything she wanted. The wagon was soon loaded. What I didn't know was that Maw's bloodline was a prominent one in northern Mississippi, Louisiana, and southern Arkansas. Maw's granddaddy was a Mr. Van of Mississippi. White and wealthy, he had a lot of children. They were all whiter than white and carried all the privileges of what white and wealth bought in the South. That store owner in Haynesville, Mr. Beer, Mr. Deb, and others knew of Maw's kin. They gave her the deference of being from the Van family. Still, I'd find out later the price Maw paid to marry a Negro.

I would take a hundred trips into town after that day, some with my siblings, even some with my daddy. But Daddy never went inside the stores with Maw. And we always sat in the back of the wagon and later in the car when we were in town. It was and is a very delicate issue for me—even after me being on this earth for well over eighty years. I soon realized what was going on.

Maw was "passing" in some kinda way that I didn't have a full understanding of then, or even now. Because this was not the passing that America knew about. Maw was not some very fair-skinned Black woman who left the confines of the segregated South for Los Angeles or Seattle, where she could start a new life as a white person. Maw was seen as 100 percent white and was probably the most beautiful white woman around for miles. She didn't deny that she was Daddy's wife, as she was living with all these caramel-colored children. But there was a deception going on. As I said earlier, this was not, in any shape, form, or fashion, an abandonment of love. Me and my siblings felt nothing but deep love from Maw and Daddy. But to say that my mother's color had no effect on her life and our life as a family would either be naïve or a lie.

Looking back, I think Maw had an on-and-off switch. She was white when she needed to be. And my family benefited from it. But over seventy years later, I still have questions. Did Daddy have an on-and-off switch, too? Was he seen as her driver, since he didn't go in the store with her?

But I really tussle with how Daddy felt. He had to know Maw's skin opened some doors. But did he know the extent to which Maw played the dual role of a white and a Black woman? And did whatever advantage he got leave him unmarked, or did it leave a scar on his spirit? And if so, was it a tiny blister that you could pop to relieve the pain or a large, open wound that never fully healed? So I wonder.

Of course, it would take me decades of learning before I could think about this with some kind of wisdom. My people's struggle created a little war within us Black folks. As a boy I couldn't understand how that war was so much bigger than my, Maw's, and Daddy's little world of Claiborne Parish. But time would teach me that the battle started when my ancestors were ripped from their families. Loaded on massive boats, chained, and laid down like slabs of meat—traveling for months, thousands of miles across the Atlantic in their own piss and shit. The crew threw overboard the dead ones. The ones that survived were raped of every form of their humanity.

But that crucial history would come later. It would be taught to me by teachers in school, teachers in life, and what I would be willing to teach myself.

The Beautiful Gifts

One thing about coming up in the country when I did was that bloodlines didn't move very far away from where they were born. It was just the natural restriction of life in the Deep South. But like every other limitation in American life, this was even more true for us Negro folks. We were forever poorer, sicker, and more restricted than white or Creole people in where we could go. If you knew someone who had been on the train that went anywhere—he was as like an astronaut that had been to Mars and rocketed back to Earth. If someone had been to a place as close as New Orleans or, God forbid, as far away as Birmingham, Alabama, you would sit around and listen to them for hours as they spun tales of what the big city was like. We needed those stories to remind us that there was a world beyond the cotton and sugarcane fields in the wide-open spaces of northwest Louisiana.

But within the close bounds of Claiborne Parish, many sons and daughters would marry someone from a family that you had known all your life. And then they would raise their kids within a few miles of their original homestead. So I had first, second, and third cousins all around me. But you had to be careful. You had to make damn sure that when your sexual hormones kicked in, the girl you were liking wasn't some cousin you didn't know about! All the old folks put a fear in you that sexual activity with some cousin you didn't know could produce a one-eyed baby.

Daddy's brother, Scott Ellis, had a boy named John. But everybody called him "Son Scott." Son Scott took a liking to me early, because even though I was almost half his age, my outgoing personality drew girls close. During the summer months, he'd bring his guitar around and I'd play it. I wasn't really good, but I'd figured out a little diddy or two, and girls would gather 'round. They would giggle and eventually do a little jig. This made Son's nature happy—if you know what I mean.

One fall, around 1943, I saw Son walking towards the house toting a big croker sack on his back. "Emmett, come 'round back wit' me," he said. Out of view of everyone, he pulled a guitar out of the sack. I wondered: *Why all this secrecy?* All we were gonna do was find some girls for him to mess with.

"Take dis here geetar."

"Oh boy, thanks. I'll bring it back to you."

"No, no, you can have—go on, take it."

"Ya sure 'bout dis, Son."

"Ain't nobody playin' it. I reckoned you may want it," he said.

"Me?"

"Yeah, you always bouncing 'round about sumthin'."

I was in a bit of shock. Where I come from, people were always giving stuff to others, especially kinfolk. But this was different. This felt unique. This felt sanctified in a way. Son, sensing my reluctance, held the scratched-up, brown Kay brand guitar to the sky. The instrument looked like it blended in with the backdrop of the naturally changing autumn landscape.

Louisiana has a different kind of fall season. Depending on the parish you're in, autumn can be as green as an Ohio summer or as burnt orange as the trees of the Blue Ridge Mountains of Virginia. That fall, however, in Claiborne Parish, the leaves were a rare light brownish-yellow color, just like the guitar.

I finally took the guitar from his hands, cradled it for a second, and hit a few strings. All I could say was, "Thank you, Son, thank you." I can close my eyes now, over seventy-five years later, and remember that feeling—knowing that the guitar was mine. For wherever I would go in my life, I would often return to this autumn moment, knowing that so many beautiful things start with a gift.

It's a blessing to remember to remember.

Sing It Again, Daddy

I knew for sure I wanted to hide the guitar from Daddy. Daddy didn't have a full-time church. But he might as well have had one. He was the secretary of the Freewill Baptist Association in that part of Louisiana. Seemed that every Black church I ever saw in Louisiana was Freewill Baptist. So folks looked to Daddy for all the things a pastor would do: praying for the sick and leading prayer meetings in people's homes. They would sing old a cappellas and sometimes they would get to shouting and find the Holy Ghost. But Daddy's stature as a Freewill Baptist leader wasn't just limited to the things of God. He would help people read important documents and explain things to them. He would organize the sharecroppers for the benefit of all. So he carried all the standing of a righteous man.

I didn't know that in all kinds of hollers in the American South there were quartets singing old spirituals accompanied only by a guitar. I also didn't even think so much about the guitar in country music. Which I know sounds odd. Those six strings only represented one kind of music to me—the devil music of the blues.

So I hid the guitar from Daddy in the barn's loft under some hay. With every spare moment I got, I'd sneak up the ladder, looking over my shoulder with every step. Digging the guitar out from under the hay, I'd sit on a small barrel and just tinker with it—trying to squeeze out a bluesy lick or two. In those first weeks, with every climb up to the loft, I was falling deeper and deeper in love. I didn't even know how to tune it fully. So I just got it in tune with itself the best I could. Then I found a riff or a chord that just sounded cool. I can't put into words what I felt when I was getting a riff under my fingers. It was more than a feeling of accomplishment. It was like I was making a promise to myself.

To get better.

To keep on keepin' on.

Northern Louisiana is not as humid as the southern part of the state closer to the Gulf, but even in the fall the humidity can get muggy. Consequently, the neck of the guitar started to gradually warp, rendering it less playable month after month.

Even with that, I kept crawling up the ladder, knowing I had my secret love safely hidden under the hay. So it was a great shock when Daddy said to me, "Boy, go git that guitar and let me show you something."

Daddy's words paralyzed me. Did I hear him right? Did he actually know I had the guitar? He must have. He knew where it was—and this scared me. "Go on now, git. Do what I tell you." Now, "Do what I tell you" was as close as you got to the line with Daddy. So without hesitation, I went and got the guitar. Walking back from the barn, my mind raced. I did not know if Daddy was going to whip me, break the guitar in two, or preach me a sermon about "the devil's music." When I walked in the door, he said, "Now bring me that thing and let me show you how to play it, boy."

What? Does Daddy know how to play? How could he? The guitar belongs to the blues. I couldn't believe it. But I handed the warped guitar to him. He strummed the strings up and down a few times, and then he started to tune it. Now I'm really curious—I can't believe he knows how to tune it. Still, I was sure he was going to play "Amazing Grace," "Precious Lord," or some other churchy song.

"Now, Junior, let me sing ya a song that I use' ta sing to a little girl when I was just a wee bit older than you." *Okay*, I thought. *Now I got it.* I knew that he was going to sing a song about Maw. Boy, was I in for a surprise.

"Me and my gal went chinkapin hunting,
She fell down and I saw something."

What? Daddy just up and blew my mind. I was so excited, so tickled, I shouted with joy, "Daddy, sing it again!"

"Me and my gal went chinkapin hunting,
She fell down and I saw something."

He smiled at me with a wee bit of a mischievous grin, knowing his song juiced me up something good. I couldn't help myself. I said yet again, "Daddy, please, please sing it again!" He thought I wanted him to repeat the same line. I did not. I wanted him to sing the rest of the story—as in what happened next. I wanted to know what Daddy saw when his girl fell down! So I started in on him with the questions.

"Daddy, how big was she?"

"Aw, boy, she was fat—real fat."

"How fat was she?"

"She was 'round three hundred fifty pounds."

"Daddy, what did she have on?"

"Nuttin' but ah itty-bitty dress," he said.

A big fat girl with nuttin' but a tiny dress? Now my boyhood sexual curiosity was stirred up. Daddy must have seen that stuff that the older boys talk about—meaning her coochie. "Daddy, Daddy, please. Sing it again!"

Just then I heard Maw go, "Ahem," clearing her throat as if to say, "Don't sing that kind of off-color stuff to Junior." But by now Daddy was into it. He wanted to show me he knew about music. With Maw in the kitchen cooking, and he and I standing in the hallway, he gave me one more taste. I faced the kitchen, but his back was to it. He artfully cocked his hat to the side, poked out his lips a little to entertain me more, and sang:

"Me and my gal went chinkapin hunting—"

But just as he was about to sing the other line, I saw Maw look around the corner of the kitchen doorway. I kicked Daddy and whispered, "Here come Maw!" He looked over his shoulder and saw Maw glaring at him. With that, he toned down the line:

"Me and my gal went chinkapin hunting,

She fell down and I kept running."

Daddy lifted his head back on his shoulders and laughed hard. He gave me the guitar back and said, "Go on now, git that thing from 'round here, boy." As he passed me the guitar with his long outstretched arm, I grabbed it ever so quickly and looked up at him. Our eyes briefly met, and he slightly grinned at me with a sparkle in his eye. There was a message in his grin and twinkling eye. Maybe an approval of some sort. I didn't have the maturity or wisdom to know what it was, but in the fullness of the good Lord's time, I would understand what Daddy was saying to me—by not saying it.

Something in the Soil

As sure as the sun rose in the east and set in the west, my musical waters started gradually rising after finding out that Daddy could play the guitar. There was a stirring in my spirit because, again, Daddy was everything. If he knew how to play, then playing just could no way be about the devil. After taking the guitar from his hand, I scurried out of the house, singing the little cornfield diddy he taught me. With every repetition I sang, I felt more and more of the rhythm, the rhyme, and the country humor of it. This joyful feeling hooked me. My music fire had been lit. It would burn down any other childhood ambition I may have had. And soon it would be inextinguishable.

That fire has remained hot for over seventy years. My life as a professional bluesman has taken me all over the world. And wherever I go, the young bluesmen ask me one question: "What was it like to grow up in Louisiana?" For sure, the Bayou State carries a musical mythology of sorts. But it ain't mythology, it's reality. And the truest story you've ever heard. For the blues, country, jazz, ragtime, soul, rock 'n' roll all have their roots in Louisiana and Mississippi. Maybe even in the spirit world—there is indeed something about the water, dirt, air, and the ghost of Louisiana that sings a song all by itself.

But in terms of my particular story, I was born in the perfect place to do what I do. I can't overstate the power of growing up in northern Louisiana. With New Orleans Dixieland jazz to the south of me, the Mississippi Delta blues just to the east of me, and the country twang of the Texarkana area to the west, I possessed the essential ingredients that make up my American musical story. When Daddy wasn't around, I listened to the Grand Ole Opry. They would announce performers with gusto followed by applause: "Ladies and gentlemen, Mr. Roy Acuff," or "Ladies and gentlemen, Ernest Tubb." Hearing those announcers was like a bloodsucking tick embedding itself into my skin.

As a matter of fact, the first song I wrote was taken from the melody of "The Crawdad Song." Some people believe the first folks to sing "The Crawdad Song" were slaves building levees to prevent flooding on the Mississippi River. As time went on, I heard other versions that had a sexual innuendo. Be that as it may, the song is as old as America itself.

You get a line, I'll get a pole, honey
You get a line, I'll get a pole, babe
You get a line, I'll get a pole
We'll go down to the crawdad hole
Honey, baby, mine

With its standard country/folk melody. I created a thousand little song ideas in my five-year-old head. It would be years before I would put together complete song ideas, but it all started with that simple folk musical story. And it is only fitting that I planted my songwriting roots right there. Because I'm a true-blue country boy. I talk like one. I play like one. I am one. It ain't no use in me faking who I really am. And I got it honestly in the soil and ghost of northern Louisiana.

The Money of Nature

The soil of Louisiana gave away a lot of lessons: lessons about safety and danger, lessons about loss and gain, lessons about hoaxes, and lessons about hustles. A lot of my song ideas are just a play on words from the natural-world lessons of my boyhood: "Camel Walk," "Porcupine Meat," "Chicken Heads," and others. We lived so close to the countryside that the joys and pains of the land became our joys and pains.

Around 1944 or 1945 foxes were multiplying like rabbits. Problem was, most had rabies. Soon the foxes were biting the dogs and transmitting the virus, and that virus was some serious-ass business. Stories of people dying (whether true or not) spread like wildfire. Coming from church one day, Daddy explained to me the reality of rabies.

"Emmett, can you tell when a dog has rabies?" he said.

"No, Daddy."

"Well, son, the easiest way is that he's slobberin' at the mouth. But the surefire way is to stand in front of him. If you stand in front of him, and he doesn't look right or left—his gaze stays straight—then that dog has rabies. He won't run from you—he just stares straight. And if you get out of his path, he won't bother you. But if you're in his path, he'll come right for ya."

"Won't he bite me?" I said.

"He may try, so you got to be prepared."

"Prepared to do what?" I asked.

"Be ready to hit him with a stick—it's you or him."

"Ain't it better if I just git out the way?" I said.

"Junior, like many things in life, you got to face things head-on to get at the truth of a situation."

Daddy never wasted an opportunity to get a bigger point across to me.

I never forgot those words. *"You got to face things head-on to get at the truth."*

Soon we little boys learned. When we'd approach a house, we'd throw a rock at dogs, and if they got out of the way, they didn't have rabies. Still, rabid dogs remained a terrible threat because they lived so close to us. With all the children he had, Daddy had to be on guard. He could spot a rabid dog from thirty feet away. One cool fall afternoon in '43, Daddy saw a dog dart under the porch and plant himself under the house.

"Don't go near there; he's got rabies!" Daddy shouted.

Daddy ran into the house, quickly grabbed his shotgun, and lay flat out on the ground. He shot the dog dead. As soon as he fired, he shouted at us: "Get back, get back. There's another one!" Just then, a large, grayish, scruffy mutt came up from under the house and darted straight for Daddy, missing him by two feet. I had never seen a dog run like that. Head down, moving hotfoot—with a purpose. He didn't bark, growl, or anything—just hauled ass across the yard, heading straight to the woods. But Daddy was a sure shot with a quick trigger. He quickly recovered from the dog's failed attack, got up on one knee, aimed, and shot the dog dead not a foot from the forest tree line.

I can't remember being more scared in my budding life. My fear was magnified because Daddy took it so seriously. Yes, rabies could kill you, and since a doctor wasn't around the corner—by the time you got your medicine it could be too late. And the way you had to take the drugs complicated the treatment. First day, this—second day, that—third day, this. So getting healed wasn't straightforward—especially for poor country folk. The danger felt real. I would have nightmares I was playing guitar and a rabid dog would come and eat my guitar. I guess I mixed up my joy of playing with the threat at hand.

Rabies got so bad in Louisiana that the government started a program where they paid 50 cents for each fox you could kill. Yes, rabies was a devil of a menace, but that money was a savior of surprise. Everybody

30

who was hunting gators for their hides and meat turned their attention to foxes. And soon everybody else got busy hunting foxes; there was too much cash to be made. If you managed to get eight fox hides a day, that was four dollars—real good money in 1945.

Daddy's brother O. B. Ellis was a rough man—tough as shoe leather. He was the kinda man you didn't mess with. He had a slow drawl and yet he was a fast talker—know what I mean? He was crass but creative.

Uncle O. B. quickly figured out that there was a lot more money to be made here. If he found a pregnant female fox, he didn't kill her—he let her have her babies. In a month and a half he'd have a litter of six to eight pups. In about six months, he'd sell those young foxes. But Uncle O. B.'s enterprising ways didn't stop there. Soon he was putting male and female foxes together in pens made of chicken wire. The females got pregnant, and before you knew it, he'd be taking twelve foxes a day to the white government man in Haynesville for cold hard cash! Those white men were left scratching their heads. They couldn't figure out to save their lives how my Uncle O. B. killed all them foxes!

Soon the fox rabies scare was over. We wiped them out, and Uncle O. B. was flush with cash. It was a hustle.

But Uncle O. B.'s windfall did not change anything in our house at Christmas. We got a quarter slice (yes, a quarter slice) of an apple or—if we was lucky—a quarter slice of an orange. We had to share a one-cap gun. We always got a little bag of niggertoes. Which is what we called Brazil nuts.

That was Christmas year after year.

Mule Hustle

I had a cousin named Bobby who was rough. But we were all mischievous. All money came from nature, including the hustled kind. Cousin Bobby, my big brother Alvin, and I found out that Mr. Yuke Wise would pay one dollar for every mule we returned to him if they had gotten loose out of his corral. That 33 cents for each of us was some wanted change. Mr. Yuke (which is what everybody called him) knew one little boy couldn't collar a mule, but the three of us was believable.

Mr. Yuke was a white man who was well-off. His daddy had left him and his brothers a lot of land in Claiborne County, and he had lots of people working for him. But Mr. Yuke was deaf. You'd have to stomp real hard on the joints of his front porch and knock loudly to get his attention. You could hear him talking to himself as he got closer and closer to his seemingly always freshly painted white front door.

Everybody needed mules. Dependable in every way, mules were used for wagon pulling and anything else that you needed to have moved. From plowing fields to lugging cotton and sugarcane, to pulling logs or anything else out of the muck, their strong backs seemed to be able to carry anything. Mr. Yuke had lots of mules. Pretty ones, too. They ranged in color from the usual gray and black to brown—a few even had beautiful, big white spots. After we found the first one that escaped, we stomped on Mr. Yuke's porch. Although deaf and unable to speak, we could communicate with him somehow.

"Mr. Yuke, we got one of your mules." As we pointed at the mule to add to our message, he just nodded and said, "Ahuh, ahuh, ahuh, ahuh, ahuh, ahuh . . . Ahuh, ahuh, ahuh, ahuh." He kept nodding his head the whole time to say thank you for bringing his mule home. He then reached in his pocket and gave us coins for a good deed done. Walking down his steps, he grabbed the rope around the mule's neck and guided him back to the corral. "Ahuh, ahuh, ahuh, ahuh," he said, waving and saying thank you again.

A week or so later, we were wishing we had enough money for pop, so we got to thinking.

"If only one of Mr. Yuke's mules was loose."

"Let's let one out."

We stalked through high brush to the farthest end of Mr. Yuke's mule corral. Hunched down like commandos invading enemy territory, we knelt real low and cut that fence. We then clicked our tongues to draw a mule near, carefully looking around to make sure we weren't seen. That old mule walked out. Alvin put a rope around his neck while I sealed back the fence by twisting the wire together.

Taking the long way around, we were soon at Mr. Yuke's door, pounding our feet on the porch. Same result. "Ahuh, ahuh, ahuh, ahuh, ahuh, ahuh . . . Ahuh, ahuh, ahuh, ahuh," he thanked us and gave us a dollar. We did that a few times a week. It wasn't right, but we didn't feel it was too wrong, either—with the wealth they had inherited and all them Negroes they had working for scraps.

Joe Jesus

During World War II, we didn't have much but had more than most. One thing all us colored folks had was pride in one man, and it wasn't FDR. It was Joe Louis. For as long as I can remember, the name of Joe Louis was like Jesus himself. I was told by my older sister that the only reason we had a radio in the house was so Daddy could listen to the first Joe Louis–Max Schmeling fight in 1936, which Joe lost. By the time I was born, Joe Louis was already the first Black American hero. My early memories are littered with someone saying the name "Joe Louis." As I grew, I would understand what that name represented. And that was hope.

In our little home with no power, Daddy had put a car battery under the house, ran a wire up through the floor, and connected the power cord to the brown Zenith radio. It was staticky, but Daddy never missed a Louis fight. The only other thing I remember him listening to was news about the war.

When you're young, something as memorable as World War II seems shadowy. It didn't become clear to me until Maw said my shoes were coming apart. She went to her room and brought back a black leather-looking book. In gold letters it had written on it: "War Ration Book."

"Junior, since the States are at war, we cain't buy some stuff. You 'member when I sent you to the store with a piece of paper and some stamps to git some sugar?"

"Yes, Maw."

"Well, that came from dis here book."

Looking at the book in Maw's hand, they had stamps for a bunch of stuff we did not need. Stamps for butter—we made that. Eggs—the chickens laid that. Bacon—we slaughtered that. Normally with clothes, I just got A. J.'s or Alvin's hand-me-downs, with Maw buying me a new thing here and there. But Alvin and A. J.'s shoes were worn out like mine, so handing them down was out.

But you needed a stamp for shoes. They made many shoes out of leather, and many had rubber soles. But the military needed leather for combat shoes and flight jackets; they needed rubber for tires. So they rationed both leather and rubber. Uncle Sam allowed each family one pair of shoes per child. This was a problem, because with ten fast-growing children in the house, they could grow three sizes in a year. Too tight a shoe could have made you a foot cripple.

We Black folks always had to do with less, so we were constantly in negotiation with others to make do. Often Maw paid cash for stamps from a neighbor or cousin so she could buy me a fresh pair of shoes. It's Black folks' oldest blues song in America—making a way out of no way.

New

We had a neighbor, R. T. Collins, and his family were the first folks to get a TV for miles around. Now when I say *neighbor*, I mean about five miles away. I was like any other boy fascinated with the little picture and sound in the big box. So thick was I to what TV was, I thought it was a magic box, literally divine. First thing I saw was a western with Fuzzy Q. Jones, where his friend got shot. Some days later they were running a repeat of the same movie, and when I saw the guy alive, I ran home to Daddy and said, "I seen a miracle! I seen a miracle! You gotta come now! They shot a man dead, now he is alive like Jesus! Daddy, you gotta come see. Come on!" I don't remember what Daddy said to calm me down. But I know it had to be funny to him.

In 1947, two years after the war ended, a congregation called Daddy to be the pastor at St. Joseph's Missionary Baptist Church in Sherrill, Arkansas. In those days, country preachers had three or four churches. Church wasn't held but once or twice a month, so Daddy would preach back in Carquit on the second and fourth Sundays, and at St. Joseph's on the first and third Sunday. Although Sherrill is about twenty miles outside of Pine Bluff, it's kinda considered a part of Pine Bluff.

With a truck that Daddy had borrowed, and his car filled to the brim, I had to say goodbye to the only land I knew. Daddy straddled up beside me and said, "Here, Junior." He dropped in my hand his harmonica. I had been playing it more than him by now. Looking back, I think he saw his leaving Carquit as a turning point in his own life, and giving me his harp was symbolic of him leaving something behind and yet starting something new.

Sherrill

"How far is Sherrill, Arkansas?" I asked Daddy after he got behind the wheel. "About three hours." When we arrived in Sherrill, I asked Daddy, "How far is Pine Bluff?"

Pine Bluff, Arkansas, was an important place for Black people. Being near Pine Bluff would eventually change my life. But Sherrill, Arkansas, would immediately change Daddy's life.

Daddy started sharecropping for a man named E. L. Burgess. The land in Sherrill was way more fertile than Carquit. Back in Carquit, the crops were not rotated. So you could be picking a row of cotton and go ten steps and not see another boll of cotton to pick. There were stalks, but the stalks were empty—it was a starved land.

But in Sherrill the land was richer, and everything grew. After the first cotton harvest came around in November of '48, Daddy had five times the cotton yield he'd had in Carquit. We'd never seen that much cotton. Back in Carquit, we had to pick three times the acreage to get a hundred pounds of cotton. Now the cotton was easier to pick, so you went faster. And that meant way more money. As we loaded that cotton up, Daddy took out his handkerchief. I thought he was going to wipe his brow, but he put it over his eyes and sobbed like a baby.

"I'm so sorry I didn't leave Louisiana sooner. I dun worked my chil'ren and myself to the bone," Daddy sadly said.

This was the first time I saw Daddy cry. Daddy in all his wisdom just didn't know nothing else but staying in place. You worked where you were planted—you didn't think about moving your family else-where. He wasn't any different from any other Black sharecropping man with a wife and lots of kids. Moving was the stuff of single men or small families. And generally they moved far away from the South, to Chicago, Detroit, Los Angeles, New York—big places with lots of opportunity. But since we moved only 140 miles north across the state line, we were still in our neck of the woods. We continued on with the same traditions and ways of life that we had known. It wasn't a big shock to our family rhythm. But the fertile soil was like night and day compared with Carquit. The lush and fruitful dirt here made life better in every way.

Back in Carquit, Maw often worked the fields with us and still never missed a beat in being a mother to ten children and a wife to a big man. But as we fell into the new groove of Sherrill, Arkansas, Alvin felt bad for Maw.

"She shouldn't be doin' this work, Em," Alvin said to me.

"I know she still gets up before everybody and stays up the latest," I said.

Maw had a tough row to hoe on her hands. Preparing all the meals, working in the fields, and keeping us in line—it was way too much. Daddy was a kind man. I just think he was blind to how much Maw was working. Alvin went to him.

"Daddy, Maw work too hard."

"Boy, what you say?"

"She shouldn't be out here wit' us—she's doin' more work than everybody."

Daddy didn't say another word but "Mm-mm." But the next morning, and from that day forward, Maw stayed in the house after breakfast. Alvin and I had won Daddy over.

The cotton harvest was a cup running over for Daddy. Alvin and Daddy got a thought. We were used to working hard as a family, so why should we be limited to working for Mr. Burgess alone? Alvin went out to other landowners to solicit us as a family to pick cotton. It was successful. Margie May, Mary Lee, and A. J. had gotten jobs and left the coop. Between my niece and brothers and sisters, there were eight of us. Alvin charged the overseers 50 cents a head for a day's work. And soon the Ellis family was picking cotton all over Jefferson County and beyond. There was a lot of cotton to pick. Those cotton rows were so long that each person would pick one row and work that one row all day. Sometimes Alvin, Lillie, and me would pick two, as we were the oldest. From sunup to sundown.

All the burlap sacks had names attached to them, and a mule man would holler from far away, "Hey, you ready?" And if you held your hand high and waved side to side, they would come and pick up your sack. Carrying it to the scale for weight. You had to tie your sack up tightly at the top so you would lose not one boll of cotton.

But Daddy didn't trust these white folks. Watching the mule men like a hawk, he made sure they didn't tamper with those sacks. When the mule men arrived at the scale, he had Verdie Mae stand right behind him. Daddy hollered to her, "Junior, fifty pounds; Alvin, eighty pounds; Gerdie, thirty pounds; Andrew, twenty pounds," and so on. Verdie listened closely to Daddy and wrote them numbers like she was a reporter at the O. J. trial. She repeated the numbers back to him with military precision, and Verdie Mae didn't miss a beat with her numbers.

With Daddy showing that he knew numbers and was keeping righteous books, that white man wouldn't try to cheat him. We weren't his sharecroppers—we were doing a day's work. Our business with Mr. So-and-So was done when Daddy piled us in the car and we drove away. With our day's work hustle, the Ellis family gained a reputation for being very productive laborers.

Between our work ethic and Daddy's status as the new pastor of the St. Joseph's Missionary Baptist Church, he figured he could soup up this day's-work thing. He would go to the white man and say, I'll pick these thirty acres of cotton for you. Then he hired Negroes he knew (including his family) to pick that cotton. Since cotton matured at different times, the fields had to be re-picked two and three times. Daddy quickly became the biggest contractor around for miles. The white farmers turned to him because sharecropping was changing in the late forties and early fifties in the Midwest region. After we moved to Jefferson County, we saw what the future held for King Cotton.

Coming from church, there it was: a humongous orange tractor. But this tractor looked like it was from outer space. It had a V-shaped mesh basket above the engine. The basket had a dome-shaped steel hood above it. Daddy slowed the car down. With fluffy white cotton sticking out between that orange wire mesh, Daddy said, "Son, that's a picking-cotton machine. One day it will do all the cotton pickin'." Daddy's tone wasn't resentful. It was righteous—his story of the future had the vibe of those old newsreels announcing "the march of time."

But it would be years before the machines took over in the South, ending sharecropping as he had grown to know it. In the meantime, Daddy's enterprising ways made him more money than he had ever seen. I saw my daddy earn one hundred dollars a day in 1948. A hundred dollars a day! Neither whites nor Blacks were making that kind of money.

Just a Boy

Sherrill, Arkansas, just had a country school. It looked like a big old L. They had built addition after addition, accommodating more and more Negro children. With grades one through ten all in one building, I made friends with kids older and younger than myself.

On my first day in school all the kids were talking about 4-H. I'm like, *What's all this fuss about 4-H?* The teacher said, "Emmett, I know you're new, so you don't have to do anything for 4-H. Everybody doesn't take part, anyway." She talked so intelligently, I was a little intimidated. One kid I took to was Harold Willingham. He was a few years older, but we were only a grade or two apart. My friendship with Harold would be a turning point in my life. He explained to me what the 4-H club was.

"Em, it's just a contest."

"Contest for what?"

"Who can raise the biggest ear of corn, the biggest tomato, sing the best—you know, stuff like that," Harold said.

"I ain't growed nothing," I said.

"You play good—bring your geetar!"

I did. But I also brought an old big syrup can and my harmonica. I had been playing guitar and blowin' harp every chance I had. When my time came up in the 4-H contest, I put the syrup can under my arm just like Africans do, using it as a drum. I sang the hambone song and shuffled my feet while I sang.

"Hambone, hambone
Where ya been?

Round the world and back again
Hambone, hambone
Ain't cha heard?
Papa's gonna buy me a mockingbird"

I stopped and all the kids clapped, yelled, and laughed with enthusiasm. I put down the syrup can, and while picking up my guitar to sit down I told some old joke I had heard a hundred times. And the kids laughed some more. Then I played the guitar and sang. I wasn't too good of a guitar player yet. I played in only one key—but I knew about four or six songs. It was quiet at first when I started to sing, but all the kids started to clap. And the clappin' got louder. Then I told some jokes that were spicy, but ones that we kids understood. Everybody laughed—even the teacher. I pulled out my harp and did the train and the dog race. I told a story about how a dog bet a train that it could beat him in a race. The train said, *Oh no you can't.* I started playing the harmonica to sound like a train starting down the track. *Chuchu—chu—chu—chu,* getting faster and faster. Then I did the sound of the dog—and that melody was whiny and quick. I went back and forth between the two sounds. Showing in musical tone how the dog won the race.

They applauded and laughed noisily. Between my syrup can drumming, singing, dancing, playing harp, and telling jokes, I had put all my talents together. This became the moment of me understanding what a performance truly was.

It came natural to me. I didn't know it then, but in that 4-H contest, I had put together my first act. I rehearsed nothing. My performance was born by hearing the inspiring sound of the applause. I was just a boy when all this happened. But in time I would learn that what came naturally would have to be developed—sharpened. And that development would be the difference between me being an amateur and a professional.

Pictures in My Head

WLAC from Nashville played what at the time was the new sound—
rhythm and blues, or R&B. At 1510 on the radio dial, the station's
50,000 watts of power could be heard all over the South late at night.
WLAC's "John R." became the first DJ that I would wait for. He was
white, but he sounded Black. He came on the radio with a bang.

"Yeah! It's the big John R., the blues man.
Whoa! Have mercy, honey, have mercy.
John R.—way down south in the middle of Dixie.
I'm gonna spread a little joy.
You stand still now and take it like a man, you hear me, baby?"

In the late '40s, before R&B would get a new name called rock 'n'
roll, John R. would play mostly jump blues. The jump blues were small
big bands. The big band sound of the '30s and '40s was dying out on the
radio. The jump blues bands were hot. And no one did it better than
Louis Jordan.

Louis Jordan is the godfather of what I do. As a matter of fact, Louis
Jordan is the godfather of what everybody does. He changed music.
His sound was completely new. There was a bounce to his songs. The
music was fast, swung like jazz, and had a boogie-woogie feel but with
a backbeat that really made it pop. His lyrics were more like real-life
stories, and most of those stories were funny. No one had combined the
elements of groove and storytelling like him. He became my obsession.

Louis Jordan's music built my musical daydreams. There were no albums, so each song was a building brick. And brick by brick, he built a musical house for me to live in. Songs like "G.I. Jive," "Is You Is or Is You Ain't My Baby," "Caledonia," "Beware (Brother, Beware)," "Choo Choo Ch'Boogie," "Ain't Nobody Here but Us Chickens," and many others were the walls, windows, and roof of my imagination. Before Louis Jordan, what a professional musician was, was just imaginary pictures in my head. His sound and incredible storytelling skills became my soundtrack of those pictures. His songs were like the outlines in a coloring book, and my imagination drew in all the assorted colors.

His music was the key that unlocked my natural, God-given gifts of music, comedy, and storytelling. His music put my imagination into overdrive. I put myself in his songs. He mushroomed my fantasy life. I started imagining I was performing everywhere I went—even at church. I wouldn't be listening to the sermon—I'd be observing the style of the preacher. The hand gestures, the rocking back-and-forth movements, the various changes in his voice, the emotion. In my mind, I became whatever I consumed. I was the preacher—and bringing home the word. I was Louis Jordan singing those stories.

My Uncle O. B. enjoyed Saturday nights in juke joints more than Sunday mornings in church. Although he was way more worldly than Daddy, Daddy truly loved his brother. And Uncle O. B. loved Daddy's children just as much as he loved his own. He'd come over often, and when he did, I'd start in on him.

"Uncle O. B., where you go last night?" I said.

"Why you wanna know, boy?" he said.

"'Cuz I wanna hear 'bout the music."

"Junior, went to the Gala Room to see Louis Armstrong."

"Louis Armstrong?"

"Told you I was at the Gala Room Club."

By the wide smile on his face, I knew that Uncle O. B. was enjoying my wide-eyed interest. The Gala Room was more than just another Pine Bluff, Arkansas, nightclub. It was where the biggest stars came to perform in the city. Pine Bluff was the hub for Black folk for a hundred miles around. I kept on pushing questions on Uncle O. B.

"What did he have on?"

"Ah you know, black tux wit' a red carnation."

"What was his first song?"

"Don't remember that."

"How many people did he have in his band?"

"Six or so."

"Was the stage far from the dressing room?"

"Ah boy, I don't remember all that."

"Let O. B. relax," Maw said.

I asked him one more question: "Uncle O. B., what did you wear?"

With pride he stood up, using his hand gestures to show me his obvious style. "Junior, I had on my gray pinstripe suit, brown tie, and brown wingtip shoes. I looked good!"

"Uncle O. B.! What did—"

"Junior! Didn't I tell you to leave O. B. alone?" Maw shouted.

"Boy, go on and do what your Maw say. Next time, I'll tell you 'bout the time I saw Cab Calloway!"

My head exploded—Cab Calloway! Uncle O. B. gave me more outlines for my mental coloring book. His stories had me scurrying away into more visions. I wanted myself in the shoes of a grown-ass entertainer. I went and got a box of matches. I lit about six of them and quickly blew them out—leaving the charred tips unbroken. I stood in front of Maw's chifforobe mirror and artfully drew me a mustache above my upper lip. Suddenly I was an adult. Grabbing my guitar, I looked in the mirror imagining I was a guitar player in some band, or Louis Armstrong, or Louis Jordan, or anyone under the bright stage lights in my dreamed-up nightclub.

Trust and Choices

A wagon and mules were like a Cadillac to a farmer. That's how Daddy would move the goods around that would make him money. If he said it to me once, he said to me a thousand times, "Junior, I'd shoot a man dead if he tried to take my mules or wagon." Nuff said. So for Daddy to entrust his wagon and mules to anyone was a big deal.

But he did with me.

In the summer before I turned twelve years old, Daddy said, "Tomorrow, Junior, I want you to take some of dis cotton over to be ginned at Mr. Bill's place." I must not have heard him right. *Me? No way.* I still had an older brother living at home. And a wagon full of cotton was like a truck full of live chickens—valuable chickens. Not to mention Mr. Bill's was over twelve miles away. Also, this wasn't even cotton-harvesting time, but I guess he needed some money to tide him over.

Daddy looked down at me, square in my eye. He must have seen the doubt in me. Wondering if I could handle it. He read my eyes right.

"Now, Junior, you ask that man 'How much is cotton selling for today?' and if it ain't high enough—you bring my cotton right back chere."

"But Daddy, howz I to know what the price is?"

"Junior, think about this now—you was with me to sell cotton before. What's a good price in your head?"

Mane, I didn't want to give Daddy the wrong number. Not that he would whip me or anything. I just didn't want to be wrong—never wanted to disappoint him. Looking back on it now, he was trying to teach me to trust myself. So I looked up to the sky and said, "Daddy, I thinks about fifteen to nineteen dollars."

"That's right, Junior!" His approval meant everything.

"Now what would be too low?"

With more confidence in myself, I quickly said, "Twelve dollars."

"See, boy, you know more than you think you know—'memba, that—always 'memba that."

Next morning, right after sunup, Daddy tightly pulled one more piece of rope over the cotton to secure it down even more. He pushed about two dollars in coins into the palm of my hand and patted me hard on the top of my thigh. He said, "Lord be with you, son." I wasn't scared till he said, "Lord be with you, son," which meant that Daddy took my trip seriously. I ain't saying it put the fear of Jesus in me—but it made me wake up to that I was representing Daddy, Maw—all of us. And that was a mighty big bag of responsibility I was toting—and I don't mean the cotton.

In a couple of hours I was at the gin. It was busy there that day. I jumped off my wagon to go get a drink of water out of the pump. It's funny, all of us Blacks and whites were drinking out of the same ladle. I guess thirst was different here than in Montgomery, Alabama—or at least on this day. Heard some white men talking. "Next week, cotton comin' down some kinda hard." I thought to myself, *I better change my notions 'bout this price.* After that bit of news, I unhooked one mule and walked him over to the trough so he could drink. That old mule lapped up that water like a champ. I kept my head down but my ears up as I listened to everyone I could, trying to get some info about the prices that day. I was a boy, but I kept my hat down over my eyes as if I were an old man not to be fucked with.

When it came time, Mr. Bill offered me $12.90. I said okay. On the ride back home, I wasn't worried what Daddy would say. Well, that ain't true. Let's say I had a story prepared for what Daddy might say. I was coming down the road to the house around dusk when Daddy greeted me.

"How you make out, Junior?"

"I got twelve dollars and ninety cents."

"Why so low?"

"Them white men say cotton going down next week—some of them got less than me."

Giving Daddy the money, he said, "You dun good."

Maw was a different story. "You shoulda waited, Junior."

"But Maw, I—"

Daddy chimed in. "Mattie, the boy made a judgment and did just what I told him to do." Maw didn't say another word to me. I don't know if they talked about it later or not. But that was the end of it as far as I was concerned. In a few weeks I was bore out, as cotton dropped in price by about four dollars.

Daddy grew in his trust of me. I would do more and more of adult duties even though I was a boy. Which was a good thing for my manhood. What was not good for my boyhood is that Daddy asked me to drop out of school. There was just too much to do. As wise as Daddy was, he failed me miserably on that. Even though boys my age dropped out of school in their early teens all the time, my daddy knew better. I just think his farming and church responsibilities overwhelmed him, and he wanted me around 24/7. How could I argue with that? I still loved being around Daddy.

When you're eleven you really don't know how to go to bat for your future. You do what you're told, always believing that your parents know best. I did not have irresponsible parents; they were solid folk. But even though I could read well, *my biggest lifelong regret is that I didn't finish my schooling.* Over time, it left me feeling a little stunted and ashamed.

I was now with Daddy more than all my other brothers and sisters. It wouldn't be long before I was the oldest boy around the house 'cause my other two brothers had gotten jobs and moved out. I learned a lot about church business, farming, and anything that involved Daddy. I was still learning. I would look at signs, advertisement billboards, things in store windows, and if I didn't know the word, I would write it down. And by the day's end, I would know the meaning and how to say that word. I longed for school, but mostly I just had more and more chores to do. Even though my sisters were older than me, the situation left me doin' all the things a man would do.

Enormous Energy

As long as I can remember I've had waaaayyy more energy than everybody around me. I walked fast. I talked fast. I always wanted to get to the bottom of something—quick! This made me a wee bit pushy. I was never afraid to ask a question that wasn't any part of my business. And that wasn't because I was rude or just plain country—it was because I couldn't shut off my enormous energy.

So I had no problem asking my friend from school, Harold, why he always had change. I never had any pocket money, not a quarter. I knew he was more well-off than me, but when you're a kid, you may see money—but you ain't got any. Harold would always buy me a pop or something. But I didn't have transportation, so I didn't see him a lot.

But that changed when Harold turned sixteen and bought himself a car. A beautiful 1948 gray Plymouth. Even though Harold's car was new, the body had changed little from the prewar years. During the war, they made no cars in America. When the war finally ended in 1945, Detroit could have produced a frigging go-cart and Americans would have eaten it up like a thirsty dog lapping water on a hot day. Neither the Plymouth nor the Chevrolet nor the Ford bodies had changed much after the war, because the appetite was high for any new car. Detroit didn't even retool their machines. You gotta understand what a car means to a boy. Freedom, manhood, and, of course, access to girls. In them days, when a young man's car turned down a back road, drove into the woods, and parked, you had the most exquisite four-star . . . backseat motel. If girls knew you had a car, you were big-time. Harold was so generous to me that if he had eight dollars, he'd give me four and we were off to the races. Four dollars each carried us through Friday and Saturday night. We went to school dances and gradually we ventured to the big city—Pine Bluff, Arkansas.

When you're thirteen years old and from Carquit, Louisiana, the main drag in Pine Bluff at night could have been New York City. The street was all lit up with store lights, and at Christmas they'd string colored light bulbs high across the tops of electric poles. Pine Bluff was forty miles south of the state capital of Little Rock, but for Negroes it was a central hub for hundreds of miles in all directions. The Bluff would produce Black achievers in almost every workaday field of American labor. So there were stores that you could go to that were Black stores. Barber shops that were Black barber shops. Grocery stores that were Black grocery stores. Even things like the Negro Baseball League were just for us. It contained us to ourselves. I didn't know it then, but there were a hundred Pine Bluffs in America—neighborhoods—big streets run by us.

I couldn't understand how Harold got money. Not to mention enough to buy a car. I had to ask.

"Mane, how you always got money?"

"I work for my dad."

"He pays you like that?"

"He pays me whatever he pays anyone else."

I thought, *What? Harold gets paid the same as anyone else?* That seemed strange to me because whatever work I did for the white man, Daddy would choose what he would pay me. It got me to thinking.

"Harold, does your daddy need any more help?"

"You mean you want a job?"

"Yep."

"I'm sure Daddy can git you something."

Harold's daddy, Mr. Willingham, was a manager of a far-flung farm. He was short but broad and very hearty looking. He was firm about his instructions to us, but he was a friendly man who always seemed to have a smile on his face. He would always tell us boys, "It don't hurt to smile." He gave me a job and paired me up with his son and another kid. This was my first job away from my family.

The first thing I had to learn was how to drive a tractor. It was waaay different than driving a car. The huge tractor was bright orange with "CASE" written in black across the back of the seat, written on both sides of the engine compartment—hell, it was written anywhere they could place it. At that time, the J. I. Case Company was like John Deere. Climbing onto the beast machine wasn't easy. I was tall for my age, but with gigantic wheels to the left and right of me, they were almost as high as my shoulders. The steering wheel was so big that I had to extend my arms fully at ten and two o'clock to drive the monster. Harold said, "Just get it in line and then keep it straight."

Although that summer Mr. Willingham was raising mostly rice and soybeans, he had not used the land that we were plowing in years. So the dirt was rock-hard and in spots had weeds and briars. Harold drove one tractor ahead of me that sprinkled water to soften the ground. Problem was, it was almost a hundred degrees that day—so the ground would dry quickly. Still, the dragging disc being pulled by the powerful tractor pulverized the hard soil. Reaching the corner of the field, there was some brush, and I just drove through it. Unfortunately, there was a bee's nest in the thicket. Those big black-and-yellow bumblebees came right after me with a vengeance. And with the big disc behind the tractor, I couldn't get off the damn thing! Them bumblebees tore me up something good! Harold and the other boy laughed as I climbed carefully off the tractor, then ran for my life.

Believe it or not, the very next day—another briar patch, another batch of bees. But this time I leaped off the tractor, my jump clearing the machine completely, but I hurt my legs as I fell to the ground. I ran as fast as my hurt leg would take me. Harold said I danced like a crazy man to get them bees off of me.

But when the eagle flew on Friday, it was all worth it. Mr. Willingham put almost twenty dollars in my hand. Twenty dollars! I ain't never seen that much money for a week's work. He paid me almost 50 cents an hour!

Leaving Home

Almost a month later, I was back working with my family picking cotton. At the end of the day, I didn't go to the car and wait. I walked behind Verdie Mae and Daddy to settle up with the white overseer. I didn't say anything. When we got home, Daddy gave me 50 cents for a day's work. I was upset, but not about the amount. I just wanted to collect my own money for the work I did. At thirteen, I wanted to be my own man.

"Daddy, I want to get my own money."

"Boy, what you mean?"

"I want to go to the white man myself with my own cotton and get paid like any other man."

"Junior, you ain't no man."

"Other boys my age get their own money."

The conversation was getting heated. It scared my siblings. I was scared. "No, Junior."

"I'm man enough to work. I'm man enough to get my own."

"I'm through wit' it now," Daddy sharply said.

"You ain't taking my money no mo'," I said to Daddy.

"If you cain't do what I tell you to do, then you don't live here."

I left.

I swear, I swear, I swear I didn't want to cross Daddy in any way whatsoever. I just wanted to collect my own money. I didn't want to deprive the family till. I just wanted to put the money in my hands before I gave it away. I don't know why in the devil it was so important to me, but it was.

What's Left Unsaid

After I left home, I went straight to Mr. Willingham and said I wanted more work. Which he gave me. I got a room to rent. Still, it was almost like I never left home, as I would stop by often. It seemed that the confrontation between me and Daddy was forgotten, and we never ever talked about it again for the rest of his life.

Looking back on these early days after I left home, sometimes I get a troubled feeling. If it had been my young son, and he was out there in the world, no matter how we parted, I know I'd wanna know how he was getting along. I wondered then and I wonder now, seventy-plus years later, why Daddy never said:

"Where you go, boy?"
"Where you been?"
"How you eatin'?"
"How you survivin'?"
"What you been doin' wit' yourself?"

But Daddy never asked. In my quiet times, I wonder, was he mad that I seemed to make it on my own? Was he happy not to have another mouth to feed? Was he trying to teach me a lesson? Did he think I was gonna run back home with my tail between my legs? Since I will never know, all I can do is wonder. If I look at it negatively, it hurts. If I look at it positively, I say he trusted me and my abilities to find my way. Either way, I would learn that oftentimes the questions that are left unanswered are the very questions that egg us on to do better.

Shot

I found a better fit for me than the room I was renting. I partnered up with a guy and we rented an apartment in Pine Bluff. But this arrangement didn't last even four months. My roommate had a brother named Preacher. He came into the bathroom, where I was styling my hair.

"Where you think you going?" he said.

"Ah, mane, I'm just about to go out and git wit' this girl," I said.

"Uh-huh, you think you really something, don't you?"

"Man, what'chu—"

And just then, *BAM!* with a bright flash of light—he'd shot me. I must've struggled with him after he shot me, as I was told there was a lot of blood inside the bathroom that had been smudged on the floor. But somehow I almost made it to my car, and that's the last thing I remember. Some angelic soul drove by and saw me facedown with my car door open and got me to Pine Bluff Hospital.

I woke up in a very white room. Maw and Daddy were there as I opened my eyes. Even though the wound was in the flesh part of my leg, they said I was lucky, as I almost bled out. I had cheated death. Maw took my bloody clothes home. My sister Gerdie told me how Maw put those clothes by themselves in the washpot, which was a big black cast-iron round tub she kept outside. She built a fire under the tub and with a big stick turned those bloody clothes of mine round and round. She washed them again. And again—till it boiled all that blood out of the fabric.

I was in the Pine Bluff Hospital for around three days. On the last day, as I was putting on my clean-as-a-whistle clothes that Maw had boiled, Uncle O. B. came to visit me, with only one question.

"Who did this to you, boy?"

"Preacher," I said.

"Where does he live?"

"Somewhere near the tracks and Pecan Street."

"Okay," he said and left.

As he walked out the door, he mumbled under his breath, "He won't do nothin' no more to my nephew." What I didn't know was that Uncle O. B. had previously begged Daddy to tell him who had shot me. But Daddy, being a preacher and all, didn't tell his brother one thing. Daddy knew his brother was a hothead and that he loved his nieces and nephews almost more than he loved his own children. It's not that Daddy didn't want justice for me, he just didn't want trouble for his brother. He finally told Uncle O. B., "Don't get yourself in no trouble. Leave it alone—he won't be 'round long." But the real truth was that Daddy and Maw believed in witchcraft—Louisiana voodoo. They had a network of folk who, either through herbs, rituals, poisons, or charms, could cast spells of protection or harm.

To this day, I don't know why Preacher shot me—another unanswered question. I never had an argument with him. It wasn't about a girl. Nothing. It was a short, mild conversation until he pulled out that gun. Hell, I never really seen Preacher but three or four times. It could have been about my talent. It could have been about skin color, because I was light caramel and Preacher was black as night. But I don't know. It wasn't two months later that they found Preacher dead in a burned-down house. I didn't ask questions. I didn't have to.

In terms of Preacher's demise, my money was on Uncle O. B. and not on some Louisiana voodoo. Even after I got shot, I did not move back to Daddy and Maw's in Sherrill. The city of Pine Bluff had too much to offer.

A Drive to Tutwiler

I wanted to be in music so much. So when I saw Boyd Gilmore strolling the streets of Pine Bluff, I looked at his guitar as much as I looked at him. Taking a likin' to me, he showed me things. Boyd could play slide like no one I ever heard. He was the first slide player I saw that held on to the note and then wiggled his finger—squeezing out that howling twang that I had only heard on the radio. Even with all the Black folks that were making money in Pine Bluff's thriving Black businesses, after meeting Boyd I knew I didn't want to be no farmer, no factory worker, no janitor, no bricklayer, no deliveryman, or no barber. I wanted to play my guitar. Perform. Write and sing my songs. I know that made me a dreamer. But Boyd Gilmore gave me just a lil' taste, and that was all I needed. Period. I just wanted to do what I wanted to do.

Boyd was from Mississippi, but it seems he was always in Pine Bluff. Because of the number of juke joints and clubs, he could make money. He took an interest in me and he would let me play with him. And I would grow significantly as a musician. When we started jammin' together, I learned so much in those first jams—which would be with me for the rest of my life. The big lesson was the use of space. How to play a lick, stop—wait some time, and play again. But the big schooling was that when you stopped, even your silence had a groove—but you would not feel that groove until you started playing again. *So the time in between the notes was just as important as the notes you played.*

Boyd Gilmore was the first big-shot musician I got to know. Even though he sometimes stayed in an abandoned house and never seemed to have a dime, his name connected him to people that were actually on the radio. So despite appearances, he was still a star to me. I didn't know what name-droppin' meant then, but when he would say the name "Sonny Boy," I got a thrill.

Sonny Boy Williamson was the bluesman of the air. He had been a regular on the King Biscuit Time radio show on KFFA in Helena, Arkansas. As leader of the King Biscuit Time Entertainers, everybody knew Sonny Boy because KFFA had a wide signal that covered most of the Mississippi Delta, Louisiana, and Arkansas. Most Negroes in the Delta were sharecroppers. The King Biscuit Time radio show came on at 12:15 daily. Sonny Boy would blow that harp over the airwaves, and it was like a church bell ringing for a call to worship. Sharecroppers, who got up at sunrise, took needed breaks to listen to the thirty-minute show. Adults and kids would stand around, and we just bopped our heads. Some from side to side, some up and down. Sonny Boy's voice and harmonica were the loudest things comin' out the radio, and did it cook. I didn't know it, but so many of my future friends like Ike Turner and B.B. King would listen just like me to King Biscuit. The show became so popular it would inspire musicians all over the Delta. Those cats would come to sing the blues themselves or be the first stars of R&B. They would flock to Helena, Arkansas, hoping to get some kind of break and be heard on the radio. Since Helena was only an hour and a half from Memphis, it became a stopover for all the cats trying to git to Memphis to hatch a record.

Hearing Sonny Boy's songs on Daddy's radio planted seeds in me. See, Sonny Boy had a bit of a lisp. Even on the radio you'd hear that slight spit in his voice on his s sounds. And it sounded a little funny to me, but it sounded cool, too. Much of the tunes Sonny Boy sang on the air were kind of takeoffs of songs I'd heard before. These little cornfield ditties that were a mix of the blues, gospel, and country rhymes. The ditties were mostly sung in the field while picking cotton.

However, Sonny Boy had a unique take on this tradition. He'd create extra words and often write these long lines of melody that didn't fit in the song—but he made them fit. Mane, it was some genius in that. Everything that would come after that—Little Richard, Fats Domino,

Lennon/McCartney, Johnny Cash, and everything in between—was right there in Sonny Boy's phrasing. His art became a part of his songwriting magic. Between the seeds of his lyrical gifts, voice, and humor, I fell deeply in love with his songwriting.

But that's only half of the story.

Sonny Boy Williamson was the best damn harp player that was—till I later discovered Little Walter. Sonny Boy combined the melodic things you could do with a saxophone with the boogie-woogie groove of a piano or rhythm guitar. Let me try to explain this. See, when you play the harp, especially solo, you're playing a melody. But in between that melody, you're playing in a lower pitch—a "chug." That repetitive chug is keeping a groove going. So it's a percussive and a melodic thing. Since Sonny Boy had such a command of his instrument, he'd mix up long and short grooves on the low-pitch chugs and play beautiful melodies on the higher-pitch end. He was the first I heard that made the harp talk to ya. Sonny's playing was so good it was like a juicy conversation—full of gloomy truths and joyful lies.

Sonny Boy's legend wasn't just about his groundbreaking radio gig or his harp playing. In those days, in the world of musicians, you were also judged by how well you took care of the other musicians you played with. Sonny had an awful reputation for running off with the money before he paid his band. So he couldn't keep a band together for long. He had taken club owners, too. As much as Sonny was a mentor, I knew I didn't want to be that kind of cat. I wanted to be a stand-up cat with my commitments.

Nevertheless, Sonny Boy Williamson was one of the brightest lights of the blues. Sonny Boy was born in Tutwiler, Mississippi; so was John Lee Hooker. Because of folklore surrounding a story that W. C. Handy first heard the blues there, many consider Tutwiler (along with a lot of other towns in the Delta) the birthplace of the blues.

Every two or three years, I'll jump in my car and throw in a couple of Sonny Boy's CDs. I'll head north on I-55 from my home in Jackson and drive two and a half hours north. I'll stop in Yazoo City or Indianola (where B.B. King was born), have lunch, and get back behind the wheel blastin' Sonny Boy's music the whole way to Tutwiler, where he was laid to rest. At the gravesite is a beautiful tombstone where a picture of him is inlaid in the marble. Players from around the world sojourn there and leave harmonicas on his tombstone. Standing there, I said a prayer of thankfulness because Sonny Boy taught me almost everything I would need to be a writer and a solid bluesman. By just being who he was.

You Gotta Git

Boyd Gilmore continued to feed me stories that whetted my appetite for music. It didn't hurt that he was living the musical life. "Boy, I gotta get over to Little Rock to play with Ernest Lane." Ernest had learned piano from Pinetop Perkins and was the up-and-coming cat. I was excited, jealous, and horny for a musical life. As I walked with Boyd to the Greyhound bus station, he let it fly.

"Boy, you gotta git," Boyd said.

"What'chu mean?" I said.

"Move around. Go see everybody. Play wit' everybody. Move around."

"I hope I can."

"I know you just a boy, but you gotta hang in the right joints."

"I know you is right."

"Listen here, my cousin Elmore is coming to the Jack Rabbit Club next week. Tell him you know me and to let you in."

That next Saturday afternoon, I stood across the street of the Jack Rabbit Club and waited—till dusk. I saw an old brown beat-up Buick pull up and three cats get out. They opened the trunk and took out a bass drum and snare. *This must be them.* I didn't know what Elmore James looked like, but one cat's whole vibe said he was in charge. He had on a classy light-brown suit and these thick glasses that made him look like a schoolteacher. Had an eyeglass protector case clipped neatly to his suit pocket and a tiny gold pin in his lapel. Oh yeah, that had to be Elmore James.

"Mr. James, your cousin Boyd told me to ask, could I play with you tonight?"

"Son, call me Elmo."

He looked at me with suspicious eyes and said, "How old is you?"

"I'z fourteen." (I was really twelve.)

"Boy, you cain't come in here, they serve hard liquor."

"I can pass."

"Yeah, but not wit' me. I'll tell you what. You come to the Jitterbug next Friday. And I'll let you in there."

In my life, I've said to myself over and over again: *"I ain't gonna let it beat me."* So I was deflated but not defeated. And I damn sure wasn't going to depend on Elmo James to let me in that night, either. I did the same thing I did as a boy back in Louisiana in front of Maw's mirror. I lit about twelve matches and quickly blew them out. Taking those charred tips and rubbing them gently between my thumb and first finger, I carefully brushed in a mustache above my upper lip. I had one of Daddy's apple caps that I put on and cocked it to the side, putting it a little over my right eye as the young men were doing back then. And with my five-foot-ten-inch frame, I looked down and had no smile on my face. I walked right into the Jack Rabbit with no problem. I started lying about my age as a rule. Soon I was clever at it. I couldn't let anything like being underage prevent me from what Boyd Gilmore told me I had to do. And I wasn't gonna go through what other kids had to. Getting pushed through bathroom windows by your friends—shit like that. Hell fucking no. I had to get in every joint I could in the Pine Bluff/Little Rock area. Like Boyd said, I had to *git*.

The Jack Rabbit jumped that night. Elmo was one of those blessed cats whose first record was his biggest success. "Dust My Broom" was a remake of a song by the father of the guitar blues, Robert Johnson. But Elmo's version was red-hot. The song showcased his slide guitar style in a big way. That's the sound that he would be known and remembered for. Elmo had an acoustic guitar with an electric pickup. And tonight was rocking the house. You really had to have lung power and a command of your sound to play what folks called juke joints.

I didn't talk to Elmo that night. But I showed up at the Jitterbug the following Friday with my fake mustache, a nice suit, my guitar, and Daddy's cap.

"Well, well, well. Look at you, boy—so you dun growed in a week, huh," Elmo said with a laugh.

I just laughed back and asked, "Do you think I can sit in tonight?"

"Let's see how it go."

At the Jitterbug that night, Elmore James did the same show. Unfortunately, he did not let me join the band. Can't blame him. He didn't know me, but he soon would.

What a Life

It was 1949. For many of us Black folks, 1949 seemed a world away from ten years earlier. In '39 the war started, we got into it in '41, and now five years after it ended, some Negroes felt they were moving on up.

But before the war, during the war, and after the war, some things remained the same. Black, white, and Creole folk never lost their appetite to be distracted. And we ate our entertainment like a hog eats slop—happily. For us Black souls, we wanted a moment to be taken away from white folks' shit. So when the Rabbit Foot Minstrels would come to town, people got excited. Their appearance felt like the arrival of a carnival. When I was younger, the clowns and the animals made me smile. Arkansas saw a lot of the Rabbit Foot Minstrels shows. It wasn't a thing where they went around Pine Bluff and put up posters; instead, they would have a small parade-like band walk through the town center and announce their arrival. And that's all they had to do to advertise. Because from the city square we passed by word of mouth news of their upcoming show like a big bowl of potato salad at a church homecoming service.

Raising their big tent up high to the sky, it looked like a big city church—a cathedral. On the inside there was a wooden stage that they put together piece by piece. Football stadium bleachers were on the far right and left of the tent, and they set up maybe five hundred wooden folding chairs in the middle. All this stage stuff arrived on big white trucks with banners dramatically painted on the sides:

The Greatest Colored Show on Earth
Rabbit Foot Minstrels
To-Nite

I started seeing the Rabbit Foot Minstrels when I was eight or nine; my age limited me to seeing stuff that little kids see. The elephants, the acrobats, the contortionist, the freak show, and magicians. But by the time I was eleven I was seeing the musicians, the singers, the slapstick adult humor, and the girls. Lawd have mercy! The girls! When you're a boy coming into your manhood and you see for the first time beautiful brown and bronze adult women in short skirts that flew up revealing their butts, you could barely hide your excitement below. Their bikini-like tops left little to the imagination.

Still, for a young man like me who knew he had a gift to stimulate a crowd, the Rabbit Foot Minstrels, or, as everyone called them, the Foots, represented one thing: the life of a professional entertainer. I want to emphasize *entertainer*. Yeah, they could sing and play their in-struments with the best of them, the dancing was as tight as a drum, and the comedy was too funny. But their overall showmanship made people come back year after year. They played, sang, and danced not just for the sake of the glorious music—they performed to captivate you. To comfort you. To delight you—through your ears, eyes, and mind.

The high tent represented a holy place where I could perform and learn from the best my people offered. A place where I could learn how to charm an audience of five hundred. After seeing these super-talented performers do their thing, I knew I could contribute. So after their last day of performing, I hung around as they got ready to move on. I watched them take down the big tent and pack up. I asked one work-man who was also a performer a few questions.

"Where do y'all go next?" I asked.

"What city is this?"

"Pine Bluff," I said.

"Oh, I think Helena is the next stop, then Hot Springs, then Little Rock," he said.

He then picked up a big thick rope and started to wrap it around his arm as he walked away gathering more of the rope with every step.

It surprised me that he didn't even know what city he was in. I kind of thought of that as sophisticated and citified. That's when I first understood a part of the show business life. You went to so many places, saw so many different faces, that it could blend together in your mind. The show you did every night was just the show. The city where you were was just an afterthought. I thought, *What a life!*

The Way In

You got to understand something about Black Southern folks. We all believe we are talented. Almost by birthright. However, some can just carry a tune and some can really sing. Pretty much all of us could dance a little, but there is a gap as wide as the Grand Canyon between a little dancing to being a real hoofer. But if you wanted a life in showbiz and you were in the South, the Rabbit Foot Minstrels were the way in. Consequently, people who had talent or thought they had talent were eternally auditioning for the Foots. As a result, when they came to Pine Bluff, a few folks would stand outside the office tent to see if they could join the Foots. By now, Elmo James knew: though I was still a boy, I had the right stuff.

"Bobby, the Foots is hiring," Elmo said.

"What I got to do?"

"Come on down wit' me. I gonna join up for a few months—it's good money."

"I cain't."

"Why not, boy?"

"My daddy would find out."

"Your daddy?! Boy, you better forget 'bout what your Daddy sez."

"I cain't."

Even though I had moved out of Daddy's house, there was no way that I could've signed up with the Foots in Pine Bluff and Daddy not know about it. No way, no how. There was a network of the churchy folks, and word would have gotten to Daddy quick that his son was down there with all them fast women. Elmo must have sensed my gut grinding and my sadness 'cause he said, "Boy, forget Pine Bluff—we'll take the bus down to Port Gibson and try out there. Your daddy won't know nothin' 'bout it. If it don't work out, I'll put you back on the bus myself." Today, we Christian folk talk a lot about the favor of God. And I believe in that. I also know God chooses people to bless our lives, and Elmore James was one of those blessings for me.

Elmo, who married before he left to join the navy, lived down in Canton, Mississippi. It was about an hour and a half from Port Gibson, where the Foots were headquartered. The Greyhound bus cost about four dollars. Arriving in Port Gibson, Elmo and me made our way to the Foots' headquarters. Now Elmore's talent was known around. At least to me, who by now really worshiped him.

When we arrived at the Foots' office, there were two or three other people wanting to audition. I placed myself on a wooden bench to the right of the opening slit of the tent. We were all sitting there, and Elmore went in first.

You could hear him singing and he sounded good to me. After one song he popped out of the tent and all the white judges said, "Good job." But they popped back in the tent and I overheard them saying just the opposite: "That was a mess." Their disapproval was harsh. I was stunned. Their negative response repeated itself with the next talent and the next. Now I was scared because I knew for sure I didn't have Elmore's talent—not even close. But I could do the hambone. Hambone is a thing where you sit and slap your thigh, then chest and knee in a quick, catchy but tricky rhythm. The chest, knee, and thigh all have distinct tones, so it mimics drums. There's an art to it, and I was as good as anyone. Putting my guitar down on the floor, I made a split-second decision on how I would audition for the Rabbit Foot Minstrels.

The men emerged from the tent, looked me up and down, and said, "Hey, boy, what you doing here?"

"I'm here to audition, too."

"Sam, come look at this little man; he wants to audition," he said, almost mocking me.

"What do you do?"

"I do lots of things. Play guitar, sing, dance, and more."

Waving his arm, he invited me into the tent. I went into the ham-bone slappin' and singing. After that, I jumped into a dance and quickly stopped and told a joke. My audition was over in less than five minutes. When I stopped, they applauded. "You're hired. Just pull together a three-piece band. But do that hambone thing every show."

I hired Elmo James and some others that were turned down that very same day.

Although I didn't work for the Foots for more than three months, I learned so much about how to hold an audience's attention. The Foots had what television would later call a variety show. The show started with the beautiful, sheer-stocking-wearing chorus line girls. You can't imagine how pretty those sisters were, and they all could sing and dance in sync. Then you had one of the toughest jobs: the comic. He or she had to walk out there—and not tell just funny jokes but tell the absolute funniest jokes. Then a solo dancer and a solo singer. It was an experience of a lifetime. Playing mostly cities in Mississippi and Ala-bama, I was really glad that I had left home. As the youngest thing with the Foots, I would have had a hard time explaining to Daddy and Maw about the scandalously clad girls that I saw and even became close to.

Being a country boy, I wasn't thinking about how the Foots would train me in the fundamentals of entertainment. At thirteen, I was just glad to have a job. As one of the beautiful chorus girls said to me as she rolled her stockings down her long legs:

"Boy, do you love doing this?"

"Oh, yeah."

"Well, that's good, but remember, this is a privilege."

"What do you mean, beautiful?" (Calling her "beautiful" was my first attempt to show her I was a man and not a boy.)

"Getting money for doing what you love."

I would learn later that musicians crowded the boulevard of bro-ken dreams. And to be able to earn money with something that you were gifted to do and enjoy is like winning the lottery. But at my age, I wasn't studdin' about money and music. Money is something that only came from hard labor: picking cotton, shucking sugarcane, slaughter-ing hogs—farm stuff. Earning money from the land is all I knew—and

I deeply believed that this was the only way to feed myself and maybe later a wife and a family. Entertaining folk gave me so much joy it would take me quite a while to equate it with making a living.

Performing with the Foots was fun. I saw how it gave people a release from their daily lives. This carried a joy all its own.

Still, with the money I earned from my short stint with the Rabbit Foot Minstrels, I bought me a new Silvertone guitar out of the Sears & Roebuck catalog. In them days Sears probably sold more guitars to young boys with musical dreams than anybody. They had many models to choose from. But I had to buy what I could afford. They called it a "Grand Concert size flat-top guitar." It had a brown satin finish. They advertised it as having a "sunburst effect." Included was a book of songs, a pick, and an instruction book. The strings were all high off the neck, as it wasn't a good guitar, but it was new and it was mine. It was the first investment I made in myself.

‖‖‖‖‖‖

Despite earning money, I didn't know that some early Rabbit Foot Minstrels performance styles would later be seen as negative. Starting with white folks painting themselves black with burnt cork and big lips—to when Black folks took it over and performed in ways demeaning to our image. But what we must not forget is that the audiences of the Rabbit Foot Minstrels were mostly Black, not white. This meant everything. Entertainment meant for us by us did not carry the negative weight as when other minstrel shows were performed for white audiences. And so many Black entertainers cut their teeth under the Rabbit Foot tent, because it was the only way in. Many became legends, and many I admired. Ma Rainey (the mother of the blues), Bessie Smith, Louis Jordan, Rufus "Funky Chicken" Thomas, and others.

As a boy, I didn't have a clue about the ramifications of the beautiful and ugly history of the minstrel shows. It's a can a worms. But here's the big truth about it: every Black person who sings, dances, or tells a joke for a living with a smile on their face is playing into a stereotype. Why? Because the smiling Black entertainer is at the core—literally in the DNA—of American entertainment culture. It deserves to be examined by people much smarter than me.

But just like we invented jazz . . .

And just like we invented rock 'n' roll . . .

We also invented, through the minstrel shows, the modern-day entertainment structure. Minstrelsy became Black vaudeville. Black vaudeville became white vaudeville. And along with my Jewish brothers and sisters, white vaudeville stars like Jack Benny, Abbott and Costello, Bob Hope, Burns and Allen, and a thousand others, became the stars of early movies and television.

And I'm a product of that tradition.

The greatest of the great entertainers honed their craft with the minstrel shows. Many of them did it all—sang, danced, played an instrument, and told a joke. These talents are at the very heart of American entertainment culture. And I ain't studdin' anyone who judges through a 2021 lens the women and men who took the stage in the Rabbit Foot show. The Black vaudeville world was the most important bridge for Blacks in the South to learn how to become professionals. Probably the greatest one-man entertainment powerhouse of a generation, Sammy Davis Jr., got his start in Black vaudeville. Sammy's gifts and hard work personified much of the talent needed to succeed in Black vaudeville.

Sammy could spin like a ballet-trained dancer.

He could also tap dance as good as anyone.

He could sing as good as anyone.

He could play the drums like nobody's business.

He was one of the greatest impersonators of our time.

So he was Gregory Hines, Michael Jackson, Art Tatum, and Rich Little rolled into one, and he came out of the Black vaudeville world.

I've Gotta Name

After my time spent with the Foots, I had a new confidence in my ability to entertain. And I was proud of it. I had a lot of energy, and I still felt that I hadn't fully shown what I was capable of. The world hadn't seen me at full tilt—with my energy point-blank and wide open. I caged up all this juice inside of me. It couldn't hold back for too long, as I felt like a volcano waiting to spray its hot lava everywhere. People could feel it as I was now becoming that boyish face with a guitar walking around Pine Bluff, Arkansas. Folks kept saying to me, "Slow down, boy," as I always had a vibe like I was in a hurry to get something done.

Feeling a little more comfortable with who I was and who I wanted to be, I realized that I did not want Emmett Ellis Jr. to be confused with Rev. Emmett Ellis Sr. Daddy's shadow was large. And the places I knew I would have to hang out in were places where a man of God's name should not be heard, talked about, or, God forbid, seen. I needed a new name.

All the blues and early R&B stars had names that were hooky. Little Richard, Muddy Waters, Big Joe Turner, Howlin' Wolf, and others. I knew nothing about what syllables were, but I knew I wanted a name that flowed together as one word.

In 1950, no other name flowed as one word like PresidentEisenhower. Those seven syllables sounded like one powerful word. So I thought of naming myself TrumanRoosevelt. Good idea, but it wasn't cool. Thought about Emmett Rush, T. B. Rush, or Clearwater Rush, as I was always rushing somewhere, so that seemed to fit my vibe. All

I wanted was something that had a groove and a pop to it. I wanted a sound in my name, so when you heard it, it felt like T-Bone Walker. My older cousin Bobby, who was as wild as a tornado, had died young because of his hot head. I always liked his name. But Bobby was so common—it didn't have a ring to it. But when I added Rush to it—that felt right. And Bobbyrush definitely felt like one word. I had that name in my head for months before I started telling people that I was Bobby Rush. To this day almost everyone glues my first and last name together as one. No Bobby. No Rush. Just Bobbyrush.

Going to a House Party

I started playing house parties as Bobby Rush. Just me, my guitar, my harmonica, and my big-ass feet. You gotta be a magnetic and powerful man to sit down with people talking and drinking around you to command their attention.

The world gets the wrong idea of what the blues is. They like to think that it's just some Negro picking his guitar and hollering. That's not even close to the truth. The blues is shy and simple. But to do it well requires an incredible amount of unique skills. How to get an audience up, then take them higher. How to bring an audience down, then take them lower. How to make them shake their hips and how to make them think. How to make them laugh and how to make them cry.

One of the first house parties I played was in Ladd, Arkansas, about ten miles southeast of Pine Bluff. This wasn't the Apollo Theater in New York, but tonight this was the Apollo to me. This was it. My proving ground. They had about a ten-inch-high, four-foot by five-foot wooden platform that raised me slightly above the crowd. I started my show by just stomping my big feet and playing harmonica. Within a few minutes everybody was facing me. By the time I launched into my first song with my guitar, all you could hear was me singing at the top of my lungs, strumming my guitar very hard and the scratchy sound of people sliding across the dusty wood floor in hard-heeled shoes. Them folks' raspy sliding had a swing to it—a beat. But it was a swing I was creating. That was a mighty powerful feeling. Along with the snapping of fingers and clapping popping in and out, the combination of sound filled the room with a groove. I was swinging and so were they. Couldn't have been over twenty-five or thirty people there. But to me, as I looked over the dancing and bopping heads of the crowd, it might as well have been a thousand folks. This was a house party, but the scene wasn't too different from the juke joints that I would perform in for the next seventy years.

Juke

The good Lord had planted me in the right place. For Pine Bluff, Arkansas, had lots of juke joints. There was Sturdik's, the Elks Lodge, Drum's, Nappy's, the Jack Rabbit, and Jitterbug, where I got to first know Elmo James. In the early '50s some juke joints had improved in the way they looked, while others looked like they hadn't been touched since Negroes built them. Some didn't even have indoor toilets.

Most of the jukes in Pine Bluff couldn't hold more than a hundred people. Many were in the woods, off the beaten path. This was so the bootlegging and gambling and—sometimes—prostitution could take place freely. 'Cause the four Bs—the blues, booze, broads, and booty (money, not boo-tay)—were the magical mixture of people spending their paychecks, and that was the lifeblood of the juke joint hustle.

Still, music being the central attraction for most, we Black folks raised Cain to get into the juke joints. With delicious music, there was a feelin' in the air of livin' it up. Everybody is enjoying everybody else. Men picked up women and women picked up men. Some people were fully liquored up, and some just a little tipsy.

Segregation was a way of life for us. But in juke joints we fixed onto being segregated. Being in the thick of ourselves with our own groove. The sights and sounds, the tastes and smells, were ours and ours alone. There was freedom in these places. But it doesn't mean that jukes couldn't get rowdy, especially on the weekends after payday.

||||||||||

But I would make a name for myself at Nappy's and at a jumping spot in Altheimer, Arkansas, called the Busy Bee Cafe. Nappy's was the first place I performed with a band, a microphone, and an amplifier. Just a drummer, upright bass player, and me. Nappy's sat behind a big old sawmill. And like most juke joints, it didn't look like anything from the outside. Just a frame dwelling with a front door and a back door. No windows. There were three of us, each paid 75 cents along with a plate of chitlins, a hot dog, and a hamburger. I sold my chitlins and my hamburger for 50 cents and ate my hot dog. I had $1.25. I was happy.

In my first gig at Nappy's I was just that teenager with personality that could get the house goin'. Even though I was playing 90 percent of every song I knew in the same key, with a hard-finger-playing bassist and a drummer who could really snap, we grooved. And I played enough of the hits of the day to keep the party going. Louis Jordan's "Saturday Night Fish Fry" and "Caledonia," Johnny Otis's "Double Crossing Blues" and "Cupid's Boogie." I blazed through Charles Brown's classic "Trouble Blues" and Memphis Slim's "Messin' Around." Those were great party songs. And with a few of my own ditties thrown in, I had a pretty bouncin' set.

But this was late 1951, and there was one song that came out earlier in the year that I had to play in my set. And that was "Rocket 88" by Jackie Brenston & His Delta Cats. But for all intents and purposes, this was an Ike Turner record. It was his band and, although not credited, he wrote the song. That record changed everything. Most people say "Rocket 88" is the first rock 'n' roll record, but as Ike Turner told me repeatedly for over forty years, "Bobbyrush, everybody knows that that's a damn R&B record."

R&B was very boogie-woogie influenced early on. But in terms of what they then called pop or popular music, that boogie-woogie sound was the opposite of the very calm and stuffy hit parade tunes. Hell, the big pop hits of 1951 were songs like "The Tennessee Waltz" by Patti Page, "Too Young" by Nat Cole, and "If" by Perry Como.

"Rocket 88" just turned the world upside down. Just like ten years before when the snap and pop of the jump blues sound swept young folks off their feet. The distorted guitar and sexual innuendo dripping from "Rocket 88" was too much for young Black and white kids to take.

You felt that shit in your bones. It made you horny in a way that wasn't all sexual. It had heat. It was literally a fresh feeling when I played that song from the stage. But no one could deny the smokin' energy of "Rocket."

I took Boyd Gilmore's advice when he said, "You gotta git, boy," and made it my religion. I went to every gig by every artist I could in Pine Bluff and the surrounding area. Saw everybody. From guys performing on the street to stars performing at big nightclubs and the little juke joints. I would do a lot of soaking at the Townsend Park Recreation center, or, as everybody called it, "Big Rec."

Big Joe Turner was the first artist I saw at the Big Rec. This was before he had his hit record with "Shake, Rattle & Roll." But he had popular songs everybody knew, like "Piney Town Blues." Most of his grooves were boogie-woogie, and back then that was irresistible—you couldn't help but bop your head. People that didn't (or couldn't) dance would just wiggle their first finger in time as he sang. The boss of the blues was light-skinned like me and had a flawless slicked-back haircut. He looked to be three hundred pounds or more. Joe Turner wasn't an outrageous performer; he just stood there and pointed every once in a while. But his voice was so commanding you couldn't help but to focus on him. And when he'd stretch both of his arms far out to his side, he looked like a giant T. Big Joe was so big—it was as if he was wrapping the entire room up in his outstretched arms. I immediately copied that move into my performances. I also tried to copy something else.

To get my hair like his.

As all the people were filing out of the Townsend Park Rec, I struck up a conversation with a lady who had the baddest hair in the joint. A big and shiny pressed curl on the top of her head, with a white thin sash wrapped around by the back of her ears and tied into a large bow at the top of her hair. In the back, her hair was long and hot-combed smooth into big wavy curls down her neck. She was clearly older than me, and I don't know if she thought I wanted to get with her when I said, "How can I get my hair like Big Joe Turner?"

"Let me tell you what to do, handsome. Go get you some Tuxedo Club Pomade, it comes in a little red can. Get a hard brush, a soft brush, and a stocking cap. Before you go to bed, brush your hair straight

to the back with the hard brush, then put a about the size of a quarter dab of pomade in your hand and rub it together till it thins out.
Rub it all over your head, especially on the sides. Then with the soft
brush, brush your hair straight back and as much as you can. Put on the
stocking cap before you go to bed. Do that every night for a week and I
guarantee you'll have them waves like Joe Turner."

The lady stranger was right. I hadn't conked my hair yet, but the
side of my hair was wavy. More time in front of the mirror. I looked
good.

Mud, Walter, and Jimmy

After Big Joe Turner, the next person I saw at the Big Rec was Jimmy Reed. His performance had a profound effect on me. I had never heard a group that had Jimmy Reed's band's feel. There was a mysterious chemistry between the drummer, bassist, and guitarist. They were playing behind the beat—almost dragging—but it was still tight as a tick and hypnotizing. Ya couldn't help but fall under the spell of that feel. A few years later, in 1957, you'd hear that vibe on one of his signature songs, "Honest I Do."

But it cost me only 75 cents to change my life. 'Cause that was the ticket price to see Muddy Waters at the Big Rec. Little Walter was in his band. Muddy, with that moon face and twisted mouth, sang from the Rec stage like he was trying to tell me something. Raising his eyebrows high and low while he sang, he really let his band shine. Often he'd look at one of his musicians and say, "Play that thing, boy." With Little Walter blowin' that harp right behind him, he gave praise up a lot. Like most young musicians, you learn by watching others. I soaked up every one of Muddy's musicians that night. Going back and forth with my eyeballs, I was a sponge. And I would do a lot of soppin' first time I saw Muddy Waters.

After seeing some greats perform at the Big Rec, my dreams felt possible. Because there they were, standing right in front of me. The greats came down to earth. What remained in outer space was recording and songwriting. I wanted to know more. And in my case, that was the basics. I started to listen to music, more like a doctor examining a patient. I checked out the lyrics. I learned what sets the verse apart from the hook, word-wise. I was figuring out what made great guitar riffs and the power of repetition that created a bass line. Still, I just kept putting my pennies together, working little jobs, and booking little gigs. From gig to gig I went, just trying to survive. This sounds crazy, but I didn't know what I was doing—but somehow I knew what I was doing.

This was 1952, right before the dam burst with what would be the birth of rock 'n' roll. But don't get it twisted. As Ike Turner and a hundred other Negro musicians would soon say to me: that rock 'n' roll is nothin' but R&B.

The Kid

"I don't give a rat's ass how much that nigger lost," said Old Folk. Then two men threw a drunk man right out the front door of Jitterbug, where he landed facedown in a puddle. The top dog at Jitterbug was a guy everybody called Old Folk. I didn't know why they called him that, cause he was a little guy—almost like a midget. But he ran everything for Jitterbug. The gambling room, money box, and problems with cats who got too drunk too early. Despite his size and who owned the Jitterbug, he was the HNIC (head nigger in charge).

Old Folk knew my age and would let me in through the back door. Lookin' back at it, Jitterbug didn't probably give a damn one way or the other—they just knew I could entertain folk, and that was my way in. And as I said earlier, that was the lifeblood of the jukes. But I knew I was a minor and probably a little paranoid, so I didn't want to take any chances.

One of the few pictures I have of myself as a young musician is me holding my guitar behind my head like Jimi Hendrix would make famous years later. But this was 1952, and I was copycatting T-Bone Walker. Still being that sponge. His moves were unique to the blues. He could do a full leg split (with his guitar) where his crotch would be all the way down to the floor. Nightclubs would plaster pictures of him in various gyrations on light poles when he was coming to town.

Every musician and entertainer that came through the Negro neck of the woods of the Bluff, I tried to bend their ear. I would learn much from the voices of those entertainers and especially their musicians. Got to understand more about what I would later know as the Chitlin

Circuit. Got to know the power of the promoters and bookers. Got to know the power of the Arkansas blues scene. Pine Bluff, Hot Springs, Little Rock, and Helena were the Arkansas entertainment loop. If you played in one of those four cities, you probably played in them all. There were many joints for Negroes to play and—just as important— places to stay on the Arkansas swing.

My entertainment loop was in the juke joints and nightclubs in and around Pine Bluff; I was now that kid performer everyone knew. Even though I was underage, I was hanging out every moment I could. Just like at Jitterbug, it got to where doormen would just let me in. As the American Express commercial says, "Membership has its privileges," and I was a member in the fraternity of musicians. I was the local kid who had talent and was proud of it.

Benefits of Being a Bullshitter

I had a first cousin, Curtis, who was a foreman for GWL Construction. They were expanding the Pine Bluff Arsenal and needed men. He gave me a job. They started me at 56 cents an hour, but that was upped to 75 cents when they saw I was good with my hands. I've always talked a good game, so when the foreman (not my cousin) asked if I could lay bricks, I said sure. (I ain't never laid a brick in my life.)

He told me to pick up where this other guy had left off. I said, "Mane, I gotta run home. I think I left somethin' on the stove." I was lying—I hadn't left anything. I clocked out, came back around, and watched them bricklayers. Saw how they mixed the mortar, which was two to one—two parts sand to one part mortar. That was easy, but since my mouth was bigger than my skill, I also told the man I was a corner man—which was the hardest thing to do. A corner man got paid more 'cause he could lay corners of a building or steps, and the other guys were line men, who filled in the bricks in between the corners.

There's only one way to lay bricks, and that's perfectly. Well, I screwed up them corners mighty bad. Still thinking I fooled the man, I was feeling good until he pulled me aside and said, "You lyin' son of a bitch. You ain't no motherfuckin' corner man—you told me you could lay sum damn brick—hell, I don't even know if you're even a motherfucking line man." He stopped. He was cussing me out with such gusto, he had to catch his breath. He pulled out his white handkerchief from his back pocket and wiped the beads of sweat from his forehead. With his hands now on his hips, he took a few seconds to stare me down.

Then he smiled and said, "But somebody that got your basketball-size balls? I need you 'round here. I'm gonna make you a foreman."

I've bullshitted my way a few times in life, but this was one time where I was promoted because of my bullshit. This was one of the best things for me, as it was perfect for my God-given gifts—and that I learn very fast. I learned not only to lay corner brick from the guys under me, I also learned to lay brick around a chimney pipe—in a circle. But my learning didn't stop there. I was always handy. But with GWL Construction, I got the know-how of plumbing and electrical work—all because I wanted to. One old boy asked me one day, "Man, why you learnin' all that stuff we ain't never gonna work on?" I said, "'Cause I just wanna know how to do shit."

I was making forty-nine dollars a week. I gave my daddy thirty dollars a week. Yes, I wasn't living at home, but I knew Daddy needed it. It was a pattern I would continue for the rest of his life.

PART 2

PART 2

Chicago, by Way of Memphis

Where I come from, age was nothing but a number. Girls sometimes married at thirteen or fourteen, and some boys struck out on their own in their early teens. I was one of them. A huge turning point came in 1953 when my brother Alvin and his wife moved to Chicago. With my big brother in the Windy City and knowing I had a place to stay, I made plans to get there.

Caught a Greyhound bus headin' for Chicago by way of Memphis in the spring of '53. Think the ride cost me about three dollars. Went to Memphis first because I couldn't afford the entire journey—and I wanted to explore—and I wasn't afraid. Arriving on a Saturday, I had my guitar and a few clothes in a croker sack—I must have looked as country as three dozen brown eggs. I had lots of ambition and even more energy. And I think it was oozing out of me because right there on Beale Street, Rufus Thomas took notice of me.

Taking a quick liking to me, Rufus was old enough to be my daddy, and he led me around like he was. As I told him about myself, he lit up. I told him I had worked for the Rabbit Foot Minstrels. "Boy, I worked for the Foots, too," he said. I didn't know anything about the deep Rabbit Foot Minstrels' history, but I think me being young, Rufus saw me as somebody who wanted to be like him. And looking back, I guess he was as right as rain. Because he saw things in me I couldn't see in myself: my rascally humor, my love of people, and my ability to entertain. And Rufus had all those qualities in spades.

Rufus was a cat who loved people. Felt he could entertain anyone at any time—Black or white. When I met him, he was already a Beale Street legend. He had already put out a record, was an occasional MC at the Palace Theatre, was part of a comedy duo (Rufus and Bones), and had a radio show on WDIA, which was THE station for Negroes in them parts.

But here he was talkin' to me like he had known me forever. "Now, boy, let me show you how to work this thang here." With that, he threw his hat on the sidewalk and started singing and tap dancing, and people just started to drop money in the hat. A small crowd quickly gathered, and before you knew it Rufus had around eight dollars. He said, "Come on, boy," and we walked one street over to Peabody and did the same thing; however, the police quickly came and said, "Move it along." Negroes really couldn't hang on Peabody Street.

I didn't know it then, but Rufus also had a job at a textile mill—a job he kept even after he came up. So it made sense to me, only in my rearview mirror, when he'd said to me, *Ain't no shame in doing what you gotta do to get where you wanna be.* Those are words that would stay with me for the rest of my life.

Once Rufus showed me how to "work that thang," I sang and played my guitar and that got me around six dollars my first day there. Stayed at Hotel Clark right on Beale Street. When we parted, Rufus wrote down on a brown paper bag every phone number he had: the radio station, the textile mill, and his home. I don't think his home number changed in thirty years. I didn't spend more than a day or two with Rufus, but just in that itty-bitty amount of time, he became a close, lifelong friend.

I worked enough to get money to go to St. Louis—really Lovejoy, Illinois, just across the river. Went to this suburb because Albert King told me if I was ever in Lovejoy, to stop by. Lovejoy was a mostly Black town and a small one. So all I had to do was ask a stranger, "Where do Albert King live?" Which is what I did. To show how there was a brotherhood in the blues, Albert King opened his door to me like I was his blood relative. He let me hang with him and play with him on his next gig, right in St. Louis. And he paid me! Had enough to get to Chicago with about fifteen dollars left over.

I would start about a year-and-a-half process of going back and forth between Pine Bluff and Chicago.

Cityfied

I stepped off the silver Greyhound bus in the spring of '53. They stunned me—all these huge buses in this cave. Greyhound had just opened a brand-spanking-new station at Clark and Randolph Streets in the heart of downtown. The buses came and went from this underground dock or cave. As I took the shiny escalator up to the street level, stone columns greeted me with mile-high ceilings. This new station was a huge, open space that looked as big as an indoor football field. In the very center was a circular desk and the shiniest floor I've ever seen. Shops with bright lights and people scurryin' around trying to catch buses to go all across America. No one lollygaggin'. I felt like I had stepped into the future. I felt cityfied.

I made my way to Alvin's doorstep, where he threw open the door and gave me that hug that only a big brother can. I quickly got a job at a gas station where I would make just enough. I first pumped gas. But after two weeks, when I told the owner what I could do, he quickly made me the oil-change guy.

It was a big day when I walked in Sears with Alvin and bought a brand-new Sunburst Silvertone archtop guitar. It had one pickup, which was important because in the blues electric guitar was "where it was at" in 1953. Also got a little Silvertone amp. It was green on the side and beige on the front. The controls were at the rear. My brother was so kind to my dreams. I literally practiced all night long, and I know he and his wife could hear me. He never complained once. Every blue moon he'd tap on my door at three a.m., on his way to the bathroom, and say, "I like that one you just played." Alvin is a true big brother.

At Boyd Gilmore's suggestion, I went down to the legendary open-air market on Maxwell Street. It was called Jewtown by many because of the Jewish immigrants that had establishments there. I loved the go-getting vibe of the people selling and the people buying. No item was too small, big, odd, or ordinary that you couldn't find it. Seemed to me you could buy anything.

They had storefronts with little bandstands where cats would play. In my memory, this end of the street looked slummy. But in my sixteen-year-old heart it felt like heaven. I had met so many bluesmen back in Pine Bluff who talked about getting their hustle on down on Maxwell Street. They said it was wonderful, dangerous, and fun. The only warning Boyd Gilmore ever gave to me was: "Don't hang out at Jerry's, someone always getting cut up there." Jerry's Cozy Shop, smack-dab at the corner of Maxwell and Morgan Streets, was a sketchy place. My first time approaching the joint, some white EMTs were rolling some bleeding Negro lickety-split out on the stretcher. I didn't go in—that night at least.

And even though this was the early 1950s, you didn't hear early R&B on Maxwell Street; you heard mostly Mississippi and Louisiana blues. There were so many good harp players, and when I saw all their hats and tip jars full of coins, I knew I could make some money.

My Fake Cousin Otis

I was a kid, but I was no longer the cute, funny, talented kid from Pine Bluff. I was Bobby Rush, and even though my Illinois driver's license said I was a twenty-year-old named Emmett Ellis, I was really seventeen. I had been calling myself Bobby Rush for some time. Yet after a year in Chicago, I had yet to sit down and talk to who many people thought was my older brother, Otis Rush. He knew who I was, as we were introduced by, I think, Little Walter. I was concerned that he felt I was piggybackin' off his name. There's a rich tradition of that in the blues. There's Washboard Sam and Washboard Willie, Mississippi John Hurt and Mississippi Fred McDowell. There are a ton of Little Somebody This or Little Somebody That. It went on forever.

So when I walked into Lee's Unleaded Blues and saw him, I was a little scared. Lee's didn't have a fancy stage, and like many blues joints it just looked like a vacant brick building from the outside. I got a ginger ale and stood towards the back wall as Otis put his guitar over his head to start his set. As he adjusted the microphone stand, he talked to the audience.

"How y'all feel tonight?" Otis says.

Some folks softly said, "Alright."

"I said, how y'all feel tonight!" Otis said much louder.

They shout loudly, as if to say, "*You have our attention.*"

He then says, "There's a young fella in the house tonight that may be related to me. That is Bobby Rush. Give him a hand y'all." A few people clapped, and Otis counts off his song. That's when I officially, officially, officially became Bobby Rush.

It was like me getting a diploma.

Hazel

Back in 1949 I met Hazel Adams at a school basketball game in Pine Bluff. As far as I was concerned, it was love at first sight. She was tall for a girl, but with high-yellow skin and coal-black hair she could have been a runway model today. So pretty and shapely. Wasn't anything gonna keep me from that. Six or eight months passed before I saw her again at a school dance. We talked the whole night. I can honestly say she strongly attracted me sexually and as a friend. And that was a first.

I wasn't old enough to drive back then, but Daddy would let me take his car on Sunday afternoons after church. But I'd have to have it back by dark. It was nothing but God's grace that I didn't crash or get caught speeding as I drove like a madman to Hazel's home. Picking her up, I'd find a secluded place to park and we fooled around. I wasn't a virgin, but with her I might as well have been, 'cause she stirred up feelings I ain't never had before. In those days, if you felt like Hazel and I felt, you got married. It really helped the whole situation that her parents, Felton and Lulu Adams, really took to me. I was like their son. So after getting settled in Chicago, my first order of business was to catch a Greyhound bus back to Pine Bluff. I got my car fixed; we got married and drove back to Chicago.

When we arrived in Chicago, naturally we moved in with my brother Alvin. He and his wife were gracious enough to let me and my new bride stay with them. I was still finding my way as a provider, and Alvin often brought groceries for us all. I don't think I would be in music today if it wasn't for Alvin. He lovingly put up with so much of my joys and pain of me getting into music.

Howlin' from the Heavens

Daddy taught me biblically, through the Old Testament, that it was an act of superiority to name something. And it was an act of submission to take the name shelled out to you. I know history gets written by the powerful. And white folks were trying really hard to take what we'd cooked up and make it theirs. But the fact remains that the only thing that white folks did to create rock 'n' roll was Alan Freed giving it the name rock 'n' roll. And with white folks being in power in every layer of American society, there was an immense power in that naming.

So even today, I hear their voices screaming in my memories and howlin' from the heavens: the voices of Ike Turner, Big Joe, Little Richard, and they all are shouting the same thing: "It ain't motherfuckin' rock 'n' roll! To hell with that. It's rhythm and blues."

But the change from the name R&B to rock 'n' roll happened so fast.

Less than a year and a half earlier, I was playing only one R&B song in my set. That was "Rocket 88." But by my second official year in Chicago, in late 1955, that had all changed. I was playing songs like "Ain't That a Shame" by Fats Domino, "Maybelline" by Chuck Berry, "Shake, Rattle & Roll" by my friend Big Joe Turner. But it was "I Got a Woman" by Ray Charles that seemed to shake that thing. Moving music forward with its gumbo-like mix of gospel and blues. All them songs were catchy and almost irresistible. All they needed for this good-ass, feel-good, change-your-life music was a white face to sing it.

Then like a dump truck full of clear water, they started dumping in the radio—re-recordings of R&B with white faces. Hoping that dumping that water in the muddy waters of the Mississippi River would turn it clear. But after Chuck Berry, Little Richard showed America how to "do that thang." Only the real funk could satisfy. Imitations couldn't compete with that.

Yeah, I know you'll say it: "Well, it worked out pretty good for Elvis." And you'd be right.

Chitlins

Just like Chicago's windy streets, the blues scene was blowing just as strong. It's hard to explain how much blues music was a part of Chicago back then. Like Nashville is to country music, Chicago was to the blues. When you drove the streets of the West Side or the South Side with your windows down, it was like you were changing the dial on your radio. Different sounds. Different songs. Different voices as you passed by club after club. King Drive, Forty-Third Street, Thirty-Ninth Street, Madison Street, and many more. Hell, on Roosevelt Road I could go there at 11:00 p.m. after I played somewhere else and visit ten spots. I'd sit and watch everybody. Cats who were friends and cats who would become friends. And everybody knew everybody.

I can't tell you how many clubs there were dedicated only to the blues. The greats hung 'round like furniture. Between Green Mill, Lee's Unleaded Blues, Mister Kelly's, Theresa's Lounge, and too many others to mention, I fell into a world of:

Musicians who could play their asses off.
Singers who could sing their asses off.
Songwriters who could write their asses off.
Performers who could entertain their asses off.

I would grow and learn so much from all these talented folk. But the start of my career would not only be in the multitude of clubs in Chicago, I started down a path of working in the same type of joints I had in Pine Bluff. This is where I would make a name for myself. Right

95

in the small and large Black night spots between Chicago and the Mississippi Delta. Joints known for being on the Chitlin Circuit.

The Chitlin Circuit ain't nothin' but a place where we Negroes could go and have a good time. The Circuit is another arm of the Black neighborhood. Along with the little hotels and boardinghouses that we were allowed to stay in, these were places of comfort and retreat. Just like chitlins themselves, where we took the shit-filled colon of the hog that the slave masters threw our way—we cleaned up these venues and seasoned them into a delicacy. These Chitlin Circuit club owners made an oasis for us Black people from all the shit we were taking on the outside world.

White folks had their big theaters, big nightclubs, big country clubs. And what we got? These little places. Down South, some Chitlin Circuit clubs weren't anything more than a nice shack. So in the refuge of these Chitlin Circuit clubs, you got the uncut funk of Blackness. Who we were, who we are—and, ironically, all the spirit that white folks wanted from us: our music, our resilience, our heart, and our soul.

Today I'm called "The King of the Chitlin Circuit." And I'm proud of what that means in terms of me being a survivor. But apart from that, I always felt that whoever cooked up the name "Chitlin Circuit" got it wrong. And I'm capitalizing *Chitlin Circuit* to amplify that they got it wrong. "Chitlin Circuit" sounds like you are sneering at it—something low-class, something you're disparaging. And by making it low-class, it makes the circumstances that made it all happen sound dirty.

And it wasn't. It wasn't dirty at all.

How can you think of something dirty that gave to the world the best art the good old U.S. of A. has ever produced? Outta them Chitlin joints—big and small—you got to see the talent, the faces, the personalities of Count Basie, Little Richard, John Lee Hooker, Duke Ellington, B.B. King, and others. What they now call American treasures. But at one time, those American treasures could play nowhere but for us Black folk.

I think we have forgotten that in so many cities we were just trying to be seen as legitimate men and women—human, if you will. And in these places that belonged just to us, it was akin to our Sunday mornings at church—no white folk around. And just like the church where we could freely praise the Lord, the Chitlin Circuit nightspots were where we could praise our talent, celebrate our humor, and tell our stories to one another. Occasionally throwing in a few devils like drinkin' and sex, these joints strengthened us to fight another day—we needed the release. These were places where you got support and love. Where you could have a funky good time. To make the most out of your life. If we didn't have that, I don't know what would have happened to us.

White Devils, Green Money

Thanks to the television, the world was just starting to see how devilish white folks could be against Black folks. And not just in the South. For all the Negroes in Chicago, just outside town, you'd think you could have been in Birmingham, Alabama. In '51, two years before I moved there, a mob of over three thousand people tried to block a family from moving into an apartment in Cicero about twenty miles outside of town. When they moved in, they stormed the family home, threw their shit out the window, and burned all their belongings. A riot broke out and the governor called in the National Guard—it was one of the biggest riots in America for a while. Not in Mississippi, not in Alabama, but in the 'burbs of Chi-town. That family, the Clarks, a WWII vet and his two kids and beautiful wife, didn't spend one motherfucking night in Cicero.

Bobby Rush and the Four Jivers played in those Chi-town burbs and even joints farther away. The farther away you got, the more white it was, and with that came more problems. Again, just like the South. When you were down there in Mississippi, Alabama, or Texas, even in 1955, you had to know the places to stop that would serve us food or motels to spend the night. You didn't want to stop over in some off-the-beaten-track kinda place. If you did, you could land in jail for absolutely nothing or facedown in a ditch if you ran up on the wrong set of evildoers with guns.

About an hour and a half east of Chicago is the tiny town of Mendota. Bobby Rush and the Four Jivers played a three-night stand there.

We could leave after the show and get home to our own beds. Less expense. Less trouble.

On the first night, the all-white patrons were lovin' my music. I was playing some Louis Jordan song, and I guess the groove got to this white man something bad. In a pinstripe suit with a carnation pinned to his collar, he stumbles to the tiny stage and says:

"Goddamn, niggas, y'all sure can play! I love you damn niggas. Goddamn, you black niggas can play!" He was almost having a Holy Ghost experience fueled by the music and the liquor. I just ignored him and went into another song. But my guitar player, Willie James Lyons, wasn't havin' it.

"Man, Rush, I'll handle dis goddamn cracker for you," Willie whispers to me on the stage.

"Mane, be cool. Let's just get through the gig and we go," I said.

"He better shut the fuck up—I 'on't care where we is."

"You want yo' five dollars and fifty cents?" I said.

Willie chilled. He damn sure wanted his $5.50, and I wanted my $7.00 as band leader. Willie James Lyons was a hell of a guitar player and a bit of a rebel. We was all conkin' our hair, and don't think I ever saw Willie without a neat, natural afro. But Willie had another pride thing going on that night, too. His wife was sitting in the front row—and she was as white as Ivory soap. So on this night, the word "nigga" cut him even more.

After we played some song that got to this pudgy white man again, he said, almost with tears in his eyes, "Niggas, play that shit again." But this time he puts something in my left jacket pocket. I knew it was a paper bill and assumed it was a dollar. That was enough for me to crank up his favorite again (remember, I'm making $7.00 a night). Again he cried out, "Goddamn, niggas, y'allz can sure play that damn music! I love you niggas." And he keeps putting more dollars in my pocket. He did this about four more times.

At the end of the Friday night gig, I pull out the crushed-up bills in my side pocket. Looking down, I untangle the cash and see hundred-dollar bills. I quickly straightened out the cash and I've got five hundred motherfuckin' dollars! I ain't never seen that kinda money in one night in my life. Saturday night, same thing! Now I got me around $800.

I never told the guys what I got, but on Sunday afternoon I gave them each $100. Willie was especially overjoyed. Happy to where when we were playing the last night there, he saw the nigger-lovin' white moneyman over there playing pool. The cat was into his game, hard. Had his jacket off and you could tell he was really tryin' to beat this cat. And after we go through his three favorite songs, Willie can't hold it in any longer. He jumps to my microphone and calls out to the moneyman at the pool table, "Hey, the niggas is over here playin'!" Willie was trying to get that money.

What a difference a night makes.

Heard and Not Seen

In rural Illinois I got an offer to play a gig by a friend of mine, J. B. Lenoir in Harvey, Illinois, just outside of the city. J. B. had a regional hit on his hands with a ditty called "Eisenhower Blues." But old Ike was so popular that no white folk wanted to hear nothing disparaging about Ike. His label made him re-record the thing as "Tax Paying Blues."

J. B. was a politically minded cat—white folks shied away from him. So when he offered me this gig, I suspected there was a catch, but I didn't care. I was gonna make eight dollars after I paid the band.

But there *was* a catch. A racial one. We had to play behind a curtain. This was one of those small theater-like joints that had two heavy velvet curtains. We played there for three nights and I guess we'd impressed the man. He said on our last night that he was gonna introduce the band. They opened the curtain; we took a full bow, and they shut that thing so fast—by the time we were coming up to stand straight, we felt the wind of that heavy velvet curtain clamping shut. The white folks couldn't stomach looking at our brown faces for too long. We were to be heard—not seen.

Sober Living

Jimmy Reed knew me from his many visits to Pine Bluff. I was that kid who just wanted to hang around the cats, and he was nice to me. Mostly every story (*including mine*) you'll hear about Jimmy Reed is about him being drunk. However, I ain't proud that I cheated Jimmy one time. He gave me a dollar to get him a little bottle. A pint of liquor wasn't but 50 or 60 cents. Sending me back to the store three or four times this night, I started cutting his liquor with water—saving the real thing to sell to him later. I made almost 50 cents by the time we ended the night. Again, I ain't proud of it. 'Cause there were other cats who cheated Jimmy waaaay more—getting him to pay for big shit twice, takin' his pocket money.

Still, Jimmy was my boy. He showed me a few guitar tricks. He had hit records but was exploited by his inability to read. Chuck Berry, Elvis, Tina Turner, and others covered his songs. I'm sure someone is re-recording one of his songs for some commercial right now. I hope whoever is supposed to be getting Jimmy's royalties is getting them. And not some grandchild of some dirty-dealing white man, because some motherfucker who didn't have a damn thing to do with Jimmy's songs was the one who stole them.

Jimmy was a whiskey-head for sure. But on the blues scene, everybody drank. Young and old. Famous and unfamous. And frankly, Jimmy's drinking didn't bother me until I saw the toll it took on his face. Seeing him as a boy in Pine Bluff, he seemed so vibrant, so bright-eyed and bushy-tailed. But as time went on, he was like a big flashlight that when you leave it on, it just gets dimmer and dimmer and dimmer.

Even in my world of the blues joints and bars, nobody ever gave me grief for not drinking or drugging. And I ain't never fake drunk either, pouring two fingers of ginger ale in my glass to act like it was whiskey. My deep feeling about getting drunk was always that I didn't want anything to rob my energy. But as time went on, I stayed dry for an old-fashioned reason, too: "Don't Start No Shit—Won't Be None." None of my crowd called me out for being a stick-in-the-mud or a fuddy-duddy—and many would grow to respect it. Bobby "Blue" Bland said something to me late in his life that surprised me.

"You know, Bobbyrush—you dun saved a million dollars."

"Then why don't I have half?" I said in my joking way.

"Seriously, I'm tryna tell you something."

"Sorry, Bland; go ahead."

"By not buying all that dope and spending half your life looking for it—you dun saved a million dollars!"

Looking back, I think my country-boy way of talking gave me some blues cred or, I dare say, a drunk cred. I was cool with everybody—they saw me as one of them. 'Cause when they were drunk I laughed just as hard, cut the fool, and told just as many jokes as they did. But I was as cold sober as a Sunday-school teacher on Sunday morning.

The Bottle, Papa Charley, Daddy, and Me

I can't say for sure what made me remain clean when I was a boy. But I remember an incident in Pine Bluff back in 1950 that may have cemented me from not tilting the bottle.

We called Daddy's father Papa Charley. Even Daddy called him Papa Charley. He had all his hair—only one tooth missing. Had eighteen children by one woman. He always carried a loaded WWI-era Colt .45 pistol. Papa Charley wasn't more than one hundred and fifty pounds wet. The biggest thing on him was that gun and his big-ass feet—that I gratefully inherited. I always remember that when he'd visit and have breakfast, after he was done eatin' he'd take his buttered hands and wipe his face for lotion. Now, Papa Charley drank wine or whiskey seven days a week—so he always had a bottle with him. Wasn't a secret to us kids 'cause that's the way we always knew him.

Papa Charley turned ninety in 1950, and Daddy wanted to give him a birthday party. So we milked the cows and churned an extra amount of butter, as Papa Charley loved him some of Maw's biscuits with tons of butter. Maw cooked a spread, and Daddy invited all his preaching and church buddies over for the celebration. They came out of respect for Daddy.

With the table prepared almost in a way I had never seen it, these church elders stood to say grace. Only problem was, Papa Charley wasn't there.

"Papa Charley, we's waiting on you," Maw said.

"I'z coming."

He plops himself down while everybody else is standing. We were waiting for Papa Charley to say grace over the food. I know Maw and Daddy wanted him to stand. But at ninety years old, I guess they said it was okay. Now all of us kids knew Papa Charley was tipsy. Still, he managed to say some kind of blessing, and all those preachers sat down. Maw said, "Y'all go 'head and help yourself." But with it being Papa Charley's birthday, we waited for him to get his food. Maw had a big bowl of butter sitting right in front of Papa Charley. The butter had softened in the late summer heat. Papa Charley grabbed a big serving spoon and with one quick motion raised that spoon high and came down in that soft butter smack-dab in the middle—like he was splitting a log of wood. The butter splattered up high. Maw quickly cleaned the mess up and said to Papa Charley, "Now, Papa, just take a lil' bit of the butter from the end." Papa Charley then announces in front of all those preachers:

"Why in the hell iz I gonna start out at da end when I'm going to eat all the motherfucking butter up anyway."

Of course, Daddy and Maw were rattled, but we kids weren't—and we had the tiniest chuckle we could muster. We had to hold it in— not embarrass Daddy or Maw any more than they already were. But as startled as those country preachers were, they took it in stride. 'Cause in the country, who ain't got a relative that loves the bottle? Also, the food in front of them was too enticing for them to focus on anything else. But when Daddy left the table that afternoon, he glanced at me with this look. It was not a look of shame or embarrassment. But it was a look.

I know for sure that Daddy loved Papa Charley, as he always made him feel special when he moseyed up to our door. Still, what was the message of Daddy's look? Looking back, I think it was a look of tenderness and regret. I think he saw how vices, although they can bring you joy, can cut you down. Daddy never said a word to me about Papa Charley's drinking or what today we call alcoholism. All I know is that not long after Papa Charley's party, Daddy stopped smoking, using snuff, and chewing tobacco.

Maybe nuff said.

Integrate? What's That?

"I'm willing to do whatever has to be done to survive" was my motto.

I went down to Bourbon Street Bar, located right there in the heart of Rush and Walton Streets where there were several clubs. Bourbon Street was a burlesque and cabaret club. Big joint with a big stage for the girls and a pit in front of the stage for the band. However, they had a big sign out front that said No Colored Allowed. Knowing this already, I went in with three white guys and auditioned, as they always needed musicians. I showed out. All the folks that were there early in the day—cleaning crew, bartenders—applauded. They hired me on the spot. The guy in charge of things was this stocky Asian man named Kunch.

Kunch took a liking to me and said to me after my audition, "Bobby Rush, this gonna be great, 'cause we finally are going to integrate this place! See ya Wednesday."

As a country boy, I didn't know what the word *integrate* meant.

I arrived with my real band—three Black guys—and I strolled in, making my way across the club to the band pit. Kunch dashed towards me and said, "Where's the band?" I said, This is the band, pointing to my three Black guys. He said, "Oh no, no, no, no, we can't integrate that far. When I said integrate, I meant just you—you and the white guys."

There's that word again that I don't know—*integrate*.

It was quarter to nine, and show time was in fifteen minutes. Kunch just started rubbing his head from front to back, back to front. There was no time for me to get any other guys. He looked in pain. He paced a few steps back and forth. He said with some anger, "Just get in the pit—just get in the pit. I gotta figure this out."

This was a burlesque house. So the girls had an hour-long set. But they divided it amongst twelve girls. One set of four girls had fifteen minutes, then another set had fifteen, and so on. The band played for the girls for the full hour, then we played an hour-long set in the pit, giving the ladies an hour break.

Kunch said, "This is what we gonna do. Bobbyrush, you call those white musicians that you auditioned with—and tell them to get their asses down here by the second hour of the show."

So that was the plan: my Negro band would play the first hour with the girls, and then I'd swap them out for the white guys. I don't know why Kunch let me, a Negro, play and lead the band. Well, I was yellow, so maybe he thought I was Creole or some blendation. There was a strikingly beautiful showgirl, an Italian woman with short dark hair and the most shapely plump legs in the world. She grabbed me and pulled me into the dressing room. She said, "Boy, we gonna integrate this place tonight!" Now I really started to feel good about this word *integrate*. I thought integrate meant, like, I was going to make out with this woman!

Anyway, she said, "Look, I'm gonna get sick and cut my last set short. That way you'll have a chance to show your stuff—alright?"

So just as the beautiful dancer promised, she left the stage early. And I jump on the stage, leaving the band in the pit. I go into my gyrations and do my best version of Chuck Berry. The crowd went wild—they ain't never seen a Negro, even a high-yellow one show his stuff in the Bourbon Street Cabaret. Needless to say, I never called the white musicians.

It's 2 a.m. And on the loudspeaker comes a command: "Bobby Rush, Bobby Rush, come to the office." So I figured they were gonna fire me for my antics—but I didn't care 'cause I knew they were still gonna pay me and the band for the night.

When I entered the office, on one side of the door there was a guy with a machine gun. On the other side of the door, there was a heavyset guy with a bald head and a .45 strapped to his side. Sitting behind the desk, there was a wide gentleman with a fat stogie in his mouth.

He said in a low, scratchy voice, "Hey, boy, you afraid of me?"

"Oh, no sir," I replied.

He then told the two menacing-looking guards, "Hey, you guys, go. Go. Go. This kid is okay."

"Sit down, kid, sit down." He waddled from behind his desk and slapped me on the knee and sat down.

Laughing a little, he said, "I like you, kid; you alright. You got nerve. You got real nerve trying to integrate my place."

There's that word I don't know again—*integrate*.

Then he picked up his big black rotary dial phone and said, "Kunch, Kunch, come in here." Kunch came in the office, and the wide gentleman said, "This is my kid, okay. Okay. You don't pay him. I pay him 'cause he got nerve." Giving me his card, he said, "Kid, you take a my card—you wanta anything, you come see me, okay?"

I found out later that I was working for the Chicago Mob and didn't even know it. But they took care of me 'cause I was workin' there four—sometimes five—days a week. And I was only one of two Negroes that were working as musicians on Rush and Walton Streets.

JB

In 1957, I was making $7.50 a night at a joint called Walton's Corner. That was top dollar for me. Walton's Corner had a gigantic neon sign in the shape of a T, with WALTON's in the top of the T and CORNER in the stem of the T. With SHOWPLACE written at the bottom, it was impressive-looking for the neighborhood it was in. That bright sign stuck out like a church steeple. It was one of the better blues spots around. In the fall, I invited Sonny Thompson over to my show. He loved it. I was just hitting my stride with a show that was well paced with just the right number of blues, slow songs, and early R&B hits. I wanted to impress Sonny 'cause he was kinda like the Chicago hookup to King and Federal Records based in Cincinnati.

"Bobby Rush, man, I been telling James (Brown) about you. I'm bringing him tomorrow night."

I was excited. James Brown had not become James Brown yet, as in the Godfather of Soul, but music folks knew him far and wide as a dynamic performer—with some badass hair and a badass band. "Please, Please, Please" was out on Federal Records—but it wasn't that big signature song of his yet. James showed up with two other cats from his Famous Flames band. The drinks were flowing and the conversation lively. After my set, James only had one question. "Bobby Rush, what do you put in your hair?" I said, "A little bit ah conk and a little bit ah love!" Everybody fell out laughing.

Sonny Thompson always knew I was seeking some kinda break— maybe even to get on King Records. So in trying to be a big shot that night, I told the bartender that I would buy a round of drinks for them.

My happiness was short-lived, for I found out that James had put three more rounds on my tab. My bill was $112. It would take me months to pay back Mr. Walton. That pissed me off. Real bad. When I saw James, maybe a few days later, I said, "Mane, y'all put me in a trick Saturday night." I didn't threaten him, but I was trying to squeeze some sympathy and maybe some money out of him. James said only one sentence to me.

"Mane, if you can't stand the heat, get out of the kitchen." He laughed.

"What do that mean?"

"Mane, if you can't stand the heat, get out of the kitchen." He laughed some more.

But it wasn't funny to me. Not at all.

Years passed and I guess I opened for James Brown maybe ten or twelve times, and we became friends (not close friends, but friends). We talked about remaining as independent as possible. And women. James had lost two or three fortunes over his career to the usual suspects: poor management and, of course, the old favorite, the IRS. In 1968, the IRS said James owed them $2 million.

Fast-forward to 1991. James was getting ready to be released from prison. He served three years of what was a six-year stretch for aggravated assault and running from the cops. Pervis Spann, who was his friend and all-around good guy, came to me with a proposition. We would produce "James Brown's First Show" out of a prison in Atlanta, Georgia. It required us to put up $30,000. Fifteen from me, fifteen from Pervis. I didn't have money, so I went to the bank to borrow it. If we filled up a little more than half the venue, we'd be in good shape. I could double my money—easy.

But James screwed us, and I lost my shirt. I felt stupid—so motherfuckin' stupid. When I called James, he said, "Mane, if you can't stand the heat, get out of the kitchen." The same line he had said to me thirty-four years earlier. I lost my respect for him after that—because he showed me no mercy at all. Maybe he shouldn't have—hell, I put up my own money, and in 1991 I should have known better. As the years passed and the sting of that lesson wore off, I do have fonder memories of James. He would always say, "There's only one James Brown and there's only one Bobby Rush. So don't do me, just do you."

I knew in life that sometimes you're the windshield and sometimes you're the bug. Still, I always took chances—flying close to the edge. I called it having hope or investing in myself. But hope can be like a hen that lays too many eggs. Losing that bread over James Brown was a hard motherfucking lesson. I would have to learn to take chances on things I had more control over. And the only thing I had control over was me.

The Little Rock Talk

In Little Rock, Arkansas, spring comes early and hangs around to fall, which can hold its mild-weather grip till December. On one of those warm fall nights, I think in '56, I got my biggest break so far. A chance to open for Big Joe Turner at the Morocco in Little Rock. Even though this wasn't Chicago, New York, or Kansas City, Little Rock was a Midwest center for the blues. One hundred and thirty miles east you had "Little Chicago," or West Memphis, Arkansas, that was just across the Mississippi from Memphis, Tennessee. Two hours southeast you got Helena, Arkansas, home of KFFA and King Biscuit Time—the most important blues radio show in the South. And just forty miles south you got to my second hometown of Pine Bluff, with its healthy Black population and juke joints.

Black folks called the main drag where we owned the business "The Stroll." There were strolls in damn near every American city that had a lot of us. Ninth Street was the stroll in Little Rock, the bosom to pretty much all the Black nightclubs. And Little Rock had quite a few. The Dreamland Ballroom, the El Dorado, Chez Paris, and The Morocco.

To understand what a big deal this was for me, you gotta understand: B.B. King ain't real big yet, and Chuck Berry's 1955 "Maybelline" was blastin' everywhere. But in '56 my heroes were T-Bone Walker, Louis Jordan, and Big Joe Turner. Just a few years back I'd been at the Big Rec in Pine Bluff, standing at the foot of the stage, looking up and watching Big Joe—now I was opening for him.

As they say, I showed in and showed out. I was doing everything I had learned from the Foots to the jukes of Pine Bluff to the Chicago nightclubs. I played my guitar behind my head like T-Bone Walker. Played more of Louis Jordan that night 'cause with Jordan's music you could always get the crowd going. His songs were irresistible. I also was imitating the new star of rock 'n' roll, Chuck Berry, by doing his duck walk. I got a standing ovation.

"How come I ain't heard of you, boy," Big Joe Turner said to me backstage.

"Well, Mr. Turner, I been around."

"What on earth you mean, 'around'? Where you from—how old is you?"

"I'm twenty-two [I was nineteen], from Pine Bluff—but I live in Chicago now."

"Sit down, boy."

Big Joe's enormous frame was sprawled out in a wood folding chair. Leaning back, his legs spread wide apart—so big and high reachin' that it made his black pants look like curtains as they hung down over his frame. He talked to me for over an hour. Over an hour—that impressed me so. One thing I love about us—if a Black bluesman saw something in you, he wanted to talk to ya. Tell ya something. Leave you with some wisdom. It's a mighty beautiful thing, I tell you. It's a noble tradition of us.

"Rush, you got a thing—make sure you watch your friends."

"I will, sir."

"I don't think you know what I'm telling here. Don't let nobody meddle in your business—'specially your woman."

"Okay."

I thought that was odd. Only later would I understand that Joe was speaking to his personal situation. But the opening for Joe Turner in Little Rock became my night at the Apollo. Not because anything drastically changed for me on the outside, but it changed me on the inside. It was like a stamp of approval. Joe knew Duke Ellington, Ray Charles, Chuck Berry; they all looked up to him. I felt by sharing the stage with him and him talking to me as a peer, I was rubbing elbows with the big boys. I felt I'd done good.

Last thing Big Joe said to me on that big night was "I'm going to Australia next year." To this country boy at nineteen, the word

"Australia" sounded like he was going to fucking Mars. Over the decades, I would get to know Big Joe better. And I don't think things ended so well for him. But what is a natural, absolute fact is that I don't think there is any other person like Big Joe Turner in history. His music life ricocheted around like a silver ball in a pinball machine. Bounced from jazz to jump blues, boomeranged to R&B, and jumped right into rock 'n' roll. What most folks say is true—that there ain't no rock 'n' roll without him. And he was part of a night that changed my life right there in Little Rock.

Just next year, in September of '57, the image of Little Rock, Arkansas, changed around the world. The governor commanded the Arkansas National Guard to prevent Negroes from integrating the high school. It would take President Eisenhower putting the Arkansas National Guard under federal control so the Little Rock Nine could integrate Central High School. As the racist crackers showed their asses on TV, it told the world that, contrary to its image, Little Rock, Arkansas, was not like the slow and peaceful river that ran through it. It was a dark example of America in the 1950s. Full of good ole boys with pickup trucks ready to fight to keep America white and evil. The pictures on TV were as clear as the moonshine they drank. And white folks could get plenty drunk on their hatred of Black folks.

Little Walter

In 1957 my first child with Hazel was born, Valerie. Hazel, I, and the baby moved from my brother Alvin's home to the 1100 block of Troy Street on Chicago's West Side. Little did I know, on the next block over, on Albany Avenue, lived Little Walter. Our back doors were catty-corner to each other.

I learned harp from Daddy and then from listening to Sonny Boy Williamson. But that learnin' was elementary school and high school. Hangin' with Little Walter was college. When Walter had his first hit with "Juke" in 1952, everything changed for the blues harp players. The song was like a breath of fresh air for the blues. In terms of the harp, that record "Juke" was like before Jesus and after Jesus in the Bible. Because after it, everything changed for the blues. One of the old repeated stories is that before "Juke," you could buy a harmonica for 50 cents. After "Juke" they were three dollars 'cause everybody wanted to play one.

It pushed the harp out front in a fresh way. "Juke" was just a regular old boogie-woogie, but it began with a harp lick that would become famous. When you're a young musician, if a lick on your axe becomes something that every ear has heard, you better learn that lick and learn it good. So every harp player including me had to know how to play "Juke" from top to bottom.

Everybody wanted to take the credit for the song's opening riff, and pieces of it may have been ripped from other songs. But despite what Junior Wells and a bunch of other harp players said, that shit belongs to Little Walter. And even if the opening lick was ripped from someone else, all his playing through the song made it a hit.

I knew a pretty good amount about playing harp, but Walter talked to me about gettin' a sound, a certain tone. Taught me more about the basics of tongue-blocking. He said, "That's how you git it dirty—make them notes bend. If your tongue ain't hurtin' after you've played for half an hour—you ain't shutting the door hard enough with your tongue." That technique, along with a few others, gave Walter his one-of-a-kind sound. Walter could make that thing weep like you were burying your Mama or he could make that thing praise the goodness of the Lord. He made the blues harp become like a saxophone, where he could produce cool mellow moods or hot screams and shouts. No one on the harp could do what Walter could do.

I could walk right out my back door and be at Little Walter's back door in fifteen seconds. He worked a lot on the road but was never gone too long. He'd be out there four days, then back home for three. Sometimes he went farther and would be gone for a week or more. But most times he was at home, especially Tuesdays and Wednesdays. From the time I first saw Walter onstage with Muddy, I knew he was something. Now, as neighbors, I saw him in full bloom. He had some money and dressed like somebody. He had a lot of hats and suits! Mane, he had beige, brown, gray, pinstripe—black. Between that slicked-back conk hair and reddish-brown skin, he was a handsome cat when he wanted to be.

Little Walter was nice to me. But he was a complicated man. He was a little guy, and maybe he had what they call a Napoleon complex. If he felt you were above him in any way—education-wise, socially, had a cuter girl, anything—he'd have a problem with ya. He was like a guy who couldn't read or write thinking everybody was writing bad things about him.

He'd always start some kind of rumble. Something was never right. I'd walk to his back door many mornings, knock, and say, "Hey, let's grab some grub." We'd go to some hash house, and he'd be in good spirits. We'd be laughin' or talkin' 'bout music or women. But it wasn't long before something wasn't right. Eggs weren't right, bacon wasn't hard enough, coffee wasn't hot enough. Just penny-ante stuff. It got so bad that if the toast wasn't right, I'd say, "Aw, come on, Walter, take my toast." It was like you were always putting out these fires over absolutely nothin'. It was hard for people to understand how someone like Little Walter—with so much talent, handsome as the devil—could be so touchy. But he was.

I didn't shun Walter. Why? Because he was Little Walter. A living legend on the harp. And I was Bobby Rush, still trying to make a record and get people to take notice of me outside of Chicago. With the success of his hit record "Juke," Walter had left Muddy's band. Muddy said nothing to me personally about whether he was pissed at Walter, but all I know is that even after he left Muddy's band, Walter still played on just about everything Mud recorded in the studio.

I, on the other hand, was trying to get my own record deal. It would take some time, but at least I had gigs. And sometimes I had more gigs than folks who had records. I hustled hard.

"Bobby, what'chu doin' tonight?" Walter said.

"Ah, mane, I ain't doin' nothing—but you know me. That means I'll be doin' something."

"Man, come on wit' me to Waukegan—got a nine o'clock gig at the Cat and Fiddle."

"Cool. Leave 'round seven?"

"Naw, 'round three thirty."

"Why so early?"

"Man, I wanna cat around a little."

"A'ight—I'm in."

I may have had five dollars with me. Walter had a pocket full of money. He probably only had thirty dollars, but it was all in ones—so it looked like a wad to me. And frankly, thirty dollars was a lot of money to me anyway. As Walter and I walked into the joint around five, the girls were there already and, mane, they were something else. All kinds of beautiful sisters of every color dressed to the nines, hair all done up. Fine, fine, fine.

Walter said, "This is my little brother, Bobby."

"Ah, he's cute," one of the ladies said.

Walter ordered three quarts of beer for everybody—then another round, and before you knew it the girls were sitting on my lap, drinking, rubbing my hair, and kissing on me, just like they were stuck like glue to Walter.

I was having the absolute time of my life!

Now remember, I ain't drinkin', but I might as well have been 'cause my head was spinning from all the affectionate attention I was receiving. The voice in my head said, *Damn, Walter, you really are a superstar.*

Walter said, "Man, I almost outta money." I thought, *No, no, no, Walter, not now. Please not now. I'm enjoying the hell out of this scene here.* But he said, "Let's go," and with my nature looking like a big top tent through my pants. I was thinking we would drive back to Chicago. But he walked around to the rear of the car, popped the trunk of his Caddy open, and it was a mountain of money. It was all in one-dollar bills, so it probably wasn't more than $500, but it was just loosely laying there in the trunk—it looked a million dollars to me. It just blew my mind—all that money. I even forgot about the girls!

He said, "Get you some." So being polite and not greedy, reaching down I grabbed one fistful. Couldn't have been more than twenty dollars or so. Walter was so drunk that when he slammed the trunk, some of the loose bills stirred up in the blast of air and they got stuck between the trunk and car body. They're sticking out of the seams like confetti. So I pulled out the ones I could and stuck back in the ones that could be pushed. I was plucking and pushing those bills like a thirsty man in the desert looking for water.

As we were walkin' back to the club, I was thinking: *Walter's got to be selling dope. Ain't no way he's making money like that playing music.* So I just straight out asked him, "Walter, how you git all dis money?" He shot back without missing a beat, "Blowin' harp, maaannnnnn. Blowin' that harp. I'm a harmonica player!"

The pride in his voice even with the liquor came through: "I'm a harmonica player!"

Stood out to me. And so did the money.

Around this time I was playing a lot of guitar and bass. But after that, I really started to blow the harp on more songs and with more gusto. I felt the power of it—I also thought about that pile of money. Little Walter was a rock star. Crazy, yes. Hot-headed for sure. Warm when he wanted to be. Definitely. Most folks rightfully say he's the Jimi Hendrix of the harp—pulling out unique sounds of the harmonica nobody had heard before; and that's true. It's also true he lit my fire.

Muddy

I was lying on the couch half-asleep when my wife, Hazel, nudged me awake. "I thought said you was goin' to Muddy Waters's birthday party tonight?" I said, "Oh shit." I jumped up, washed my face, put on a suit, and hightailed it over to Lake Street, where he was giving the celebration. As I walked up to the building, there was Muddy's brown moon-looking face hanging out the window. "Hey, Blood, I been waiting on you—told everybody you was gonna be here—come on up here, boy." It was after eleven, and the party had wound down, as those cats probably started drinking around six. When I came in the joint, it was Muddy, some other dude, and around fifteen ladies. They all had low-cut tops and short skirts where you could see everything but the sunshine. Women in their mid-thirties and early forties. At eighteen, I felt like these were some old-ass broads. Stupid-ass me. I didn't want to taste what they were cooking—know what I mean? After twenty minutes of some pussyfoot flirting, I snuck out the back door.

What Muddy Waters saw in me, I'll never know. I didn't smoke. I didn't drink. I didn't even chase women (not to the degree they did). But he took a liking to me, always calling me "Blood." He gave me advice and talked to me about things as if I was his son going away to college.

"Blood, beware of someone telling you you cannot do something that you know you can."

"Mud, I got it. I'm a can-do mane."

"Whoa, whoa, whoa—wait a minute, I ain't finished."

"I know, Mud—"

"Blood, also be careful of some Negro tellin' you that you can do something when you know damn well you can't."

I didn't at first understand the full meaning of what Mud was trying to say to me. It wouldn't be long before I knew what he was saying to me. It was the often-used phrase "know your strengths and your weaknesses." I took his words to heart, and I've tried to live what Muddy was trying to teach me. But I think I wanted to take it further. For I knew one of my strengths was entertaining, but just like there are plenty of good guitar players in the world, there are only a few Albert Kings, Buddy Guys, or Chuck Berrys. I wanted my entertaining chops not to be just good—but to stand out from the crowd.

Respect the People

After Muddy told me to play to my strengths, I didn't study on it too much. Till one night I saw Jackie Wilson and two other acts I don't remember. Gorgeous George was the MC. Every time George walked on that stage, he had on a fresh set of clothes. He changed suits maybe four times that night. That impressed me. What people don't know is that George made those clothes. That's why years later, out of Atlanta, he was a stage clothier for just about everybody, including me.

He had a scratchy, resonant voice, almost like Otis Redding, but mostly Gorgeous George had a gift in style and charm. Everybody knew him. He would soon put out a few records in the early sixties and have a tiny recording career. But in that small career, a young Jimi Hendrix played in his band. That's where Little Richard found Jimi, and the rest is history.

I never ever saw Gorgeous George unless he was dressed to the nines, and he was the cream of the crop of the MCs. George conked his hair like we all did. But he put a part high on his head. Then he feathered his hair around that part. So when he shook his head, either telling a joke or singing a line or two, his conked hair whipped and bounced right along with him. The women loved that shit. I mean, he was somethin' else. He was an MC, but he was like a part of the show, too.

I took what dollars I had and went to Fox Brothers on Roosevelt Road. Fox Brothers was the hip spot for threads near and far. Legendary. Everybody got their clothes from Fox Bros. First it was the jazz cats: Duke Ellington, Billie Holiday, Sarah Vaughan, Miles Davis, Nat

"King" Cole, and many others. The first suits I got from there were not just any suits. They were getups that popped out—white, yellow, lime green, purple.

This is where I began my long-standing practice of changing clothes many times during a performance. Gorgeous George helped me see a value in it. It gave my show a kind of pizzazz. In the small and big joints I played in—but especially the small juke joints—it was like I was paying value to the audience, too. Mostly these were just regular, hard-workin' Negroes stepping out for a night of joy. The fact I cared enough to dress up several times for them made the people love me more, because I respected them as an audience. And they respected me back.

Hot Dog

In 1960, my firstborn son, Donell, was born. Hazel seemed happy, and Donell's birth overjoyed me. Maybe a year later, in late 1961, Hazel, Valerie, and I took my youngest to see Daddy and Maw. My parents had left rural Sherrill, Arkansas, for Pine Bluff. When we arrived, I felt something was wrong. Pulling me into their bedroom, Maw gave me the news.

"Junior, your daddy's going blind."

"How?"

"I don't really know. All the doctor said was it could be a fast or slow process. But we may need some more of your help."

I had always sent Maw and Dad a little money. But the news put things in a new light. The urgency to make money as a bluesman was always knocking at the door, but now, with two children, Daddy's failing eyes, and no record deal in sight—I had to up some kind of game.

I was making money playing in juke joints and clubs. But not a lot of money. And I was really playing only Thursday, Friday, and Saturday. Sometimes I would pick up a dance show on Sunday afternoon, but by and large I didn't have a pot to piss in.

I needed more money. The kids needed coats. I had to pay the rent—on time. Everybody had to eat. That is why I spent $62.50 on a rolling hot dog stand with a trailer hitch. It was used and beat-up a bit, but still nice. Once I polished the white metal and small black wheels, it shined. It had the usual silver top compartment for the dogs and buns, a place to hold the dispensers of ketchup and mustard. Not as large as the ones you see in NYC today. But large enough. Most carts were charging $1.25 for a hot dog. I was charging 75 cents.

My first couple days in business were so-so. But as in real estate, the three words that matter are location, location, location. One of my most profitable spots was right in front of Cossomer's Lounge. The magic was that I would also play there. No one knew that the hot dog stand was mine, as I had a friend run the thing. All the while I was inside acting like I was in show business. But I really was in the hot dog business. Because I made $17 with the Bobby Rush Show and over $50 in hot dog sales.

I started selling out of hot dogs after three hours. On early Monday mornings I'd be at the wholesale butcher buying as many dogs as I could with the money from the weekend's activities. Most times if I bought twenty dollars in dogs and buns, I'd have eighty dollars by Thursday afternoon. I was tripling my money. This became one of my first of many side hustles. And it was good.

But the main hustle was always music—or I wanted it to be. Still didn't have the hit record and the popularity that came with it. So I didn't have clubs seeking me out yet on a grand scale, and that kept me close to Chicago. I had to rely on my tried-and-true, and that was giving the best damn show I could. What was good for me was that all my buddies knew I was a born entertainer.

Rock Island

I had a pretty talented band and show in 1960 and '61. Earl Hooker, one of the all-time-great slide guitarists, told me about this club in Rock Island, Illinois.

"Bobbyrush, there's a club there called Baggerbar, and they would love what you do, man."

"What'chu mean, Hooker?"

"You know—your show. Your moves. Your clothes, the way you talk to an audience. Them jokes you tell. You know—your show."

That was high praise comin' from Earl Hooker. 'Cause Earl was a one-of-a-kind musician. Played with everybody that was great: Sonny Boy, Bobby "Blue" Bland, B.B., Junior Parker, and everybody in between. Nobody played slide like Earl. He was the recent version of Elmo James but had more technique. A stutterer at times, he also was a sufferer of tuberculosis. I think his ailments kept him humble. Life ain't fair. He was a prince of a man and musician.

I had already been playing gigs in Peoria and Kewanee, Illinois, so Rock Island was just another town close to Chicago. What was good about Rock Island and Peoria was that they were far enough away from Chicago that club owners and audiences looked at me as an import. Like I came a long way to grace their joints. Rock Island was about three hours west of Chicago.

I threw away the name Bobby Rush and the Four Jivers 'cause there were a few groups that called themselves the Jivers: "So and So and the Two Jivers," ". . . and the Three Jivers," ". . . and the Four Jivers." What I started calling the Bobby Rush Band, I took over to Rock Island. Earl and I opened for the Ike and Tina Turner Revue. It was a blast. A memorable night all around. Ike and Tina's show was hot. Blew me and Earl off the stage. We weren't mad about it, because we all liked each other. I don't think Ike and Tina were married yet, but their performance couldn't be denied. They had this stage play thing between them that was perfect for the Chitlin Circuit. Their give-and-take was cute, suggestive, and funny all at the same time. It was like watching a movie.

Ike was a different cat. Rough around the edges but had a head for business. He knew what so many of us Negroes didn't back then—that being on the *business* side of show business was more important than being in the *show* part of show business. Because of all the craziness with Tina, Ike has a tendency to be forgotten. But he brought into the spotlight many of the greats of the blues: B.B., Bobby "Blue" Bland, Little Milton, and others.

After Ike and Tina's show, Earl introduced me to the owner of Baggerbar, and he invited me back in two weeks. Playing there three times in a month and a half, I had become friendly with the club owner, who said to me, "Bobby, why don't you be my house band, come down and work for me Friday, Saturday, and Sunday?" This was great, as I was making thirty-five dollars a night, and after giving twenty to my band, I could clear as much as forty-five dollars for myself in a weekend. Hallelujah!

This was great for me, as I drew a nice-size crowd. And I understood why Earl thought I would thrive at the Baggerbar. The people liked to dance, but they also liked—more than cats at other clubs in the Midwest—to sit at a table and order drinks and watch a show. And I was more than willing to give 'em a show. The owner said to me, "Bobby, your show is so good and you're bringing in so many people, we need an MC or a comedian to open up for you."

I said, "I got a funny cat for you."

"Will you get in touch with him?"

I said, "Sure."

I called Pretty Bopp.

William "Pretty Bopp" Franklin was one funny motherfucker. He was one of those guys who could make a joke out of anything. He would later work in all the top Black clubs in Chicago as an MC, comedian, and later a ventriloquist. He would appear as an opening act for lots of musical greats like Stevie Wonder, the Temptations, and Ray Charles.

"Pretty Bopp, I want you to go to Rock Island, Illinois, with me."

"Bobbyrush, how does it pay?"

"Thirty, and they pay for your room."

"What time you gonna pick me up?"

"Friday morning, 'round eleven a.m."

I called the club owner up and lied through my teeth. "The mane say he wants fifty dollars and you to pay for the room."

He said, "Tell him I'll give him forty-five dollars and pay for the room."

I said, "Okay, you have a deal." However, come Thursday night, Pretty Bopp calls me with the blues.

"Bobby, I can't do it."

"Ah, mane, why not?"

"Boy, my wife is in a bad way, and she don't want me to leave."

"Mane, you putting me in a trick."

"If she feels better, I'll let you know. I'm so sorry, boy."

"I'll call you in the morning."

Friday morning came and I called Pretty Bopp and nothing's changed. He apologized. But I'm screwed, and I wasn't thinking about his performance, either. I was thinking about that extra fifteen dollars I was skimming off the top.

And I needed that money. I paced the kitchen floor. Hazel said, "Baby, what's wrong with you?" I said nothing but kept repeating under my breath, "I don't know what to do, I don't know what to do." Then it came to me.

I shouted, "I got it!"

My wife said, "Got what, Bobby? Got what?"

I said, "I cain't talk right now," and dashed out the flat.

I went to the Goodwill store downtown and bought some overalls, a big floppy hat that kinda covered my eyes, a big shirt, and a big suit. Couldn't have spent over five dollars. I practiced hours in the mirror doing a comic routine in this getup. Arriving at the club, I avoided the owner. When it was showtime, I had on this big black Goodwill suit. I said, "Ladies and gentlemen, we got an MC from Chicago and a great man and comedian, so give a big hand to "The Tramp." The audience clapped as the band played "When the Saints Go Marching In." I walked off the stage and dropped that big suit to reveal my country overalls. I popped on a fake mustache and a hat, and I strutted out on that stage in less than thirty seconds.

I told jokes, jokes that I've known for years. Country jokes, racy jokes, fat jokes, drunk jokes, talking about people in the audience. They were in stitches. I just killed them.

Then I said, "Ladies and gentlemen, it's star time. You're here to see Bobby Rush, right?" They yelled loudly, "Yeah!" "Ladies and gentlemen, let's give it up for Mr. Bobbeeeeee Rush!" They applauded and the band started and I dashed backstage. I stripped them overalls off, pants already on underneath. I snatched off the mustache. I had a fresh shirt and a new jacket—I brushed my hair, and in under a minute I was duckwalking out to center stage and going into "What'd I Say" by Ray Charles.

I did that a few times before the man found out. And when he did, he was furious—for a moment. He got right in my face and said, "Bobbyrush, youz a lyin', low-down motherfucker." I put my arm around his shoulder, and all I could say was "Mane, you got me." He said, "But you're damn good. Don't let no other motherfucker know it but me." And he kept me there for almost one year.

Someday

"Jerry-O ain't to be trusted," Albert King said to me.

"Yeah, but he can get me to the majors," I said.

"How can he get you somewhere he ain't got himself?"

Guess he had a point. Jerry J. Murray was a singer, music business guy, DJ, and promoter. Some would say he was a jack-of-all-trades and master of none. Known by everyone as Jerry-O, his auntie and cousins were friends of mine. I met him while I was playing at the Birdhouse nightclub on Dearborn Street; not long after, he moved to Chicago, around 1961. Jerry-O was flashy and was one of the smoothest talkers around.

"Bobby Rush, can't nobody put on a show like you!" he said.

"Jerry-O, this was an off night; you shoulda seen me last week in Peoria—I had 'em fainting."

"Man, I can get you a contract with Motown."

"Motown! What I gotta do?"

I was hungry to make a record.

No, I was starving to make a record, and Jerry knew just what to say to get me salivating. Motown. I believed with all my heart that if I got to share my shine with all those Motown writers, producers, and engineers, I knew I could get a hit. All Berry Gordy and crew had to do was to see my show. If I could get them in the room. I knew—by my pure will—they would dig me. After all, I had the good looks, the height, the hair, and I had a million songs and song ideas that I had collected. And even if they didn't like my blues music, they could see that I had the energy.

In my head everybody and their momma had done a record but me. And I felt inferior as a professional with my friends. Especially the close ones who had been making recordings for ten years or more: Albert King had put out records in '53. Bobby Bland, since '51. Rufus Thomas, since '50. As a matter of fact, Rufus, who was the closest thing to kinfolk I had in the business, was having the biggest hit of his career with "Walking the Dog." "Dog" was an international hit. So big Rufus quit his textile mill job.

It was 1963, and I ain't done even one under my own name.

Jerry-O was always well groomed and had many beautiful suits. Never a hair out of place, and if he wasn't wearing a suit, he was wearing something cool. He always had some kind of ensemble on. And as a good dresser myself, I admired that quality in him. Maybe two or three times when he was around me, he called Berry Gordy or somebody at Motown. Now I never spoke to Berry Gordy myself. And whether it was truth or lies that he had him on the other line, the possibility seduced me. Jerry was from Detroit, so his so-called relationship with Berry Gordy seemed real.

But Jerry was one of those bullshit cats. He was trying to get in the door as much as I was. But he didn't tell me that. But after a couple months of nothing, he knew his constant hype was falling on my deaf ears. Jerry sensed my restlessness. "Bobby, let's record a song together, and I'll find a small independent to release it—after that I'm sure Berry will bite." That sounded reasonable to me because there were lots of independents in the Chicago area, and all you had to do was have money for studio time and money to press a record.

Jerry and I recorded two songs for the session. "Someday" and "Let Me Love You." On "Someday" I was trying to achieve that feel that Jimmy Reed's "Honest I Do" had. That same feel that had enchanted me years earlier.

But even by 1964 standards, "Someday" wasn't recorded very well. The vocal doesn't have a lot of fidelity, and the band is dragging a bit too much. To highlight how much it wasn't up to big-boy recording standards, the second song I recorded that day doesn't even have the lead vocal till the break, and then it's just way in the back. This wasn't the Motown and Chess Records musical assembly line where you had the best musicians around coming in every day—working with the best recording equipment and the best technical engineers available.

"Someday" was recorded in the back of a record store. But I didn't know any better; as a matter of fact, Little Walter's first recording was in the back room of Abram's Radio and Record Shop on Maxwell Street.

The experience left me with a bad taste in my mouth. I saw Jerry as a cat who really didn't care about music or, more importantly, me. I understand now that he was trying to get in the door as much as I was. If he had just been straight with me, the bad taste in my mouth wouldn't have lingered as long as it did. Jerry-O continued to talk a good game to anybody who would listen. Around the same time he was leading me around with snake oil dreams, he also persuaded the Dukays to record with his label.

The Dukays were a great bunch of folks, four guys and a girl from the South Side. The music business had already burned them. They had released a smash in '61, "The Duke of Earl." But the song was not pinned to them when it hit the streets. Like a bait-and-switch, the song was said to be by their lead singer, Gene Chandler. When they sold the master to another label, Vee-Jay, they had the distribution power to make it a hit. Like so many other dirty tricks in the business, it left the Dukays high and dry. But there was a lesson in it for me. "The Duke of Earl" was a smash. A million seller. It really greased the wheels of Vee-Jay, the largest Black-owned and -operated record company in the country. The songwriters Gene, Bernice Williams, and Dukays' group member Earl Edwards made out like nobody's business. Gene's royalties were tremendous. So I reckoned that even if I got fucked over, if I wrote a hit song, it doesn't matter who screws who. Because radio royalties is radio royalties.

By the time Jerry-O came a-courtin', the remaining Dukays were ready to listen to him. They released a song on his label called "The Jerk." It became a moderate hit in Chicago. For years I looked at Jerry-O negatively. But the truth was, he really wanted to be an artist more than anything else. He formed a duo, Tom and Jerrio, and released several records. They would start a big dance craze in 1965 with the song "Boo-Ga-Loo."

Barber Shop Mud

Unless you're Black and a man of a certain age, you can't know what the Black barber shop was to us. More than a bar, a church, or a nightclub, the Black barber shop was where we Negro men did more pontificatin', philosophizin', cussin', laughin', and just talkin' shit than anywhere else. It was our cigar and scotch lounge where we worked out all the problems of the world. So you couldn't just sit there—you had to have an opinion on somethin', anything.

I walked into a barber shop where I knew Muddy Waters was hangin' out. There he was, laid back in the chair, gettin' ready for a shave.

"And here come, Blood," he said to me as I walked through the door.

I just returned his greeting with "Muddy, Muddy, Muddy."

"Show Blood—see what he says," Muddy said.

A cat passed me the current cover of *Ebony* magazine. Remember, this was Chicago and home of Johnson Publishing. All the Black businesses where you had to wait for somethin' had several copies of *Jet* and *Ebony* magazines layin' around. This June '66 issue that they were trying to get my opinion on had a gorgeous chocolate sister on the cover, with a very short, neat, and tight afro. The caption read:

THE NATURAL LOOK
New mode for Negro women

"So, how she look, Blood?" Muddy asked.

"She look fine to me."

The room erupted: "Aahhhhhhh!" Apparently before I strolled in they had been discussing whether the sister with the short, tight 'fro was fine. Of course the old heads believed in long, hot-comb-pressed hair like you saw almost everywhere in 1966. But the young lions knew the new groove in what was beautiful—and they would win that war.

As Mud got up from the barber's chair, he brushed his sides off and said, "Blood, gimme that magazine—lemme show ya sumthin'."

He opened and quickly rifled through the pages and got to a feature story on Memphis Slim. The article opened with a full-length picture of Memphis Slim standing tall and smoking while the Eiffel Tower is risin' up behind him. Lemme tell ya, Memphis Slim looked like a man in high cotton. The six-page spread basically said this: the French people love Memphis Slim over there in a way America never has and never tried. The article shows him living in a grand apartment with his French wife—giving autographs, having friends over, him performing for all-white audiences. And as he would tell it, making a fucking good living for the first time in his life.

If you want to see some Negro blues greats—the founders of rock 'n' roll—go to YouTube. There you'll see old black-and-white television clips from the 1960s and '70s. Ninety percent of the videos were recorded in Europe.

I don't know when Muddy started to go to Europe regularly. But he started asking me to go with him in the mid-sixties.

"Blood, you better come and git sum a dis European love, boy."

"Mane, I 'ont know about that," I said.

"Blood, you lollygaggin'."

He was right. From the mid-sixties forward, Muddy and so many others would be beloved more over in Europe than in America. I would come to understand what Europe meant to the life of the blues—and soul. I remember in 1967, Stax Records took their stars over to Europe. Otis Redding, Eddie Floyd, and of course Sam and Dave went. Rufus Thomas was soooooo pissed that they didn't include him. "Bobbyrush, them motherfuckers can take the stars—huh. Well, there wouldn't be no Stax if it won't for this old star."

And here I was with the chance to go and didn't take it. My thinking was off. Way off. I was thinking stars went to Europe—folks with hit records. And nothin' was further from the truth. Muddy was doing folk festivals all over Europe, with people in gospel music that nobody knew. My lack of education, a manager—something kept me from looking at the big picture 'cause if I had looked around me to what was going on in America, I would have seen that Mud's big-paying gigs often had the title "Folk Festival" or even "Jazz Festival." And Mud was neither folk nor jazz; he was only the heart, mind, and soul of the blues.

I don't know why I dillydallied. Don't know if the travel scared me. Don't know if I was too proud, thinking Mud's asking was some kinda handout—which it wasn't. Me not going was a big-ass mistake.

Those European folks were sittin' in them seats for the experience of the music, not what was hot last week on WVON. So I could have gone with Mud across the pond and probably not changed the journey of my career. But I could have changed the journey of my money.

Oh Lord, What Am I Gonna Do?

I came home this mornin'
My wife wouldn't let me in
I went and peeped through the window
She was makin' love to my best friend
That's a tough titty y'all
And can't nothing suck it but a lion
Well, that's a hard pill to try to swallow
I think about all the time

"TOUGH TITTY"/*UNDERCOVER LOVER*/2003

My marriage to Hazel was good. Marriage helped me to focus on earning. And with a wife, I had to aim my heart one way. Hazel and I were so young. I was in love with my music and I was in love with her. Soon we moved into a place of our own at Sixteenth and Avers Avenue on the West Side. In 1957 our first child, Valerie, was born, and in 1960 my firstborn son, Donell. We were happy, or so I thought. But Hazel being from little Pine Bluff and now in big Chicago, I think it overwhelmed her senses. Places like Chicago and New York City could do that to folk. So much glitter, so much hustle and bustle, so many opportunities, so much light, so much darkness. It can affect your choices. But as they say, all that glitters ain't gold, and unless you're careful, you can fall for the okie doke. I had gotten wind from one guy in my band that Hazel was carrying on with another cat in my band. But a cat in my band? I couldn't imagine that it would have been someone close to me.

I didn't believe him because he was a gossip, even on Sunday. And yet I was suspicious—just a vibe I got. With that information, I kinda set a trap. I told Hazel a week in advance that I wouldn't be home after the gig on Thursday, as I was going to an all-night jam session. When the Thursday night came, I followed my suspected bandmate. He must have been really focused because he never saw me tailing him. And sure nuff, he parked at a motel on the South Side. I sat there for what seemed to be a long time, but it really wasn't more than a half an hour. I went home. I got home and found Hazel gone. I called my brother Alvin, and as I suspected, the kids were over there but Hazel wasn't. I took off, headin' back to the motel, and there was her car parked beside his. I just sat there thinking. My heart pounded. And I just cried out, "Oh Lord, what am I gonna do?"

In Chicago, having a gun is like having a snow shovel. It's a necessity. But thank God I didn't have mine with me that night. I had done all this planning and scheming to set a trap, but I didn't do a damn thing. It's funny; even with me being a real country boy, I had enough good sense to know that if I confronted them—all bets were off on what could happen. I went home.

To say that my mind was blown would be an understatement. This hurt me. I was angry, broken, and desperate all at the same time. All them feelings left me in a state of total confusion. I was not in my right mind. My male pride kicked into high gear. Of course, I fired the guy in my band, which signaled to them both that I was wise to the situation. I thought nothing about what Hazel had done—all I knew is that I wanted to win. Win Hazel back into a one-on-one relationship. But winning was more about my ego than my common sense.

Common sense would have said shake the dust off your feet and move on. Common sense would have said forget Hazel. But my pride made leaving her unacceptable. I thought I was supposed to fight for her. I loved her, but again I was fighting more to maintain my ego. I'll be damned if some dude was going to take her from me. And I wanted to keep our family intact. But the flat-out truth was that I was in such rage of maintaining my male pride that even the children were secondary to my need to win. Like a wild, free horse out on the range, I would have to have a lasso thrown around my neck and be broken—tamed to face reality.

Although the writing was on the wall, I couldn't see it—or I didn't want to see it. But in six months, what I didn't want to see would become crystal clear. Hazel would often drive me in her car to clubs because my '48 Chevrolet Fleetline was old in 1964. One summer night flashing red lights lit up the back window, and Hazel pulled over. The cop said, "Hey, ba—" stopping mid-word, seeing that it was me in the passenger seat.

Hazel smiled and gave him her ID.

"Sir, I need your ID, too," he said. Reaching across Hazel's chest, he grabbed it and walked back to his patrol car. Looking in the rearview mirror, I saw he had no partner in his car, which seemed awfully odd to me. Chicago cops always rode in twos, especially on the South Side. Returning to the car, he walked over to my side and said, "Mr. Ellis, I'm going to have to take you in—you have a warrant."

I said, "That's impossible."

"Sorry, but that's what the precinct says."

He opened the door and I turned around; he cuffed me. I said to Hazel, "Go tell the band what happened." I stayed in a tiny cell. I was never fingerprinted, nor was my photo taken. At the crack of dawn, they released me, saying, "We made a mistake." Although pissed, I was damn sure relieved.

I am not a religious man, but I am a biblical study. So many of them Bible stories are, like, the Almighty is trying to send you a message. Sometimes you hear it, sometimes you don't, and sometimes you hear it loud and clear but you ignore it. And then He has to make it plain. The good Lord made it plain for me when I saw Hazel get into a cop car about two blocks from our home some weeks later.

I confronted her.

And like a sinner seeking salvation in a confessional booth, she just started cryin' and cryin'. She came clean. Owned up to everything. It's like she turned on the faucet and couldn't turn it back off. Like a raging river after a storm flowing downstream, she could not stop crying and confessing. It all came out. Telling me, "I didn't want to do it with him anyway—he only stuck it halfway in." She went on to tell every sexual encounter, every flirtation, every time she just pussyfooted around with someone. I finally said, "Stop, stop, stop. Just stop! That's enough." I couldn't take it anymore.

"But I have to tell you one more thing," Hazel said.

"What!"

"That night you got arrested, he did that so we could be alone."

She turned her head away from me. I don't know if she did it in shame or she thought I was going to hit her. I didn't lose control, as maybe another man would have—but I knew one thing for damn sure.

Our marriage was fucking over.

There were two things I wished for after that. One, that I had told her to keep all them details to herself—'cause I think if she had lied to me, I'd have been better off. Two, I wished I could have put two and two together earlier that Hazel just didn't want to be with me. But that was a hard thing for this man to accept—especially with two children. And although I am a very confident man in most areas of my life, this breakup shook me to my core.

My God, was it a hurting feeling. It hurt something bad. All these decades later, every now and then that wound opens up and I feel that pain. But that hurt would be mixed in with some other future pains and sorrows. What I didn't have then was the self-awareness to understand what was behind that hurt. Hidden behind the hurt of her infidelity were feelings of inadequacy. My status in the world felt small. Her lover was a cop, and I was a musician who made a good living, but who hadn't had a hit record. So even though I wasn't, I felt inadequate. It was almost like I couldn't accept Hazel's indiscretion. Because to accept it meant I had loss in the game of life. The life of being a man.

I'm a dominant man, which is probably what made the knife cut so deep. I think there's a foolish inkling out there about what cheating does to women and what it does to men. I don't mean this to sound out of line, but that old cliché that "boys will be boys" has been around a long time. And it definitely should not provide an excuse for hurting someone, but it often does. But when your old lady cheats on you, there ain't no old cliché to fall back on. It's just that some man who had a bigger bank account or a bigger dingaling talked your girl out of her panties. I wrote a song years later called "A Man Can Give It (But He Sure Can't Take It)." I believe that song title is a statement of fact.

'Cause I believe cheating hurts men way more. Because it was a hurting thing to me.

Didn't Even Start Her Race

We separated. I paid Hazel's housing and expenses. She got involved with someone else—not the police officer. It was maybe eight months later when she laid it on me that she was pregnant and I was the father. I took her at her word—because I could have been. During our separation, we would occasionally carry on. But honestly, I never believed my youngest, Sherry, was my child. I took care of her and loved her like she was mine, but sincerely, I don't think she came from my seed, and that's a very hard thing to say.

It wasn't a good divorce. Neither one of us wanted to be with each other, but we didn't want the other to be with someone else. It was crazy. I told her up front that I would continue to pay the rent for what was now her place. And of course I gave her money for the kids each month. The irony was that after some time had passed we became the best—I mean the best—of friends.

She was sorry about her behavior, and, strangely, I had compassion for her. I just think she was young and impressionable. I understood how someone who hadn't been with anyone else would want to taste something different. She said it wasn't about love, and I believed her. I think it was just curiosity. But when you get too curious, you do things. Also, she had been through a lot. Within six months of our marriage, her father died suddenly; and it couldn't have been more than a few years later when her mama died.

But most tragically, our youngest, Sherry, died at age five. Sickly from birth, she had the inherited blood disorder sickle cell anemia. We kinda blamed ourselves for a while, wishing we had gotten her to the hospital sooner for a blood transfusion. Sickle cell is a very painful disease that strikes us Black folk most. The doc said poor little Sherry didn't really have a chance. Sickle cell would pop up again in my bloodline, but the sting of young death was tough. As much as it broke Hazel, I handled it with a country Black man's philosophy, lifting my shrugged shoulders, saying we'll understand it better by and by. But it was hard to have an acceptance of my child not getting to the finish line when she didn't have a chance to even start her race.

Vee-Jay

Another sad end fell. Not just on my doorstep, but on the doorstep of every Negro who wanted to be a big wheel in the music business. Vee-Jay Records shut its doors in 1966. Decades earlier we Black folks rejoiced in Joe Louis not only because he was a talented boxer, but we rejoiced also in what he represented. He was our hero just by kicking ass and being Black. He was like a big farm tractor—pulling us out of the shit ditch of second-class status in America. Vee-Jay was just another hard-pullin' tractor, becoming the biggest Black-owned record company in the world. Owned by Vivian Carter and James Bracken, they had their offices right there on Chicago's Record Row.

The reason that Vee-Jay Records' downfall hurt us so is that we were so tired of being pulled around by our ear from white record labels. Vee-Jay represented what we could do when Black business talent hitched up with good ears. They signed Jimmy Reed after Chess Records turned him down. Between Vivian's brother, Calvin Carter, looking for talent and Ewart Abner running the machine, they had a golden touch. It seemed to me that "Oh, What a Night" by the Dells was not only a hit—in time it would become a Chicago standard. "Duke of Earl" wasn't just a hit—it was a phenomenon. Vee-Jay had an in-house system of distribution and promotion. They released a bunch of gospel and jazz records. Solid-ass company. But Calvin and Abner were some hungry mofos, and they wanted more.

They wanted the white boy value pack. They were like, *White folks have been selling our talent for so long, why don't we Black folk try to sell some of theirs?* They were the first to distribute the Beatles in America.

And Vee-Jay introduced the Four Seasons to the world. "Sherry" was a No. 1 record on the R&B and pop charts.

They moved the office to LA, but Calvin Carter stayed in Chicago. "Bobbyrush, how can you leave the girl you brought to the dance?" Calvin said to me over breakfast. Calvin believed that Vee-Jay, in going to LA and recording fickle stuff like Arthur Godfrey and a bunch of quirky shit, had abandoned the very sound that got them to the top. Sky-high debts were the last straw. Vee-Jay became history, but Calvin Carter and I stayed in touch.

ꟷꟷꟷ

Little Walter died in February of '68. During a fight over a game of craps, some guy hit him in the head with a hammer. He went to bed and never woke up. I've played blues harmonica for over sixty years. And no one before or since could touch him. Contrary to folks who don't know how to play the harp, it was more than his distorted sound, it was more than the way he could make the harp cry. It was him. All that heat within him, all that noisy spirit of his came through that harp. God forbid that a young man would have to go through what Walter most times put himself through to sound like that; nevertheless, spirit is spirit. And like spirit, he is eternal.

The Best Thing That
Ever Happened to Me

I've always relied on music to take my mind away from things. After Hazel and I parted, I played more and more gigs. Sat in on more jam sessions, hung out with young cats and old cats. I worked everywhere I could. But getting gigs close to home wasn't practical. So throughout Illinois, I booked myself in Rock Island, Peoria, and a little place called Kewanee.

Kewanee had a little club that I played in on Saturday nights, but being my forever enterprising self, I also landed a gig on Sunday afternoons in a recreation hall in Kewanee. Kids that weren't old enough to go to the club flocked to the rec hall to see a show. And there I saw the woman who would become the foundation of my life: Bertha Jean Graves.

Jean was so fine, and she still is to me. Healthy in all the right places. That Sunday afternoon, I sang my songs and kept one eye on my band and my other eye on her. If she moved across the rec hall, my eyes moved right with her. I think she may have had a boyfriend. But I was a dominant young fellow. When I knew what I wanted—I went for it. I was like a bull in the pasture—I just moved all the competition out. As much as my hormones drew me to Jean, after having our first conversation I knew four things about her:

She was book smart.
She was street smart.
She was trustworthy.
She was a young woman of some serious substance.

Jean came up in rural Illinois. Racist as hell, rural Illinois. People don't get it. The raw and brutal racism of white America wasn't just in Mississippi and Alabama. Kewanee was as segregated as Nashville, Tennessee. But her parents would not bow to white folk—they were very strong-willed people. That gave Jean a whole lotta backbone.

I knew she was not only right for me as a man, but she would be a blessing to my life. You may ask: "How did you know?" I just knew. Sometimes the good Lord makes you drawn to someone like an SUV to a gas pump—it's magnetic. The Lord has to do it that way because he wants to bless you with someone that is going to be for your best, even if your dumb ass don't know it yet. And after fifty years of marriage, it seems the Lord was onto something.

Jean may have been a blessing, but she was also around sixteen. She graduated, moved to Chicago to go to nursing school, and I immediately started courting her. And it wasn't too long after that we tied the knot. Not soon after that she would give birth to our son Carl.

Now I was supporting two households. I kept from Jean how much I was supporting my other children *and* Hazel's siblings.

MLK

I was living on the West Side, 2749 West Warren Boulevard, when they gunned down MLK in Memphis. Yeah, I know it was one motherfucker, James Earl Ray, but I say "they" for a reason. 'Cause a lot of folks pulled that damn trigger. White folks who never got over the Civil War. White folks who wanted us to wait another hundred years for change— 'cause we was moving too fast for them. White folks who say they loved Negroes but were either too evil or too dumb to connect the dots, that their love wasn't real. It's like you love that chicken in your yard, but you know one day you're gonna kill and eat him. They liked us Negroes alright as long as we stayed in our place—second class. But there is no first, second, third, or even fourth class when you ain't got any power.

It's still amazing to me when you see all them pictures of a lynched Black man hung on a tree and all these white folks just standin' around drinking pop, eating an ice-cream cone, and smiling—as if it was a social event. They refused to see the evil in them even being there. Turning to the camera, saying cheese, and allowing their picture to be taken with a sense of pride.

As word got out during the night and the next morning about MLK, Chicago exploded. For two days Chicago burned hot. And it seemed the city was coming apart like a cheap pair of stockings. The Black people that owned businesses were boarding them up and writing SOUL BROTHER on their storefronts to signify that this place was Black-owned. There was a Cadillac dealership near me where I knew the owner casually. A cat just came in and shot him. But it didn't have anything to do with MLK's assassination. He was pissed that they had repossessed his car—using a genuine moment of frustration to shell out his personal anger.

Jean, who was seven months pregnant with our son Carl, was on the bus coming from the doctors' office. By the time she got to our neighborhood the city was going downhill fast. Just the next street over, it was much worse than our own. Jean was scared as she was trying to get her pregnant self to our house.

Once I got home we just stayed there in the dark, as the power was out. I was ready to protect my own if something went down. The riots made some neighborhoods look like a war zone. When the pictures taken from high above came out in the paper, some of them blocks looked like Europe after WWII. Just skeleton shells of buildings. The shit crumbled on the West Side—and maybe to a lesser degree on the South Side after that. Some of those areas didn't recover for decades. It is sad, but the people that suffered the most from the rioting and looting were us.

I can't remember what blues clubs they burned, but the blues scene shifted a bit after the riots. The interest in the blues continued to crumble with the emergence of soul. People just stopped talking about the blues as much—even amongst the cats who played it. The chatter was more about the Motown sound versus the Chicago soul sound. But it would take a while for the Rock of Gibraltar to come a-tumbling down.

Bobby's Barbecue House

After "Someday" was released on Jerry-O Records in '64, I wouldn't put out another record for three years.

Three long years.

But in late 1966, I did a deal with Sunny Sawyer's Palos label. Sunny was another one of those Chicago cats who had a hustle. But a smart one. He had this pressing plant at 2009 West Sixty-Ninth. Sunny would print up records for cats in a snap. It was almost like you could damn near bring in your tape and wait. I heard years later that he would press up twenty records for you in the daytime and forty records for himself at night! I recorded "You're the One for Me" and "Done Got Over." Both songs didn't make any noise.

I continued to play gigs, and although I was a grown-ass man, I was still that country-boy dreamer. Dreamin' of the big stage and most of all dreaming of a hit record. But reality had diluted my dreams. I had to get my hands in some other pots. Not for my music—but for my life. I had to do something big. I was determined to make it one way or the other. I remembered Rufus Thomas's words to me on Beale Street:

"Ain't no shame in doing what you gotta do to get where you wanna be."

There were so many bluesmen in Chicago just going from gig to gig. They drove cabs, worked in factories and corner stores. And even though I felt some shame, I had enough good sense that whatever shame I felt was 'cause I hung around cats who already had records out. I wasn't just another cat down on Maxwell Street playing in front of a storefront. I had an act. I had gigs. I had a following. Just no hit record. Hit records put you on the good foot.

Next to entertaining folks, one thing I could really do was cook. I took $400 and rented a storefront at 7829 Seventy-Ninth Street, right at the corner of Seventy-Ninth and Halsted, and opened a barbeque joint. The neighborhood, Auburn Gresham, was called Gresham for short. Gresham used to be an Irish neighborhood, but by 1969 the neighborhood was turning over to Negroes in a hurry. And if there was a Black neighborhood in Chicago, there was not only one but several barbeque joints. I don't care how everybody today is talking about Memphis or Texas 'que. Chicago's barbeque is a motherfucker and had a deep history in the city. But good barbeque is all about the wood. And when you grow up in the South, all I saw was cooking on a woodstove.

I took another fifty or sixty dollars and bought takeout boxes, napkins, and cleaning supplies. The place I rented already had a cash register, though I didn't use it—I just used a black metal box with a lock. When I put a handwritten sign in the window that said BOBBY'S BARBEQUE HOUSE, almost instantly I had a hit on my hands.

What helped me was that there were so many 'que joints, especially on the South Side, that there was a barbeque brotherhood between us. We were a group of Black guys who saved money by buying our meat together. It kept the prices down. The wholesaler thought for sure we were buying for some white man. But it was for us. Meeting in the freezer, we'd divide it all up, with someone wrapping our portions up in this big brown paper, labeling it with a black wax marker, and tying it up with twine. We'd take most of it over to Leon's Barbeque for frozen storage.

Not unlike a generation before, when the slave masters threw away the pig intestines and my people cooked them into a delicacy, the meat markets in the late '60s were throwing away rib tips. But not for long, because everybody was barbecuing them tips, and by the time I got my shop going those rib tips became one of the specialties of Chicago barbeque.

Like many others, I had a small joint that was only takeout. So no health department complications from indoor eating. The best advertisement I had was a line outside the store that went about eight to ten

(*Right*) Bobby Rush performing in 1958.

Courtesy of Bobby Rush

(*Below*) Bobby Rush performing in 1960.

Courtesy of Bobby Rush

Bobby Rush and wife, Jean Ellis, in the 1960s.
Courtesy of Bobby Rush

Bobby Rush from June 29, 1978.
Michael Putland / Getty Images

Bobby Rush and band performing in 1972, including Benjamin Wright on keys and Robert Plumking on drums.
Courtesy of Bobby Rush

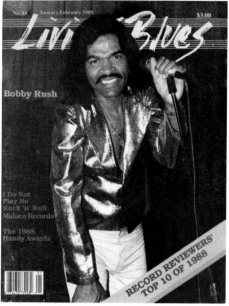

Bobby Rush with two Sunday-school teachers at church in Rock Island, Illinois, in 1982.

Courtesy of Bobby Rush

Living Blues magazine cover image, January/February 1989.

Courtesy Living Blues *magazine, photo by Laurie Lawson*

Bobby Rush with his brothers A. J. Ellis and Larry Ellis.

Courtesy of Bobby Rush

Bobby's brothers. *Left to right:* A. J. Ellis, Alvin Ellis, Andrew Ellis. Bobby's sisters. *Left to right:* Verdia Howell, Mary Lee Cooper, Gerdia Bee Crater.

Courtesy of Bobby Rush

Chicago Blues Festival, 1995. Bobby Rush with dancer Carolyn Goblet.

Robert Barclay, 1995, Chicago Blues Fest

Bobby Rush in front of his tour bus, around 1997.   *Mike Haralambos*

Bobby Rush family photo. *Top, left to right*: Bobby Rush, Sherry Ellis, Bertha Ellis,
Carl Ellis. *Bottom, left to right*: Carlos Ellis, Jean Ellis, Carl Ellis Jr.
Front row baby: Marquice Ellis.   *Courtesy of Bobby Rush*

Bobby "Blue" Bland, B.B. King, Bobby Rush, and (*far right*) Willie Martin Bland, 2010, at Bobby Bland's eightieth birthday party.

Stefan Myles—Fandy Photography—Hey! Did you see that?

Bobby Rush and B.B. King performing at the Mississippi Grammy Legacy Celebration at the Beau Rivage Hotel on June 7, 2011, in Biloxi, Mississippi.

Skip Bolen / Getty Images

Bobby Rush and Dr. John, with Roland Pritzker in the background, taken at One Eyed Jacks in New Orleans during the music video shoot for "Another Murder in New Orleans," along with Carl Gustafson's band Blinddog Smokin', in 2013.

Jeff DeLia of 72 Music Management

Bobby Rush, Dan Aykroyd, and the Roots performing on *The Tonight Show* in 2014, supporting the film *Get On Up*.

Douglas Gorenstein / NBCU Photo Bank / NBCUniversal via Getty Images

SXSW Film Festival (2014) after the premiere of the film *Take Me to the River*, with, *left to right*, Bobby Rush, Jerry Harrison (Rock and Roll Hall of Fame inductee with the Talking Heads), Lawrence "Boo" Mitchell (Grammy Award winner, co-owner of Royal Studios, son of legendary producer Willie Mitchell), Snoop Dogg, Al Kapone (leaning in front of Snoop Dogg), Martin Shore (director of the film), William Bell (Grammy-winning artist, Stax Records artist, songwriter ["Born Under a Bad Sign"]), Al Bell (former record executive at Stax Records and Motown Records), and Frayser Boy (Oscar-winning rapper). *Jeff DeLia of 72 Music Management*

Left to right: Otis Clay, Denise LaSalle, and Bobby Rush at the Blues Hall of Fame Induction Dinner, May 9, 2014. *Amanda Gresham*

Bobby Rush and Keb' Mo' both
win Blues Music Awards in 2015.

Jeff DeLia of 72 Music Management

Bobby Rush Band
at Club Paradise
in Memphis. *Left
to right*: Kenny Ray
Kights, Fred Taylor,
Bobby Rush, Mizz
Lowe, Arthur Cooper,
Erickia Henderson,
Lou Rodriguez, Bruce
Howard, Joseph Banks.

Michael McDonald

Millie Jackson and Bobby Rush
at the Jus' Blues Music Awards in
Tunica, Mississippi, in 2015.

Jeff DeLia of 72 Music Management

Bobby Rush with his dancers co-headlining the Big Blues Bender in Las Vegas, 2015. *Left to right*: Loretta "Jazzii" Anderson, Shakila "Kila" Powell, Bobby Rush, Bruce Howard. *Erik Kabik*

Bobby Rush and Morgan Freeman in Clarksdale, Mississippi, in 2015. Bobby Rush was inducted into the Rhythm & Blues Hall of Fame, and Morgan Freeman was given a Rhythm & Blues Lifetime Achievement Award. *Karen Pulfer Focht*

Recording session for album *Porcupine Meat* at the Parlor Recording Studio in New Orleans. *Left to right*: drummer Jeffery "Jellybean" Alexander, Vasti Jackson, Bobby Rush, engineer Steve Reynolds, producer Scott Billington.   *Jeff DeLia of 72 Music Management*

Bobby Rush performing with his two dancers, Erickia Henderson and Loretta "Mizz Lowe" Wilson, at the Chicago Blues Festival.   *Brigitte Charvolin*

Bobby Rush performing with his band at the San Diego Blues Festival in 2016. *Left to right*: Louis Rodriguez, Arthur Cooper, Mizz Lowe, Bobby Rush, Erickia Henderson.

Naugle Photography

Bobby Rush promotional picture for the *Porcupine Meat* album cycle, 2016–2017.

Rick Olivier

Bobby Rush accepting his Grammy Award for Best Traditional Blues Album. *Left to right*: Scott Billington (producer), Bobby Rush, Loretta "Mizz Lowe" Wilson (dancer).

Jeff Kravitz / Getty Images

Bobby Rush and his manager, Jeff DeLia, backstage at the Grammys in the "Celebration Room" talking business after *Porcupine Meat* won the Grammy in 2017.

Loretta Wilson, aka Mizz Lowe

Bobby Rush and the late civil rights activist, icon, and congressman John Lewis in 2017. *Boo Mitchell*

Bobby Rush playing harmonica during his band performance at Byron Bay Bluesfest in Australia in 2018. *Tao Jones Photographer*

Bobby Rush performing with Queens of the Stone Age at the Saenger Theatre during the New Orleans Jazz & Heritage Festival in 2018. *Left to right*: Bobby Rush, Josh Homme, Michael Shuman.

Erika Goldring

On the red carpet for the premiere of *Dolemite Is My Name*. *Left to right*: Bobby Rush, Eddie Murphy, Eddie Levert and Eric Grant of the O'Jays, Jimmy Lynch, Walter Williams of the O'Jays, and Mike Epps.

Frazer Harrison / Getty Images

Samuel L. Jackson requested and took a selfie with Bobby Rush at the premiere for *Dolemite Is My Name* in Los Angeles.

Jeff DeLia

Bobby Rush and Buddy Guy hanging out backstage at the Capitol Theatre in 2020.
Danny Clinch

Performing at the first official tribute concert to B.B. King since B.B. passed, with music director Tony Coleman (longtime drummer for B.B.), at the Capitol Theatre in Port Chester, New York, on February 16, 2020. *Left to right*: Bart Walker, Jamey Johnson, Buddy Guy, Bobby Rush, Jimmie Vaughn, Robert Cray, Warren Haynes, Ron Artis, Shemekia Copeland, William Bell, Ivan Neville. *Danny Clinch*

people deep. Cars would pass, the drivers probably thinking, "That 'que must be good." For us small guys, the competition was healthy.

For the big Black barbeque owners that had places to sit and six employees, their prospects were high. Barbeque joints were like the Black barber shops of Chicago. Folks would sit and talk at length about dirty Chicago politics or how cold it was last night. The barbeque business was a way up for many Black folks. A few would end up selling their barbeque sauce in local grocery stores. Some guys became wealthy. Some became leaders in the community.

But for me, it was just a good solid small business. As time moved on, I introduced something my daddy taught me how to do when I was a boy. And that was how to make my sausage. Jean would always marvel at how good my sausage tasted, and she said to me, "Bobby, you should sell this."

Barbeque like mine in Chicago was unique. Nobody near or far knew how to make sausage like me. It was very flavorful. This wasn't the hot links that are popular today in Chicago. But my blend of spices, especially sage, made my sausages unique. It was easy to get the casings to stuff the meat into. And I made the sausage right there in the shop. I'm sorry, but this was not a USDA government-inspected process. But the sausages were dee-lish-ish.

It was a great business. But the more successful it became, the more time it took away from my music. My highest-paying music gigs were on the weekends, but so were the most profitable days of Bobby's Barbeque House. My BBQ-sauce-covered money was crashing into my musical dreams. But I wouldn't give up either.

Frankly, there was no choice in the matter. I couldn't give up either one.

I had already bought Daddy and Maw's house in Pine Bluff for them. Just me. None of my siblings pitched in and I didn't ask them to. I stopped in Pine Bluff after a gig one morning and said, "Daddy, what they building 'cross the street?" "Aw, Junior, I don't know. I think some kinda duplex." Daddy had two vacant lots on both sides of the house. And I didn't want anybody puttin' up any kinda structure next to Maw and Daddy, so I bought both of the lots in cash. They were only $800 each; they'd be worth twenty-five times that today.

Bobby Rush's
Gotta Brand-New Dance

Even though Bobby's Barbeque House was competing for my time, it cooled me out with money. I continued to help Daddy. Paid my rent months in advance for the first time in my life and had cash to cover any gig that came up short. I've always been a hard worker, but just because I was working hard and saving a little money didn't mean my dreams were gone; in some ways I was dreaming more.

When I was sweating over that brick pit, I was thinking about how to improve my show. How to soup up my musical flair and increase my entertainment value. In Chicago we were competing with the best in jazz music that everybody knew was the top of the heap in musical expression. We were also competing with the best in the blues, and now we were competing with the best in soul and the best in doo-wop. Between beer joints that had jukeboxes, clubs that had small stages, and clubs that had larger stages with velvet curtains, we had to step up our game. Otherwise soon I'd hear, "He's just doing that same old shit he's always done."

I was playing a gig at Bonanza, down on Halsted, and saxophonist Monk Higgins wandered in.

"Bobby, you need a new record," Monk said.

"Who you tellin', mane."

"What's stopping you?"

The tug-of-war with my time, in a way, focused my music efforts more. Made me more laser-like in trying to get to the point. With that attitude, I wrote "Sock It to Me Boo Ga Loo." It's probably the tightest record I had recorded yet. I had a good thing in "Sock It To Me Boo Ga Loo." Kinda was a cross between 1965's "Papa's Got a Brand New Bag" and "Funky Broadway." Had a great band that day: Wayne Johnson and Luther Johnson. But the game changer was Cornelius "Mule" Boyson on bass, who would play with me for ten years. This was a 1960s Southern funky soul vibe. The high point of "Sock It to Me Boo Ga Loo" is the break where the electric bass solos with a walking-down funky riff. Mule played the shit out of that. It made way more noise than any other record I had put out. Although that noise was regional and not national, it was still sweet noise to me 'cause it got me more gigs. And even though this wasn't a down-home blues song, its uptown-current sound made folks take notice of me. I felt new to people—even though they knew me.

"Sock It to Me Boo Ga Loo" was another record that tried to create some kinda dance craze. And it was a good try. There was somethin' about a dance craze hit that made the dance more important than your song. But if you could catch that kinda wave, you could surf your ass onto *American Bandstand*. And in Chicago it seems someone was always floating a new dance song out on local radio.

Rufus's "Walking the Dog" had been a hit. And Rufus would make a career out of songs that created a dance like "Do the Funky Chicken," "The Breakdown," and "Do the Push and Pull," which I still play in my shows today. "Sock It to Me Boo Ga Loo" was by far the best-sounding record I had put out. But there was a misprint on the label, so "Sock It to Me Boo Ga Loo" came to be known as "Sock Boo Ga Loo." Released on Starville Records in late 1967, it broke out regionally. Starville then sold the distribution rights to Checker Records, a subsidiary of Chess Records.

With me now having a record on a label under the big Chess umbrella, I felt one step away from the big time.

Hope, Dead or Alive

This is what I always wanted. A little money in my pocket. A song that was at least known regionally. *And just the feelin'—just the feelin'* that I was close to my dreams. And I believed my dreams went through the front doors of Chess Records. Mel London, a songwriter, came to many of my shows, and though we were around the same age, he was kind of a mentor of mine. He was now working for Starville Records, the distributor that had sold the distribution rights of "Sock Boo Ga Loo" to Chess Records.

"Bobbyrush, if you want to be on Chess so bad, why don't you get Muddy to help you?" Mel asked.

That was a good question—one that I didn't have an answer for. One that would take me decades to answer. But his question was as right as rain. Why didn't I reach out for help? After all, Muddy was not only the first premier artist on the label, he was a friend to Leonard and Phil. I don't know all the dynamics of their complicated, mutually beneficial, greasy relationship, but if I'd asked Muddy to vouch for me, he would have. So would have Etta James, as she was Chess's first female star. Her hit in 1960, "At Last," on yet another Chess subsidiary, Argo Records, is still one of the greatest recordings ever. When Etta arrived in Chicago years earlier, I picked her up from the airport in a cab I was driving. She would soon come to know me as more than a cab driver and thereafter remained my friend.

Clearly I had a blind spot. I did not see that for all my high energy and assertiveness, I was not being assertive with simply asking the people who loved me for help. I swear to God, I don't know if it was my youth, my pride, fear, stubbornness, shame, or some other big word that Dr. Phil knows but I don't. But whatever it was, it kept me from getting the leg up I needed from Muddy, Little Walter, Howlin' Wolf, and especially Albert King, who would have done anything for me. I just didn't use my greatest asset—which was my friends.

Since 1957 Chess had had a storefront building at 2120 South Michigan Avenue in the heart of Record Row. But they had become so big that in the summer of 1967 they moved into the old 3M building at 320 East Twenty-First Street. With the building eight stories high, it only cemented in my mind that Chess Records had the big dick.

But less than a year earlier, in 1966, something completely random happened that changed the course of my destiny with Chess. In 1966, the two big musicians' unions in Chicago merged. Union 208, the Black union, and Union 10, the white union. Before they merged, Union 208 was one of the better musicians' unions in the country for Negroes, because there was no discrimination with the only word that mattered—scale. Our scale pay was the same as the white boys' in Union 10.

We were all in the musicians' union. Me, Muddy Waters, Buddy Guy, Bo Diddley, Howlin' Wolf—everybody. And all the jazz cats, too. We were at least thirteen hundred members strong. You must understand that the recording studio business, the nightclub business, the radio broadcast business, and the performing arts business had been thriving in Chicago for years. And the recording biz was on par with what the recording studio system would become to Los Angeles in the '70s and '80s.

But where the dirty dealing came in was where we could get gigs in Chicago. It was so dirty that it made Chicago politics look clean. They would not hire Negroes in the downtown hotels and nightclubs 'cause those hotels had mostly white patrons. But through much legal wrangling, the unions were still merged, becoming the new Chicago Federation of Musicians Union 10-208 in January 1966.

Back to the winter of 1967. Mel London, who had written tunes for Howlin' Wolf, Elmore James, Junior Wells, and of course Chess Records' first star, Muddy Waters, said he would walk me into Phil Chess's office. Mel had credibility. His compositions "Poison Ivy" and "Mannish Boy" had become blues music standards.

"Bobby, you got the big three," Mel said.

"What's that, Mel?"

"Good show, good looks, and good songs."

"Mane, thank ya, thank ya, thank ya."

"Wait now. Don't get too happy, because you always can write better songs."

Mel and I were around the same age—but he was trying to mentor me, in a way. Trying to get something across to me. That the music business was all about songs. Better songs. Craftier songs. Songs that didn't just come to you in the ether—but songs that you sat down to write willfully. In other words, *I'm gonna write a song about this today*. He was a pro in how he went about songwriting.

The day Mel and I strolled into Phil Chess's office, I felt confident. There was some cat sitting on the couch, and Mel and him exchanged some banter while Phil was on the phone. I picked up the new labor contract of the now-merged Musicians Union 10-208 that was sitting on a side table in his office. I just started reading it to pass the time. It wasn't anything confidential; I was in the union anyway, and I could have seen that contract anytime.

After reading some of the union contract, I said to Mel, "Mane, this is going to be sumthin' gooood for us." I started reading Mel some of the provisions in the contract, and Phil, now off the phone, said to his brother, Leonard Chess, "Where'd that boy get that information from?"

Leonard said, "Off your coffee table, Phil."

You got to understand something here. I know I don't speak the King's English. And I know that some might take that as me being as dumb as a sack of nails. But I could really read my ass off. So when Phil said, "Bobbyrush, read that first paragraph again to me," I looked down and quickly read word for word—all in my Southern tone—all them big old legalese-type words. Phil said to Leonard, "We can't sign this nigger—he can really read." And although everybody chuckled but me—it dejected me because I knew right then and there that my dream of being on Chess Records was dead. This was 1967.

I ain't gonna be philosophical about it. I won't give you all that hokum like, "It was for the best," or "God has sumthin' better."

The scene in Phil's office hit me as hard as a prizefighter's punch. But as I said earlier: when I was a boy, there was one sentence that guided my young life, and that was *"I ain't gonna let it beat me."* So I was again dejected—but not defeated. Also, Phil's "this nigger can read" comment wasn't exactly breaking news to me or surprising to anyone who knew him. It had a sting—but not the sting that you may think.

I didn't take it racially.

Because Phil and Leonard would routinely cuss out the musicians at Chess. Most of them felt it was funny. In sessions I attended and stories told to me over the years, most of their stinging talk went like this:

"Motherfucker, ain't you got it right yet?"

"Turn that shit up or turn that shit down."

If you were offended easily, working for the Chess brothers was not for you.

I was a country boy obsessed with Chess Records for all the right and wrong reasons. One right reason was that a big hit song could change my life. A wrong reason was believing that my chances were limited to Phil and Leonard Chess. And the hands of time can even crush the powerful. It wouldn't be a year later, in December 1968, when word got out that Chess Records, the top seed of Chicago's royal and rotten cutting-edge and cutthroat Record Row, was gonna be sold. And Record Row would never be the same.

Around the same time that Chess Records was sold, I recorded a few sides for Salem Records. Between early 1969 and late 1970, I released four songs: "Wake Up," "The Things That I Used to Do," "Let It All Hang Out," and "Just Be Yourself."

Musically, I couldn't have been happier. Great horns, bass, drums, guitar, and organ work. Band sounded great. We had great songs, if I must say so myself. The songs were right where I needed them to be. A solid mix of soul and blues. My only regret is that I didn't have money to put strings on "The Things That I Used to Do." The song had such a hard swing on it—you cannot hear that song and not swing back and forth. Had a key change that elevated the second half and fades out on a double-time feel. It's really a very well-crafted record. I was growing as a producer and writer and could now distinguish the difference between a great record and a great song. That was a part of musical maturity: that I could tell the difference between the two, and with "The Things That I Used to Do," I had both.

If those Salem records had been promoted properly—they could have had a chance to chart nationally. But my musical growth had its own reward. It was my best work so far. And that was a mighty good feeling.

Ray

I was over the moon, booked to be one of four acts opening for Ray Charles at the Apollo in New York. In those days, an act might play a whole week at the Apollo, including a matinee on Sunday. But Ray was doing three nights in a row. In those days I was essentially doing a top forty set. And I always felt that I had to switch things up to keep audiences engaged. So on the second night I had my band in there early, rehearsing before the audience was let in. I was summoned to Ray's dressing room.

"Youngblood, why are you changing your show?"

"Aw, Ray, I'm adding a new song or two, and opening with a different number."

"Boy, you got a good show—if ain't broke, don't fix it."

"Yeah, but I thought if some of the same peoples from last night show up tonight, I need to give 'em something different."

"No, no, no, boy. *Don't change your show—change towns.*"

I had a small vision of what show business was. Lesson learned. And to not change my show—move on.

Thrashin'

All bluesmen are optimists. You almost gotta be. The next record. The next big gig. And maybe this old bumpy dirt road will turn into a freshly paved easy street. From 1964 to 1971, my first seven years of recording, I had been on seven different labels. I thought about something Daddy used to say: *"Just because you're thrashin' in the water doesn't mean you're going to get across the lake."* And I was thrashing—only releasing singles. No hits. No album deals.

You can't understand why I bounced from this label to that, then to that, then to that, unless you understand the flood of small independent blues labels that were in Chicago in the 1950s and '60s. People just think in terms of Vee-Jay, Chess, Brunswick. But there was Chance Records, One-derful Records, Cobra Records, King Records, Constellation Records, and many others. There were at least fourteen distributors right on or around Record Row. And a few little guys that would press your record, plop a label on it, and throw it up in the air to see if it would stick to the magic wall called the radio.

The reason I always had a hope of something stickin' was because WVON (Voice of the Negro) had so much power. Owned by the Chess brothers, it was the first twenty-four-hour Black radio station in Chicago. I knew all the DJs: Stan Ricardo, Al Benson, Herb "The Gent" Kent, and my good friend Pervis Spann, who was known as "The Blues Man." So if you persuaded some DJ by legitimate ways or the usual illegitimate ways of payola, you had the possibility of breaking out. And in them days, a hit record in Chicago was like a spark. Hopefully catching fire in Detroit, LA, New York, or DC. So I just kept on trying.

In 1970, four years after Vee-Jay collapsed, Calvin Carter's name still meant something and the Vee-Jay name still meant something—at least to me. I saw Calvin one morning on Roosevelt Road.

"Mane, Calvin, I got a song for you!"

"What's it called?"

"Chick Head."

"Bobbyrush—you mean like a girl giving you head?"

"Yeah, mane, what'chu think it mean?"

"Bring your guitar and come on by the office and play it for me and Leo." Leo Austell was a cat who, through songwriting, working for record companies, and creating companies himself, had graduated to become one of the many Chicago music hustlers.

Arriving at Calvin's office, I sat down, tuned up, and sprang into "Chick Head," singing:

Daddy told me on his dying bed,
Give up your heart and not your head.
You come along, girl, what did I do?
I lost my heart, and my head went too.

Got through the first verse and hook and Leo said, "That's a pretty good record—a nice play on words—what's it called?" In that split second, it all came clear to me. Leo Austell was a devout—very devout—Jehovah's Witness. He even later tried to sign me up! So in the twinklin' of an eye I realized: ain't no way he wants a song about a girl giving head. So my response was "The tune's called 'Chicken Heads.'"

"Oh, I get it—you like them songs with those animal names," he said.

"Yeah, Leo. You know I'm justa country boy."

"Let's put it out!"

But don't get it twisted. "Chicken Heads" ain't lewd. It's sly. A play on words.

Even though Vee-Jay had folded six years earlier, Calvin's name still meant something, and he was a good producer.

"What's gonna be the B side?" Leo asked.

"Mary Jane," I said.

"Great, I once had a girlfriend named Mary Jane."

Holy roller, Leo didn't know I was talking about weed, and Calvin went along. I recorded "Chicken Heads" at Universal Studios in Chicago, but Calvin scammed me. He charged me $800 for the studio time. I was as dumb as a sack of hair. Why? I shouldn't have been charged anything! But because of his association with Vee-Jay and hit records, I thought I needed Calvin. When in reality he needed me. After all, Calvin and Leo were gonna sell the record and find me a distributor. On top of that, he charged Betty Everett's manager $800, too. Same day. Same block of time. By the time Betty's song was cut, there was only an hour left for mine.

Rushing and playing guitar, I showed the band he hired the song. Seems like they couldn't get it. The studio clock was ticking. I said, "Lemme try ta show ya from the top of the song." The drummer counted it off, and we played the song down.

I said, "See, that's all you gotta do."

I told the engineer, "Okay, let's record it."

He said, "It's done."

"What'chu mean?" I shot back.

He said, "I was recording your rehearsal."

The track came out great. A funky yet simple bass line with greasy guitar work and a little 1971 wah-wah thrown in. A really tight thing between the drums and bass held it all together with the hi-hat being the only thing that runs through the whole song. I didn't know then, but this was where my own style was born—folk funk. An intense, pregnant blues sound. It was as if James Brown, Bo Diddley, and future star Prince had had a baby.

That folk-funk child is all about a groove with a down-home story to tell. You ain't gotta figure out what it's saying, 'cause it's right there for you—even with my usual trick of double meanings for words. It's a primal but electrified groove right out of the heart of the Delta and the swamps of my sweet home Louisiana.

Galaxy, yet another Chicago record label, released "Chicken Heads." The song became my breakout record. Got to No. 34. And certain little markets were playing it more than others. But on the Black radio stations in the Little Rock/Pine Bluff area, they were playing it on regular rotation. So when my little brother A. J. asked me to sing it when I was visiting home, I obliged.

Daddy told me on his dying bed,
Give up your heart
But don't give up ya head

Maw popped 'round the corner into A. J.'s room and said, "That ain't it! It's . . .

Daddy told me on his dying bed,
Give up your heart
But don't you LOSE your head

"If ya gone sing it, sing it right," Maw said as she left with a smile on her face. Guess Maw knew about my moment, too. I wasn't shocked, but if I said it didn't make me smile—I'd be lyin'. Daddy and Maw never saw me play. I ain't crying on some shrink's couch about it. Just stating a fact.

Close

Even more than chart success, "Chicken Heads" put me in a Southern blues/funk direction, a direction that would put me as close as I ever would be to the mainstream Black music market. This was because in 1970 King Floyd had a crossover smash with "Groove Me." Also, around the same time Jean Knight had even a bigger hit, "Mr. Big Stuff." Same rhythm section played on both. Both had a Southern blues/funk sound. Both were recorded deep in the South at Malaco Records in Jackson, Mississippi.

But Calvin Carter screwed me every which way to Sunday. He wasn't interested in me at all. After screwing me in the studio time, he wasn't done. Registering my songs with BMI, he put his name as co-writer on my songs, and he hadn't written one motherfuckin' note.

To prevent me from killing him, I guess, Calvin Carter sold my contract to Stan "The Man" Lewis's Jewel Records for $10,000. As record men go, Stan was a fair guy. Stan is one of the untold stories of the biz. He started out by placing jukeboxes in Negro nightclubs, and then bought a record store in his hometown of Shreveport, Louisiana, that quickly became *the* record shop for a hundred miles around. In time he became what they call in the business a one-stop. Soon he was distributing records for most of the labels who were working early R&B records: Fats Domino's Imperial Records, Little Richard's Specialty Records, Chess, and others. Stan the Man also distributed for most of the independent labels in the South. You could have a regional hit if Stan's distribution network propped you up.

On his Jewel Records label we re-released "Bowlegged Woman, Knock-Kneed Man." Though not a hit, it continued to establish the name of Bobby Rush. In that frame of mind, I cut a slower bluesy remake of the swamp rock hit "Niki Hoeky." With song titles like that under my belt, my name became associated with odd, clever, and Southern-like stories.

But of course my life was not about the studio, it was about the gigs. Around 1973, right after "Bowlegged Woman, Knock-Kneed Man," a young man joined my band who would become a friend for life. Benjamin Wright was an out-of-this-world keyboardist. Ben came into my band with more equipment than anyone ever had. He had a Hammond B-3, two Leslies, amps, a Clavinet D6 (an instrument that Stevie Wonder was popularizing), and a Fender Rhodes that had just come out. He was like a white cat who came from money! But as bad as Ben was, his best playing was with his pen. Ben Wright became the cream of the crop in arranging. He would have an out-of-this-world career arranging hits for Michael Jackson; Earth, Wind and Fire; Justin Timberlake; Outkast; Aretha Franklin; and so many more.

Ben arranged for me three records in '74, '75, and '76. "Get Out of Here" for Warner Brothers; "I'm Still Waiting" and "She Put the Whammy on Me" for London Records. Full orchestra, horns, strings, keyboards, synthesizers, the whole ball of wax. These three songs were the best-sounding records I had ever cut. I was progressing.

But at what cost? Paying for an orchestra was in the thousands, and it all came out of my pocket. I had day jobs, night jobs, a hot dog truck, and a barbecue joint. I also picked up scrap iron and bottles and turned that into cash. Had worked out with Mr. Walton of Walton's Corner to play a matinee show on Sunday afternoons, where he let me have the door. As most clubs do, he still made his money at the bar. That money helped me keep a somewhat consistent band together. It was the cost of not being signed to a label that invested in you year after year.

I had always depended on my enormous energy to make it. Still, the way I handled my money was destroying my family. Jean worked, but every dime I made I saved for the studio. It created strain—not from Jean, but with myself. 'Cause you ain't a man unless you are taking care of your family. And I was still sending first wife Hazel and Daddy and Maw money back in Pine Bluff.

But with still no big, juicy hit records, I was withering on the vine. And after putting out those impressive records with the orchestra and not getting traction, I was probably a little depressed. But of course I didn't know it then. I just kept pushing, shaking the shaker, hoping the pepper comes out. What added to my frustration was that I saw buddies who had label support were really cooking. My buddy Little Milton always laid it on me about having some help in getting things done.

"Bobby, let me tell you, when I did my first album for Stax, *Waiting for Little Milton*, they let me alone and I had their studio band and the Memphis Horns—and the Memphis Symphony played on it."

And it was an outta sight record in 1973, his biggest since *We're Gonna Make It*. Of course, in the record biz world your recording budget ain't nothing but a loan. You gotta pay all the bread back. But at least Little Milton didn't have to come out of his pocket to get his album done. Hell, I had been in the business forever and hadn't even done an album yet. And I was still ponying up every dime for every minute of studio time and promotion myself.

My Kinda Song

Even though my next three releases, "Bowlegged Woman, Knock-Kneed Man," "Gotta Be Funky," and "Gotta Find You Girl," were less successful than "Chicken Heads," Southern blues/soul/funk was having a moment. Also, having a moment were some of my old buddies from the bottom who were finding their way to the top of the music mountain. Cats like Clarence Carter, a blind bluesman from Alabama, who scored a big pop hit with "Patches." The tune, co-written by General Johnson of the Chairmen of the Board is a perfect mixture of blues, R&B, country, and soul. "Patches" was an important song for me because some of Clarence's lyrics are spoken. And I would adopt some of that style later. Even though it made the song sound Southern, it also made the song honest. It tells a heartbreaking story about a farm boy named Patches. Everybody called him that because of his patched-up clothes. His daddy tells Patches on his dying bed to "pull the family though—it all left up to you." Mane, it was my kinda song.

Ike and Tina recorded "Proud Mary" in 1970. Ike in his musical wisdom changed drastically the original by Creedence Clearwater Revival. Released in early '71, it was a bluesy, rock-y, high-energy smash. The biggest thing for Ike and Tina. General Johnson won a Grammy for writing "Patches," and Ike and Tina won a Grammy for "Proud Mary."

But the earthquake in the blues came a little earlier, in 1970, when B.B. King released "The Thrill Is Gone." It became B.B.'s biggest hit and his signature song. Mane, it was a smash and recorded immaculately. But none of B.B.'s band played on that record—it was all New York studio cats. The icing on the cake was the producer adding these lushy strings to the track. Them strings didn't swamp the song—just the right pinch of salt to make the flavor of the tune come alive.

B.B.'s success spelled out how you could have a crossover blues record. However, that formula of great musicianship mixed with a tasty orchestra would soon be taken over by R&B. And "The Thrill Is Gone" is really the last pop-blues smash. But it would be enough to carry B.B. further than he thought he could ever go.

But for me, I would try to adjust to the changing times. One of the big changes came with a phone call.

"Bobbyrush, Stax don't want no more harp playing on their records," Rufus Thomas said.

"But why?" I said.

"'Cause it sounds old-timey, boy!"

I could see Rufus's big round nostrils flaring up right through the phone. Well, if harp playing was old-timey, I knew I didn't want any part of that. It would take me some time, but in the '70s I gradually put away my harmonica. I can't say it was a decision I thought about, because if I had I would have seen the writing on the wall. They glued the blues and the harp together at the hip. The harp was to the blues as the guitar was to rock 'n' roll—as close as butter on toast. So if it sounded behind the times, was the blues next?

When We Lost the Ladies

Still, Chicago blues were still thriving. Even after riots and economic dipsy doodles, most of the clubs in the Black part of town were still hanging in. We all drank the Kool-Aid, believing that people, especially the ladies, were looking to blues music for their comfort music. This was not true. The romantic side of the blues was never too syrupy. It was like that line in Z. Z.'s "Down Home Blues": *"Tonight I'm gonna do as I choose."* That was a big part of it. It was something I used to hear Howlin' Wolf say: *"You cain't buy love, but you can buy something feels a whole lot like it."* What I'm tryin' to get at here is that the romance of the blues was often about receiving love and not giving love.

But even that's not the whole story.

So much of this stuff is about what the blues is. And who gets to say what the blues is. Is the blues of the '50s the same as the blues in the '70s? Is one of the most romantic songs in history, "At Last" by Etta James, not the blues? Yes it's R&B, soul, and even pop. But its roots are totally the blues. So as music started to blend together in the '70s, the word "blues" got taken down a peg or two, plus ten.

The Chicago soul sound that started in the '60s gave way to a smoother and more romantic sound that appealed directly to women. This sweet sound would wash the blues away from the mainstream. The center of romantic soul music became beautiful and lush. Starting 'round '68 when the Delfonics came out with "La-La (Means I Love You)," it's like all the women fell head over heels in love with that stuff. Then in '71 "Just My Imagination" by the Temptations and "Have You Seen Her" by the Chi-Lites softened the sisters' hearts and ears even

169

more. By the time "Could It Be I'm Falling in Love" and "One of a Kind Love Affair" by the Spinners hit in '72 and '73, a new Black music was blooming. These were Black hits, pop hits, and what they would one day call "adult contemporary." But the Stylistics had the biggest run of this stuff all within three years. "You Are Everything," "Betcha by Golly, Wow," "I'm Stone in Love with You," "Break Up to Make Up," and "You Make Me Feel Brand New" were as sweet as sweet could be— and huge smashes. This music was not the blues.

They were all male singing groups. And, mane, had they changed from the early days. They all gave up their conked hair for the baddest, most manicured, perfect afros you've ever seen. These tall, tough, and handsome Black men sang these tender masterpieces. They were digni-fied Negroes that seemed aware and hip, too. And even in their hipness they could fall on their knees begging to their women, saying: *"Come with me, baby. Sorry I lost you, baby. There's nothing I want more than you, baby. Don't leave me, baby."*

The recordings sounded modern. All had orchestra-sounding strings and horns. This lush sound took the hearts of the sisters. The blues sounded gutbucket and moldy compared with this gorgeous music.

And *gutbucket* meant something in most of Black Americans' ear-drums that had nothing to do with music itself.

Gutbucket equals behind the times.

Gutbucket equals conked hair, not an afro.

Gutbucket equals being passive, not revolutionary.

Gutbucket equals *Amos 'n' Andy*, not *Shaft* or *Super Fly*.

Gutbucket equals 1951, not 1971.

The blues as we knew it would never fully recover.

Embarrassed and Embraced

On Southern jukeboxes and radio, I got to be known for "Chicken Heads." This is what I mean by known: when my name appeared on a poster board with five or six other acts, it read: BOBBY RUSH; then under my name in much smaller letters, it read: "CHICKEN HEADS."

In the mid-'70s outdoor summer music festivals were starting to heat up. Some people were calling it the "Revival Circuit" because most of the acts on these shows were performers who had hits in years past. Lots of 1950s acts like the Drifters (whatever version of them), Fats Domino, the Platters, and others; they all played these all-day Revival Circuit Saturday festivals.

In 1974 or '75, I along with the Meters, Clarence Carter, Billy Preston, and others I can't recall played one of these outdoor festivals in Atlanta. Headlining the show was the king, Little Richard.

Richard and I were old friends. He was a mentor—as an entertainer and as a person. I know most folk think of Little Richard as screamin' in his falsetto, "Good Golly, Miss Molly." Or with the wigs and clothes, seeing him acting flamboyantly and flashy on television awards shows. But Little Richard was really a man you could talk to about almost anything. And I know he flipped publicly back and forth between singing the so-called devil's music and gospel, but he really loved the Lord—seriously.

I hung around after my set to see a little of Little Richard's show, as I hadn't seen him perform in a while. Third or fourth song in, he cranked up "Tutti Frutti"; of course the audience was in heaven, and he ended the song with: "A-wop-bop-a-loo-bop-a-lop-bam-boom!"

The crowd rose to its feet. He walked out from behind the piano and strolled to center stage, grabbing a waiting microphone. He said:

"I'm so very glad to be in my home state of Georgia tonight. Y'all know I'm from Macon, right down the road, don't cha?" The crowd yelled enthusiastically.

"I wish I was in Macon tonight—but since I can't be, I'm so glad to be with you good people here in Atlanta. I'm also so happy to share the stage with all these great artists today. Give 'em a hand, y'all." The crowd clapped loudly.

Then, in Little Richard's classic style, he said, "HUSH!" The crowd burst out laughing. Now he had them eating out of his hands.

"Folks, I wanna let you know that today you are being entertained by two of the prettiest artists in the whole wide world—that's myself and Bobby Rush! Come on up here, Bobby, so they can see how pretty we are!"

I was so embarrassed. 'Cause he didn't say handsome! But it was funny as shit, and of course I jogged up the stairs with my long, flowing pressed hair and dashed to the center of the stage and embraced the King of Rock 'n' Roll.

Please, Lord, Not My Face

Maybe I was fooling myself, believing I could handle everything on my plate. The success of "Chicken Heads" kept me busy, and thank God I still had my barbeque joint. And it was doing good business. Had two women employees. On instinct, I felt one of them might not be on the up and up with me. One of them raced out one night at closing, and accidentally I bumped into her and heard a squishy sound. She had shrimp in her purse; it was three pounds if it was an ounce. But—surprise—this was not the one I had suspected. Also, I thought she'd been stealing money—not product! And crazily, that made me even madder.

"Doris, why you do this—ain't I been fair to ya?"

"Bobby, I'm so-so sorry; please forgive me."

"Doris, I surely do. But you're still fired."

Even though she begged, I couldn't deal with her. It wasn't even personal. I had just way too much going on. Playing gigs. Keeping the place open. Getting my suits to the cleaners. Buying meat. Calling radio stations. Hauling scrap iron. I didn't need one more drop of worry. I was barely holdin' on with my time and my common sense. Trying to have a music career and sell barbeque from my storefront. As much of a headache and a blessing that it was, I wasn't giving it up—no way, no how.

But sometimes the good Lord makes decisions for you.

In the wee hours of a Monday morning after a gig somewhere just outside of town, I stuck my key into the big metal lock of Bobby's Barbeque House. Pulled the metal gate back. I looked over my shoulder,

173

as this was Chicago, and I was always cautious about coming and going from the restaurant at odd hours.

I then stuck my other key in the glass-and-steel front door and jiggled the door open. I turned around to flick on the fluorescent light rods in the ceiling. And *BOOM!* An explosion. I remember little after that except heat and pain. I crawled a few steps, then lights out.

Waking up in the hospital, all I heard was Jean praying. Jean is a fighter—a spiritual warrior. And as the rappers say, a straight-up ride-or-die chick. They had wrapped me up from head to toe in white, gauze-like material. You could only see my eyeballs. I was in and out. I think with Jean praying so deeply, it took me back in time to my teens. I dreamed and dreamed and dreamed. Often I'm with Daddy at St. Joseph's Missionary Baptist Church in Sherrill, Arkansas. Old Negro spirituals dominated those dreams.

Precious Lord, take my hand
Lead me on, let me stand
I'm tired, I'm weak, I'm 'lone
Through the storm, through the night
Lead me on to the light
Take my hand, precious Lord, lead me home

Or it was . . .

Walk with me, Lord; walk with me
Walk with me, Lord; walk with me
Ooh, while I'm on this tedious journey
I want Jesus to walk with me

I don't know how the brain, soul, and morphine work together. But I was definitely in a land far, far away. I remember briefly waking up and hearing my sister Gerdia praying, too. My brother Larry, who was now living in Chicago, arrived, and of course Alvin.

I had severe third-degree burns. They called them full-thickness burns. The fire wiped out the outer layer of my skin (the epidermis) and the entire layer beneath (the dermis). I was charred up bad. But the pain. To say the pain was unbearable is mocking the word *unbearable*. Jean, being a nurse, understood more than me what a horrific trauma my body had been through. She was optimistic with me, but she was also protecting my spirit—giving me hope.

Found out later that a gas leak caused the explosion. If it wasn't for the glass door that blew open, I would never have gotten out to the sidewalk. I'm blessed, as I've cheated death a few times in my life. After a week or two, they took all that cheesecloth off. Large crusted scabs covered my neck, chest, arms, and some of my upper thigh. Don't mean to sound shallow, but praise the Lord, the lasting scars were to my torso and not my face!

I was in the hospital for weeks. They told me I would probably have lifetime scars. But if I wanted minimal scarring, they could brush off the scabs and dead tissue and that would probably lessen any skin grafting that may have to be done. But they didn't mince words. "Mr. Ellis, if you choose the brushing, it will be extremely painful." Again, I was concerned mostly with my neck, face, and hands; everything else I could cover up. Fearfully, I still chose the full-body brush sessions.

I had insurance on the place and got a decent check. As I lay in that bed my last week in the hospital, two things I knew for sure. They did not lie one bit about the pain of scab brushing, and I was out of the barbeque business.

Exposure of a
Whole Nother Color, Brother

Everybody that came up in the Chitlin Circuit knew Redd Foxx. We were part of the comedian's tribe. Pigmeat Markham, a good man who I met when I first arrived in Chicago; Moms Mabley, who was the queen of comedy and definitely the queen of the Chitlin Circuit; George Kirby; Rudy Ray Moore; a duo named Stump and Stumpy, who in the 1950s started to be billed as the Negro Martin and Lewis. They were all a part of the tribe. And there were many others. I played gigs with many of them, and we were all happy when Redd Foxx scored with *Sanford and Son*. And Redd, true to form, didn't forget where he came from. He hired all his buddies from the Chitlin Circuit. LaWanda Page (Aunt Esther) was a Chitlin Circuit regular with some of the raunchiest jokes you done ever heard. Redd also hired Scatman Crothers, Slappy White, Timmie "Smiley" Rogers, and Leroy & Skillet as guests. All Chitlin Circuit survivors.

1977 was the last year of *Sanford and Son*'s run. Redd really wanted B.B. King to do his show, which he did. The writers created a story that was all about B.B., Fred, and Esther—it was funny as shit. But the highlights were Fred going to see B.B. perform and a jam session at the end, where Fred and Esther (Redd and LaWanda) join in the singing. It gave fifteen million people a taste of what it was like to be sitting at a table with a white tablecloth, sipping a drink, talking some stuff, and listening to the King of the Blues, B.B. King. B.B. had been on TV a thousand times. But *Sanford and Son* was so popular that B.B.'s ticket sales jumped, and he never looked back. B.B. told me in the months after the show ran:

"Bobby, let me tell ya something. You can play in front of five thousand people. You can play in front of twenty thousand people and you say, man, what great exposure. But when you play in front of fifteen million, that's exposure of a whole nother color, brother."

Couldn't question B.B. He knew what the fuck he was talking about and had paid the cost to be the boss. He'd been all over the world a thousand times. Everywhere: Australia, Africa, Europe, everywhere. So he could evangelize about the power of TV exposure.

B.B. got to be the King of the Blues by having moments. Huge turning points. When he did his first Fillmore concert in San Francisco, produced by the great Bill Graham in 1967, he walked onstage and saw the crowd. He said to himself, "Damn, ain't nothing but white hippies." That one performance connected him to a whole different generation. Then "The Thrill Is Gone" became a smash in '71. And B.B. wasn't making more than a thousand bucks a night in 1969. But after *Sanford and Son*, he just took off down the open road in the fastest Corvette he could find. Big-time collaborations in the 1980s and '90s. Had a hit with "Into the Night" from a movie. Then came the big touring checks. Then the nightclub in his name.

Damn straight, the King of the Blues.

I'm Sure—I Hope—I Believe

Years after our divorce, Hazel, my first wife, remained a part of the family. I can't say I always liked that, but she did. She was friends with my sisters and with my wife, Jean. A big part of that is because Jean's heart and self-esteem are so big. Even when Hazel remarried, she and her new husband became members of my brother Alvin's church in Chicago.

So I already knew that my first child, Valerie, was sick. Like little Sherry—it was sickle cell. Val lived long after most people who had sickle cell back then—we was always thanking God for that. We thanked God she got the chance to graduate from high school. Valerie died in 1977 at twenty-one years old.

I don't really believe I felt grief until that moment. I cried, but not a lot. I just went into myself.

Looking back, my faith wasn't prepared. And it never could have been. One of them big questions, I guess. 'Cause ain't no one prepared to lose a child—you feel like God has cheated you. On this side of the curtain I'm sure—I hope—I believe that I'll deal with my leaving this earth better than I did losing my child.

But I'm still in that club. Parents who lose children. When I lost Valerie in '77, I wondered: *Is it me?* And knowing it was sickle cell. When you're broken, you're confused.

Rush Hour

It sounds made up. It sounds like it won't hold water. It sounds far-fetched. Down-home Bobby Rush working with uptown hitmakers Gamble and Huff? After all, Gamble and Huff gave the world some of the most well-put-together music for a generation. They had success on top of more success. And they're gonna work with Bobby Rush?

But that's just what happened. Don't think my self-esteem was low. It wasn't. It's just that I knew who I was musically in 1979. I was a blues artist. Okay, blues/soul artist, if that makes ya feel better.

Granville White, one of the great Black CBS Records men out of Chicago, cornered me at a convention.

"Bobbyrush, the blues is gonna come back."

"From your lips to God's ears!" I said.

"You just need the right producer."

"I'm open, Granville."

"You know Gamble and Huff wanna try something different—think they may be bored." I wondered: *How could they be?* Along with Thom Bell, Gamble and Huff stand alone for what they did as songwriters, producers, and entrepreneurs. The O'Jays, Harold Melvin and the Blue Notes, Lou Rawls, Patti LaBelle, Teddy Pendergrass, Billy Paul, and so many others—Gamble and Huff had either written or produced hit records for. They had their fingerprints on so many worldwide smashes—so of course I was happier than a pig eating slop.

It wasn't three months later, after I signed a deal with Gamble and Huff's Philadelphia International Records, that I was on an Eastern Airlines flight from O'Hare airport to Philly. In the air, I felt grateful to be off on a new musical road. Above the clouds, I realized this would have not happened if it wasn't for those songs that Ben arranged for me. Even though spending that money was hard, those songs were a bridge to this moment. I didn't think it would have happened without that so-called failure. Or maybe it wasn't a failure. *Mmmm.*

I learned an important lesson about partnerships. Kenny Gamble is a powerful communicator. Can talk in a way that captivates you. Leon Huff, on the other hand, is quiet. When I would see the back-and-forth between them, I thought about all those worldwide hits—success comes down to how two men interact with one another. Two personalities, one success.

I wrote songs with Leon Huff. Him at the piano, mostly. Learned so much about songcraft and music production—layering sound and building tracks. But they didn't try to make me be anything that I wasn't. That's a testament to their wisdom. When I listen today to "I Wanna Do the Do," it strikes me as funny. 'Cause Leon had me play harp, but the way he had me play it sounds like we sampled it—2020 style. He had me repeat licks that sat in the track just like a sample. Those harp licks were part of the track, almost as if someone had taken a bit from a vinyl record and sampled it in. I think that's why the hipsters have adopted "I Wanna Do the Do" as their own. We also recorded an instrumental called "Intermission" that had a sweet harp melody that then went into a bluesy funk.

These songs on my 1979 Philadelphia International release *Rush Hour* were the blues. Great bass lines, organ, and two rhythm guitars. All the tracks were funky, tight, and just greasy enough. Many of them up-tempo. My vocals were as blue and swampy.

The album came out and it was noticed. *Rolling Stone* gave *Rush Hour* high praise. As a matter of fact, in 2019 they published an article titled "10 Blues Albums Rolling Stone Loved in the 1970s That You Never Heard." I was in good company as they also honored albums by Charlie Musselwhite, Memphis Slim, Edgar Winter, Junior Wells, and others.

But what I like about that record is that it really said who I am. Because if Bobby Rush can go through the Gamble and Huff finishing school and still come out as Bobby Rush, then Bobby Rush must be okay.

Little Milton's Word to the Wise

Clarksdale, Mississippi. Where Ike Turner and Sam Cooke were born and Bessie Smith died. I'm sitting in the back of Little Milton's nice-ass bus. We're both sipping water and trying to catch up before I have to get off and he has to get going.

"Milt—how you git all this? Nice bus, everybody dressed nice—you cain't be gittin' paid *that* much more than me." He laughed.

"Rush, I tell ya, I had to become more self-reliant."

"Like what?"

"Booking my own gigs, buying a bus, promoting myself, handlin' my own business."

"Keeping other hands out of your pocket is what you're saying to me."

"Yeah, but Bobbyrush, it's just thinking 'bout business way more than music. I got the music thing down."

And he did. Milton was the most sexy and commanding of the romantic blues/soul singers. I say blues/soul for a reason—'cause he got that spot early. He had been putting out singles since the mid-fifties. Scored with "We're Gonna Make It" and "Who's Cheatin' Who" in '65. Both were more soul than blues. From Chess to Stax to Malaco, my friend never stopped sounding great. Never saw him or his band when they weren't clean as a tack. He dressed for the ladies. He would drop on his knees for the ladies. Sang to the ladies. The kind of cat women throw their panties on the stage for.

And a very gifted singer.

In the '50s, '60s, and '70s, he kept on releasing singles—later albums. Milton had more record success than I did. But by 1979 or 1980 neither one of us for sure was relying on records to earn' a livin'. Both of us had long been working the Chitlin Circuit like a bad habit.

What Little Milton encouraged me to do I already had in place. I was a completely self-sustaining operation. But Milton impressed me, because for as long as I can remember all the club owners spoke highly of him, every last one of them. I learned that the most important thing to do was to maintain some kind of integrity with the club owners, and with everyone I was dealing with, I did.

I stayed in the same hotels. I could call (without a credit card) and say, "This is Bobby Rush, and I need ten rooms—hold them for me." No deposit, just my word, 'cause I had been there before and was pleasant and tipped well. And I became, in time, one of the very few artists who would hand money back to the club owners, knowing they did not make what they intended to.

There had to be some trust for the Chitlin Circuit to operate as time marched on. One thing that Milton had that I knew was of value was a bus. Within the next year or two, I bought a used 1973 Silver Eagle Trailways bus. Now, there are old Silver Eagle tour buses—meaning converted for rock 'n' roll. This was not that. Again, this was a 1973 Silver Eagle Trailways bus—no conversion, but with row seats and a tiny toilet in the back. Plenty of storage down below and a simple-to-fix two-cycle Detroit engine. Tore out some seats in the back and put in a bed.

Just as the Chitlin Circuit of the '30s and '40s was born out of a segregated world, where we needed a place for us, with the 1980s drawing near, I realized these fans and club owners were the people who were maintaining my career.

And I was grateful.

A Different Yardstick

Things changed for everyone in the 1980s.

The music business crashed.

Reagan got elected and us Black folk knew we wouldn't be gettin' anything from him.

If I hadn't arrived in Chicago in the early fifties, I don't think I would've held on as long as I did. Never had a No. 1 pop or R&B record. I think if I had arrived in the mid-'60s in the Chicago soul music era, the lack of hits would have killed my ambitions. But the blues was measured by a different yardstick. And thank God for me, that yardstick was a question: *Could I put on a good show?*

And I really could. Almost no one knew who Bobby Rush was, but everybody in the music community knew who Bobby Rush was. People knew what they could expect from me and that I would keep my word. And I would learn that had value.

What was true about the Chitlin Circuit then (and now) was that I knew I could make a living despite what was going up and down on the blues charts. The 1980s represented the last gasp for a certain form of adult R&B artist. Tyrone Davis sent me his album produced by Leo Graham called *I Just Can't Keep On Going*, a really good album. When I saw him perform "Overdue" from this album on *Soul Train*, I said to myself, this is going to be good for Tyrone. Everybody that was chasing the mainstream was trying to figure out what was next as disco was finally dying. But his album came and went so fast, I asked Tyrone what happened. After all, he was on the mighty Columbia Records.

"Bobby, there's only so many slots and after Michael Jackson, Peabo Bryson, the Brothers Johnson, it's tough for cats my age to get any form of attention."

Tyrone had been with Columbia since 1976 and had one or two moderate hits with them. But the power of Columbia Records got him opportunities to go on *Soul Train* and *American Bandstand*. But the sand was shifting right under our feet. Even the singing groups of the early '70s that changed the tastes in Black music, the Stylistics, the Spinners, Blue Magic, the Temptations, and others, weren't having any hits.

So artists like me, Tyrone, Denise LaSalle, Johnnie Taylor, Millie Jackson, Little Milton, Bobby "Blue" Bland, Shirley Brown, Latimore, and others became more glued to this Chitlin Circuit with its Southern soul/blues sound. The Circuit was compact, but its fans were loyal. And it's not that we retreated from anywhere that would buy our records or our tickets; it's just that gradually, year after year, Southern blues became more and more under the radar of where popular R&B stood. Blues/soul just petered out—by the tastes of the times.

But there were other circuits poppin' up, too. In the early '80s the revival, or the oldies, circuit was growing. Especially those Saturday and Sunday outdoor shows during the spring and summer. Little Richard, Fats Domino, and Chuck Berry often headlined, with other oldie artists filling out the bill. And if you planned your year right, you could make a living. There was also a very much unsung circuit called Carolina beach music. It was concentrated in the Carolinas, Georgia, and some parts of Florida. Groups like the Tams, Bill Pinkney and His Original Drifters, Clifford Curry, Maurice Williams and the Zodiacs, and others dominated this circuit. But General Johnson's Chairmen of the Board would find it most lucrative as they set up booking agencies and a small record label. Often all these circuits would cross paths, sharing the stage at those all-day summer festival shows.

But what made us Southern blues/soul/Chitlin Circuit artists different was that we were still releasing records. A lot of them.

Sue

I don't know how gung ho I would have been to record a song I had
written ten years earlier if I hadn't met a cat named James Bennett.
We were introduced by one of the great unsung soul/blues singers,
McKinley Mitchell. McKinley was a cross between Brook Benton and
Bobby Blue. He had a hit in '62 with "The Town I Live In."

Now Bennett, who was originally from Como, Mississippi, had previously had a bunch of labels. He had J & B Records, Traction Records,
Retta's Records, MT Records, Big Thigh Records, and "T" Records,
and those are the ones I know about! But now he was hocking his
LaJam Records to me.

I sat Bennett down and played a few songs on guitar and a few I had
on cassette. Popped in "Sue," and within the first verse he said, "That's
it. We gotta do that one." We quickly came to an agreement to record
an album on LaJam. But right before I went into the studio, I met a
young cat who would play an important role in my recording life.

I was playing a gig in McComb, Mississippi, at the Lions Club, and
my drummer at the time, Glenn Holmes, introduced me to this young
guitar played named Vasti Jackson. Vasti, from Mississippi, had just
returned after spending time in Los Angeles. Glenn told me this cat
was good.

"Well, youngblood, wanna sit in?" I offered.

"Sure."

Before he picked up his guitar, I knew right then he could play—as
I had seen it a thousand times. Vasti just had that air of confidence that

went right up to the line of cockiness—but didn't cross it. And I was proved right, as he could play his ass off.

"Mane, I likes the way you stroke, youngblood."

"Thank you, Mr. Rush."

"Call me Bobby."

"Cool."

"Mane, we going into Malaco to record an album. Wanna join?"

"Yeah, man!"

I booked Malaco Studio in Jackson, Mississippi. That day we were in Studio B. Deke Johnson, my bass player, was late. It was my dime, and I wasn't wastin' no money.

"Bobby, I can play bass till Deke shows up," Vasti said.

"Well, then let's hit it!"

So Vasti played bass on three or four songs on the *Sue* album. He then picked up his guitar and played on several of the other cuts. We had a talented band for that record: Jesse Robinson on guitar, Glenn Holmes on drums, Larry Addison, James "Hot Dog" Lewis, Tommy Addison on keyboards, Don Thigpen on organ, Charlotte Chenault, Jewel Bass, and Thomasine Anderson on background vocals.

But the young lion Vasti Jackson impressed me. He had a lot of musical knowledge for his age. I would learn later that he played everything—guitar, bass, piano, and was an excellent arranger. Vasti was a pro.

So many of the songs for the *Sue* album came out of real shit. "Talk to Your Daughter" came out of a conversation I had with my first wife Hazel's mother in Arkansas.

Mama, you daughter been untrue
'Cause she don't love me like she usta do
Last night before she went to bed
She turned her back and covered her head.

"TALK TO YOUR DAUGHTER"/ *SUE*/1980

As much as I sang the song with my playful style, that shit wasn't funny when it went down.

Telling stories about my life in code and through humor became my bread and butter. But the story of "Sue" wasn't in any kinda code. Sue (not her actual name) was a girl that was about ten years older and way more experienced than me when it came to sex. At twenty-five years old, she turned little Bobby Rush out. When I sang "she thirty-six . . . twenty-four . . . forty-three," she was actually bigger than that. Sue lived across the railroad tracks, and even though I thought I was meeting her in secret—everybody knew. Everybody. Daddy talked to me, so did Maw, but there wasn't anything that could keep me away from Sue and our rendezvous. I was hooked. I look back now and I'm happy about my time spent with her. Yes, it was about sex, but it was also about me coming into my own as a man, because she talked to me and treated me like a man.

The single "Sue" would be my first gold record. A big hit for me. Between selling LPs after my shows and via mail order, this was the first time I made money from a recording. James Bennett paid me in product, and soon I had a mail room set up in my house. Orders would come in and I'd box 'em up and ship 'em off. Up until then, I hadn't even gotten any real royalty money. So this was a win that was sweet for my ego and wallet. The *Sue* album was a success, too—but a success through a realistic lens of what the Southern blues market could give and what it could not.

Down-Home Smash

In many ways, I was doing better than guys who had a bigger name than me. Selling more records and playing to consistently filled nightclubs. But in 1982 something happened in the Southern blues/soul world that changed the possibilities of what could be.

Z. Z. Hill's "Down Home Blues" became not just a hit record, but a spark that set off a wildfire for all of us who were in these Chitlin Circuit clubs night after night, year after year. "Down Home Blues" just seemed to get bigger and bigger and bigger. Z. Z.'s album *Down Home* hung around on the charts for two years. It was like this one record was elevating the Southern blues world. It became the song at cookouts in the summer and the one song you would always, always hear on the jukeboxes in bars. It was a shot in the arm for all of us on the Circuit.

We were all happy for Z. Z. I can say I never heard a whiff of jealousy towards him. We were an older crowd. We knew we weren't ever gonna compete with Lionel Richie or Michael Jackson. So it was important for us to support one another.

Mississippi-based Malaco Records, where Z. Z. was signed, collared up other artists who were doing a similar thing. This was the hidden record business. Far from the eyes of the mainstream. Regional and tight, they knew selling a few records focused on a small market was just as good as having a hit in the big market. You may make less, but you spend less in promotion. The expectations were realistic, and money is money. Tyrone Davis, Denise (LaSalle), Little Milton, Bobby "Blue" Bland, and others sat down at the Malaco table. Z. Z. kept on releasing records. Good stuff, but nothing had the impact of "Down Home Blues."

Z. Z. was one of us. Often wearing a fedora hat cocked to the side, he gave his audience just what they came for. He left us too soon, as the misery of the miles caught up with him. Had a car accident in February of '84 and two months later died from a blood clot—a result of the crash. Z. Z. was only forty-eight years old.

Ghost of Mississippi

In April 1983, we Chicagoans elected Harold Washington mayor of the city—first Black man to do so. Everybody in Chi-town—even us blues cats—celebrated something fierce. But not for long. Because at the end of the month, Muddy Waters died of lung cancer. Some say Muddy's death signified an end to the blues. But I think that's something folks just like to say. Because the blues ended in the '60s when artists had to pretty much stay in Europe to make a living. I went to the wake but not the funeral as I had to get back down South for a show.

Earlier in the 1950s, when Chess Records was booming, the overwhelming majority of its sales came from the South. And in these juke joints in the South, they never forgot the blues. Something about the South still held blues close to its bosom. I was steeped in that world, as most of the jobs I got were in the Chitlin Circuit of the South.

It struck me as nutty to be spending so much time in the South and on Monday morning to have to drive the bus eight and half hours back to Chicago, only to leave on Wednesday and gallop right back to the South. Diesel fuel was high, and I considered what kind of life I wanted to live. Chicago had been good to me, but the hard streets of Chicago could be exhausting. The wide-open peaceful spaces of the South were calling me. So with prayerful consideration, I chose to move somewhere in the South. Thought about Memphis, Birmingham, Nashville, Louisville . . . somewhere. I even considered putting city names in a hat and drawing one out. But I had to be more rational than that. I got a map out of the United States, took a red Bic ballpoint pen, and made these little dots on the many cities I regularly played in over the last twenty years—and it took me a while. Around two hundred clubs over seven states. Damn, I felt like that Johnny Cash song when he sang, "I've been everywhere, man—I've been everywhere." But when I examined all the dots, they seemed to circle the "City with Soul" of Jackson, Mississippi.

But memories of my childhood would cloud my journey to Jackson. For as long as I can remember, Maw always said to us, "Never go to Mississippi." Her tone always had a danger thing with it. It was like somebody flagging you down to stop the car because up ahead the bridge was out. When we came of age, she told us why she felt the way she did.

"Your great-grandmother—my grandmother—was a slave. She had lots of chil'ren. Come a point when all the kids who could walk were gathered up in the middle of the night and taken off as fast as they could git. Riding one hundred and twenty miles northwest to Eudora, Arkansas. My great-grandmother knew these white peoples there."

Maw said how this was before the Civil War started and Arkansas became a slave state. The white family she knew was sympathetic to Negroes. But maybe there was something more natural going on, as my great-grandmother started having children with this white man, Van Spivey, even though he already had at least five children with his white wife. Maw was born to one of their children, Sarah.

They set up my Black ancestors with land to farm. In the fullness of time, more and more white DNA was deposited in my bloodline till you have my mother, who looked white but not as white as many of her brothers and sisters. So when my great-granddaddy passed, and the land had to be split up, they gave the Negro bloodline the short end of the stick and told them to never come back to Mississippi. And there was a lot of land he owned in Mississippi and Louisiana. Hundreds and hundreds of acres.

Whether it was because of the shame of race mixing or they thought someone was gonna tell folk in Mississippi how Maw's great-granddaddy loved him some Black women—regardless, my maw and her mixed siblings were by force taken to Arkansas by their white relatives and told to stay the hell away from Mississippi. And that's what she passed down to us—in no uncertain terms.

The stories of my bloodline do show me the ropes of where I come from. And give me an idea about the hand that was dealt me and my ancestors. But I'd be damned if I was gonna let some ghost of Mississippi deter me from doin' what I knew was best.

So you could say me moving to Jackson was an act of rebellion to all that pain, fear, and skin shit. Maybe it was. Because it is a natural fact that after I moved to Jackson, I became way more civic-minded than I ever had in my life—and I continue to be. Raised a lot of money for sickle cell anemia research, raised money for school band uniforms and equipment, done a lot of get-out-the-vote work, and let my bus be used to get people to the polls.

If it's me trying to purify the ghost of my Mississippi bloodline, I can't say that's off. But whatever the reason was, I'm cool, 'cause I love me some Jackson.

The Big Girls

People think that the Chitlin Circuit clubs are just in the Deep South, and, yes, many of them are. But the Circuit goes down as far south as the Gulf of Mexico and as far north as Detroit. And all the way to the Atlantic coast: Virginia, the Carolinas, and Florida.

Not long after I moved to Jackson, I resurrected in my act what some people refer to as the "big girls": shapely—sometimes large— women who dance during parts of my show. Some of this was because of the popularity of "Sue" on Southern radio stations. But most of it was because it was a tradition in my kinda show business. Before my time they called 'em snake charmers, women dressed in belly-dancer-like clothes handling snakes at the edge of the stage while musicians played. When I was comin' up, they called them shake dancers. And many of the cats on the circuits had them. Louis Armstrong had them, and even some big bands (before they died out) had shake dancers. But it developed over time through the Chitlin Circuit of the '50s and '60s. I had some dancers early on but stopped it sometime in the early to mid-1970s.

But in the mid-1980s most gigs were in the South. And my audiences were mostly grown Black folks between thirty and your grandma's age. Now the shake dancers—who definitely had something to shake— became part of the stage play called the Bobby Rush Show.

This uncut Black country drama was frisky—but the emphasis is on the funny. Little one-act plays told through songs and acting. The plots are different and yet the same.

A shit-talkin' man boastin' about what he can do sexually.
A woman who obviously got the upper hand.
A man cheatin' on a woman.
A woman cheatin' on a man.

And the most important one-act play is the command that everybody is gonna have a real good time tonight. I go up to the line. I don't cross it. My risqué-ness is more about hints and suggestions than anything smutty.

When the *Sue* record became hugely popular in the South, I started doing this skit for certain crowds. I brought to the stage a high stool and a low stool. All while the band is jamming, I position myself on the high stool and motion for one of my larger dancers, you know 38-26-59, to get on the low stool so she can pleasure me.

But the Sue character in my stage play has other plans. She motions for me to sit on the low stool. She sits on the high stool—so she can be the one on the receiving end of the pleasure. Turning the tables on me, she just keeps on motioning me to come closer and closer. And me playing the role as the sheepish man, I gradually comply. So with all her junk in the trunk spilling off her higher stool and as I start to sit on the lower stool, my last words before I sit down are "Don't hold my ears, I need to breathe." Everybody falls out laughing, and that's the end of it. It's silly Chitlin Circuit satire—but it's funny.

Between my funky blues songs, me telling funny lies, and now with the girls appearing on a few songs, folks started billing me as the Bobby Rush Revue. Giving me a Vegas-y shine. I didn't mind it.

Eye for Eye, Tit for Tat

I continued my relationship with LaJam Records. My 1985 album *What's Good for the Goose Is Good for the Gander* had a single of the same name. It's a story that is often lost in the satire of my stage play called the Bobby Rush Revue. The title says it all. If you're going to do wrong by me, don't expect that same thing can't be done to you. It's a simple country way of sayin' the biblical truth of "Do unto others what you want done to you." Yes, it's addressed to men—and women love this song. It's the one where they stand up, snap their fingers, and say, "That's right, Bobbyrush—you tell 'em." I have a lot of songs in my toolbox with that same message. "A Man Can Give It (But He Can't Take It)" says the same thing.

The sound of the single "What's Good for the Goose Is Good for the Gander" wasn't new. But Z. Z. Hill's smash "Down Home Blues" definitely popularized that sound more than anyone. No one can take that away from him, God rest his soul. He influenced all of us on the Chitlin Circuit. There was a Malaco Records sound growing in the Southern blues/soul market. Grittier guitars and more use of synthesizers for string and horn punches. For me not to admit that "What's Good for the Goose Is Good for the Gander" is a part of that Malaco sound wouldn't be right.

I'm trying here to set the record straight. About the evolution of me and the evolution of the musical world that was the mid-'80s of the Southern blues sound. And there were other little blues pockets other than the Malaco sound. Alligator Records out of Chicago was signing artists and released what some call barrelhouse music, or house rocking music. Koko Taylor, Albert Collins, Son Seals, my friend Buddy Guy, and others pursued a raw and rock-bathed blues sound. Some folk even talked about a Malaco Records versus Alligator Records competition. Yes, the styles be a little different, but any talk about a competition—I ain't studdin' that at all. We's all on the outside of the big boys, and we should have respect for being together in that outsider boat.

Still, I had a big foothold in Southern blues and some of those Alligator cats had none. But unlike them I was not going to Norway, Iceland, Spain, or Germany either. So they could say they had a better thing going.

A Joyful Blues

I just shook my head and hit my hand on my thigh with joy when I heard Prince's "Kiss" in 1986. Yes, the blues had been gone from the top forty for a very long time. But Prince, in his genius, brought to life what the groove of Chuck Berry, Big Mama Thornton, Little Richard, and Bo Diddley felt like.

Here this boy is one of the biggest cats ever and is having one of the biggest smashes of his career with a twelve-bar blues in the key of A. My, oh my, oh my, oh my. That "Kiss" record was so delicious to me 'cause it was a little tongue-in-cheek, humorous, sexual, flirtatious, and catchy. It had all the edge and flavor of the blues and a Southern Chitlin Circuit song.

In 1986, my act on the Circuit was well known, and I was selling out almost every little and large Black joint between Mississippi and Michigan.

As much as the blues scene in America had become almost solely attended by white folk, there was an equality taking shape that started in the eighties but by the nineties was really on the come-up. We Black cats stopped this bullshit of prejudging a white boy before he pulled his guitar out of the case. If a cat could play, then he could play. It reminded me of the 1960s when we had to take notice of them white boys down at FAME Studios in Muscle Shoals, Alabama. They were cranking out them hits for Wilson Pickett, Aretha Franklin, Otis Redding, and more. Stevie Ray Vaughan, who exploded on the scene because of his talent, did a lot for the blues in America. Yes, his white skin could open media doors that we Black blues artists couldn't. But the blues music itself was getting exposed, and that was good for everybody. It doesn't matter who sings the blues, it only matters that proper credit is given to the men and the women who created it.

But there still was that thing where Black folks still felt a little ashamed of liking the blues. If I had a dollar for every time I heard, "My grandmama [or mama] loves you, Mr. Rush, can I get your autograph?" Then the same youngster whispers in my ear, "Your autograph is really for me—I love the blues." We still ain't overcome that stigma.

Starting in the '80s, filmmakers flocked to the South to document undiscovered bluesmen—many of my friends who kinda stayed around their birthplace and never ventured too far away. Some had done a few records, and some had done none. But by and large, they had kept their day jobs and raised their families. And as these filmmakers released their documentaries to the public, compared with us guys who were earning our living on the Chitlin Circuit, we looked less faithful to what they thought was the "real" blues.

With our tailored rhinestone-covered outfits, jewelry, and well-groomed hair, it kinda put some of us Southern blues/soul artists in a trick bag. We didn't look like the "authentic blues artist," at least the way they thought the authentic blues artist should look. Guys on my circuit like Little Milton, Johnnie Taylor, Tyrone Davis, Bobby "Blue" Bland, and others ain't going onstage in a white T-shirt and blue bib overalls so folks can feel like they done seen the real Black/blues experience. Fuck that. We had earned our stripes. We didn't have to prove that we were the real thing—'cause we knew we were. And our audiences were mostly Black.

What's Poured into Your Pitcher?

On September 11, 1988, my brother Alvin became an ordained minister. The program from his ordination read: "A Call to the Ministry." As far as I was concerned, my brother, Deacon Alvin Ellis, had already been a preacher. He had done all the prayin' for folk near and far, dropping in on the sick and shut-in—Alvin is just a good man. Preaching his inaugural sermon in Chicago, everyone was there. It was a proud day for all of us. But especially Maw and Dad.

Special occasions remind us of special people, those folks that poured something into our pitcher. Of course Daddy and Maw poured into all their children a faith. For me, when my belief is strong, I believe God is going to see me through any situation that I'm in. When my belief is weak, I count on my faith muscles that I've exercised to pull me up out of the muck of unbelief.

I'm really glad that Daddy and Maw got to see Alvin become a soldier in the army of the Lord. Because time can be a thief.

For a long time Maw would catch a cough that would get to the point where she couldn't catch her breath. We believe that's how she fell out and went to glory. Had a heart attack right there on the land in Pine Bluff, Arkansas, on October 27, 1990.

I Ain't Studdin' Ya

Somebody had the nerve to tell me the other night—
Say, Bobby Rush, you got four kids
But one of them don't look like you—

Now lemme tell you something 'bout that now

It ain't but one thing, y'all—that make me so happy
I got four kids ain't but three of them mine
But they still call me Pappy!
I ain't studdin' you

"I AIN'T STUDDIN' YOU"/*I AIN'T STUDDIN' YOU*/1991

There's an old saying: "Sticks and stones can break my bones, but words will never hurt me." We all know that's bullshit.

'Cause words can cut like a razor blade. I wish "I Ain't Studdin' You" had initially been released in the age of social media. 'Cause it has more umph in it today. Yeah, I know my little country stories ain't the stuff of PhDs; still, I wish I could teach a course to young 'uns that was called I Ain't Studdin' You 101. The first week's class lesson would be called "Stop Fucking Lying." Second week, "Get Off My Fuckin' Back." Third week, "Fuck You."

Wish I could tell some high school girl whose reputation was destroyed on social media to say, "I ain't studdin' you." Wish I could teach some boy who is being shamed by someone who doesn't even know him to say, "I ain't studdin' you."

When I was growing up in the country, Daddy taught me that gossip mongering is a sin. But the internet has made that sin as normal as a click on a mouse. It takes so much strength, so much love being around you, to resist all the gossipers and backbiters. Heard a preacher say once, "Jesus comes down way more on backbiting (gossip) than any other sin." It's dangerous stuff.

I hadn't released an album since *A Man Can Give It, but He Can't Take It* in 1988. So after three years, guess what—another record label. I did a one-album deal with Urgent! Records out of Jackson, Mississippi. In 1991 I released the album and a single of the same name, "I Ain't Studdin' You." It was the biggest seller in the brief life of Urgent! Records. I'm proud of that success, even prouder of what the country-fied song teaches.

Oakdale Prison

Like a trailer park draws tornados, Texas cops are drawn to entertainers with weed. From Willie Nelson to Snoop Dogg to Ray Price to Lil Wayne—all were busted in Texas. And so was I.

I know, I know. How did I—who's never hit a joint, didn't drink, couldn't tell good weed from bad, never had a toot—get caught up in this shit? Fair question. It could be because I was stupid. It could be because I wasn't paying enough attention to those around me. It could be both.

Lemme tell ya what I ain't told most folk. On February 6, 1985, at a bus station in Houston, Texas, I got busted with weed. My bus was out of commission, and we were catching a bus from Houston to Beaumont, Texas. The weed was in my guitar player's bag—but I was carrying his bag. I got out of jail on bond. They kept my guitar player. I went to court a couple months later. Giving them a story that it wasn't my pot, nor did I even know I was carrying it, I pleaded for probation, which I received. Whew!

I learned my lesson. The curse had been lifted. I was blind, but now I see.

Well, not really. 'Cause I was busted six years later on October 18, 1991. And this time it was way more serious.

And again it was in Beaumont/Galveston, Texas. This time for coke. A promoter I had worked with a hundred times called me at the hotel, as I had worked on one of his gigs the night before.

"Hey, Rush, my car's broken down."

"Where you at, mane?"

"I'm at home. Could you bring your U-Haul by, I got some gear to move to the club?"

"Gimme the address."

Now I knew this cat was shady, but stupid-ass me. He did a number on me 'cause as soon as I arrived, the cops swooped in. They had already been to this cat's house once, and they implicated me 'cause I showed up with a truck.

I was arrested, arraigned, and released on bond. I was stuck between a rock and a hard place. 'Cause the cats that were the bigwigs behind the promoter with the coke were some very, very bad people. And if I had told anything I knew, it would have been some hoodlum trouble for me—so I kept quiet.

My siblings all wrote letters to the judge to bear out what kinda man I was. So grateful to them for that. About six months later, I was back to court with my lawyer. Gerdia had her son drive her the 1,270 miles from her home in Michigan to Beaumont, Texas. All my siblings came. They were in the courtroom, in the lobby, and outside the courthouse.

But they never saw a judge or any testimony.

The original district attorney was vicious and wanted me to get twenty-five years. But thanks be to God, that district attorney was replaced. The judge in charge of my fate seemed to be confused on the day of my hearing. He just couldn't pull it together. As he shuffled papers, it was as if he was looking for something and couldn't find it to save the devil. Some assistant came up and helped him, and she was talking to the judge, I assumed about me.

My lawyer said it was better to plead guilty. With only Jean in the courtroom, they offered me ninety days of community service or nine months in jail. I didn't want to be seen doing community service in an orange uniform around town—so I took the time. Crazy shit, right? Who cares about a Chitlin Circuit blues singer doing some time? Nobody, right? Me not being seen and doing the time is not me saying I was highfalutin'. It's just that my name was all I had. Didn't want it to be tarred.

I didn't want to do my time anywhere near Mississippi. So my attorney arranged for me to stay at a low-security prison in Oakdale,

Louisiana, right near the Texas border. I knew this months in advance, so I grew a very, very long beard. Come September 3, 1992, I had to go sit down in Oakdale Federal Correctional Institution. I think in my months there, only ten or so recognized me.

Jean never came apart—no hissy fit. She just cut back on everything and kept steppin'. I settled in and was released in almost four months. Thank God I knew some people politically. 'Cause after my release, while still on probation, the powers that be were kind as I was allowed to go anywhere in the world—so it didn't stop my work train.

Of course, I have regret over this thing. Daddy and Maw knew, which was hard enough. And I know for sure I disappointed my wife and my siblings. And yet during my stay the thing hurt me the most was that on December 21, 1992, my good friend, and the man I could hash over anything with, Albert King, died suddenly of a heart attack in Memphis at the age of sixty-nine.

It's really the only time I felt sad. I just thought to myself, *My friend done left this earth and I couldn't even pay my respects.*

But there was a silver lining. Jean and I started a prison ministry in the aftermath of all this mess I made. And it's been really Jean who put in the long hours to keep it going for almost thirty years now. So much of Jean's ability to do this sometimes underappreciated work is because she has a gift for it, an anointing if you will. She believes in second and third chances. She believes you do not throw away people. She has changed many lives.

Old Friends

Outta jail and back on the bus. But I ain't headed to a joint in Mississippi. Going to the airport in Atlanta to fly over for a few European dates. On November 26, 1994, we were playing the 15th Annual Blues Estafette in Utrecht, the Netherlands. Backstage, I see a cat I ain't seen in forever, Luther Allison. I hugged him tightly.

"Bobbyrush, it's so good to see you, boy."

"Allison! Mane, where you been?"

"Boy, you know I been over in France eatin' that good French food."

"Allison, remember what they say 'bout that French food."

"What's that, Bobby?"

"That you gotta dig through a lotta sauce to get to the meat!"

He fell out laughing. "Rush, you ain't changed one bit—still the funniest man I know." We sat and got to talking about life, family, old friends, Chicago, the blues scene. I had a lot—I mean a lot—of respect for Luther Allison. Remember back in 1963 when I wanted to be the first blues artist on Motown? It would take ten years, but Luther Allison became Motown's first—and, I think, *only*—blues artist in 1972. He was a beast on guitar—some say he was the Hendrix of the blues, and that's not far off for me. Luther, an articulate man, was one of the first blues cats to give the middle finger to the dying blues scene of the late 1970s.

"Bobbyrush, over there in France, Switzerland, Germany, Sweden, Denmark, they don't separate live music like they do in the States. I can be on a festival with a jazz, gospel, or soul music artist—even young artists—it gives me way more opportunities to earn a living."

Luther became a touring god all over Europe. A real blues star. While in America people didn't know him from Adam. A hospitable kinda cat, he'd entertain the bluesmen who came through Paris. He was sort of a blues ambassador for us. Luther Allison was a visionary: saying fuck it and moving to Paris in the mid-'80s. He was a perfect example of Black flight from the blues scene in America.

I did my show in the late afternoon. It was not received well. And that was a hard sour pill to swallow. Vasti Jackson, who was in my band and would grow in importance to my studio life said, "Bobby, maybe you should do more harp playing and less talking." What Vasti didn't say was more important. I need more authenticity. The Chitlin Circuit show stuff, with its humor and sexy girls, came across as too Las Vegas-y and vaudeville-y.

I had always put a high value on having good music and a good show, but it didn't occur to me until now that my show may be taking away from my music.

I stayed around 'cause I had to see Luther's show. He came onstage, and people gave him a standing ovation before he played one note. Then he just burned the house down. That big rock/blues fire coming from his guitar was scorching. If you were alive, you felt that heat. Luther would play a twelve-bar solo, then take it higher and higher each twelve bars till what went from a flash turned into a nuclear ex-plosion. He musically led the crowd into a Holy Ghost frenzy of joy. That's how good he was. He didn't talk too much during his set. He just sang, played, and gave the people something so musically authentic, the audience felt like they were in Memphis, Tennessee, in 1958.

Luther gave me a blessed lesson that night. Compared with Luther's, my show sucked.

Audiences appreciated and loved Luther Allison in Europe. Still, he confessed he wanted to come home to the States. He wanted to be near his son. He accepted that Black folks, at least, don't appreciate the blues as much as Europeans. Once home, he got work on festivals, but some Black idiots complained about him having a white band some-times. Just some ridiculous, stupid shit.

They won't support the blues—don't really care about the blues—and got the nerve to talk about Luther, who found a way to carve out a career.

But Luther made it home. Sadly, he didn't live too long to enjoy it. In 1997 he died a day or two before his fifty-seventh birthday. Cancer.

New Friends

I love playing the King Biscuit Blues Festival in Helena, Arkansas. There are three or four stages and an all-day lineup. You get to hang out with old friends and meet some new ones. A lot of cats after their show stay backstage, smoking, eating, and soaking up the fellowship of other performers. And that's fine. It's just not for me. I like to walk out, get amongst the crowd—see the smiles and look people in their eyes and hear their stories. Sometimes my band or some interviewer I am supposed to talk to gets annoyed. But I love people, and frankly I need people. Their energy puts gas in my tank, especially outside on a beautiful day.

One time, after I roamed around a bit, I planted myself at a table, as scheduled, to sign autographs and sell (sometimes give away) CDs. The line was excessively long that day, as King Biscuit is a huge festival. Almost at the end of the line was this white tall drink of water with a big, thick curly head of hair and a blondish-gray goatee.

"Mr. Rush, I saw your show, and I was so impressed."

"Thank you, now what's your name?"

"I'm Carl Gustafson, and I have a band, Blinddog Smokin'."

"That's great, mane."

"But I also put together festivals."

"Mane, let me finish up here 'cause I want to talk to you later."

It sounds like bullshit, but Carl and I really hit it off—he turned out to be a prince of a dude. He invited me to come to Laramie, Wyoming. To play at the university there. I agreed. I was playing all over the country, and still Laramie was off my beaten path. But what I didn't know was that Carl had gone to all the public radio stations in the Laramie area and told people about me, and an enormous crowd showed up. My show was well received—actually the response was tremendous. Carl felt so genuine to me that I wanted to meet his family. Met his wife, kids, mother, and a bunch of his buddies. We became fast friends, and I have said of him, "He's my brother from another mother." Carl's band, Blinddog Smokin', was no joke either. Top-notch musicians with a top-notch show, all fronted by Carl. We started calling and checking in on each other. And soon a bond developed where I felt the freedom to tell him some things.

"You know, Carl, I've had it in my mind for a long time that white blues artists like yourself and me should tour together."

"I'd love to, Bobby."

"Wait, wait. I don't think you know what I'm gettin' at here. I think this would be good for our little corner of the world—to show some Black and white togetherness."

And that's just what we did. We had Sherman Robinson, Billy Branch, Carl Weathersby, Miss Blues, Zora Young, and Oli Brown (out of England)—all super-talented blues artists. We were all on one big bus and we laughed so much that if we had videotaped our time rolling down the highway, that could have been a reality show all on its own.

We played in hayfields, auditoriums, street festivals. We used one band, interchanging the bass player and drummers. With Carl's experience and my grit, we created our own rolling festival.

The Blues We Keep

My firstborn son, Donell, started singing in his preteen years. I can't remember the day he went to New York, but I knew he was in the Big Apple. Other than the usual Daddy support, Donell got his music going totally without me. If I could have helped, I surely would have. But the doors that needed to be knocked on—just to get in the room with the right people—were doors too big for me. They were out of my league. He found his way in the New York music scene in the late 1980s. He made appearances as an artist on a few dance records. Did some background sessions with Luther Vandross.

Better-looking than I was, Donell was an A-plus singer. Had that vocal gift where he could be strong and equally as tender. Just as bad, if not badder, than Luther, Jeffrey Osborne, Howard Hewett, or any one of his contemporaries. He also had a piercing high natural tenor like Charlie Wilson of the Gap Band. Signed to RCA Records in 1992, he released his eleven-song album *Comin' & Goin'*. The song "Symphony" reached No. 7 on the dance chart. I was so, so proud.

But things turned, and complications from his sickle cell jumped up. Almost thirty-five, Donell got sick and came to my house in Jackson. Jean and Donell were close, and since I was gone during his failing health, Jean took real good care of him. So grateful to her. His pastor came. Sometimes he'd wander off, driving us crazy.

On March 22, 1996, he flew home.

Sherry, Valerie, and now Donell. I felt the pull. That pull towards the darkness. The darkness of bitterness, depression—lost faith. My spirit was hardening like wet concrete in the noonday sun. I felt myself sinking down and down. Thanks be to God, at some moment I realized I had a choice. A choice to not go there. Grieve but not drown. To have a blessed acceptance. And to say: if I believe in my savior, I know I'll see them again.

We go through some things that are completely and totally baffling. But as some folks say, you're either coming out of something or getting ready to go through something. So we should show mercy to others—and ourselves.

Donell and I were as close as a father and son could be. I was gone during much of his upbringing, but we still never lost any of the warm, tender things that some fathers and sons let slip away.

There was great affection between us.

I've been to his gravesite only once.

Can't do it.

Too rough.

My daddy, in his early nineties, left this earth on December 12, 1997. When he passed—probably of old age—I thought about how he was never sick his entire life. The only time I remember him having anything was when he had a toothache—he was around eighty. He died with all his hair and all his teeth except one.

When Daddy left to go to the other side, I was tore up. But looking back, I think it was me really mourning Donell's passing over a year and a half earlier. 'Cause I had kept those blues to myself. But all I was doing was postponing the pain.

Wichita Mercy

I was playing the Riverfest in Wichita, Kansas, in the summer of 1996. I was in the middle of some song and some fella rushed the stage and tried to dry-hump one of my dancers. My natural impulse was to knock his ass out, which I was more than capable of doing. But just in the two seconds it took for me to grab him, I dialed it back. I put my arm around him respectfully and pulled him to center stage. I said into the microphone, "Come on now, we trying to do a show up here and we cain't have you actin' like that." The man got belligerent. "Get your hands off me—I'm dancing." I said, "Yeah, you lookin' good, too, but you know what? See all these people out there—these people came to see a show and you're disturbing them."

By now security had intervened and roughly escorted him off the stage. The crowd was booing loudly and cursing randomly at the man. I said, "Hey, everybody! Hey, everybody, listen, listen, listen to me. We don't know that man's circumstances, we don't know what he's been through—we don't know. He may have had some bad things happen in his life—and he just wants a little attention—'cause maybe nobody's given him any—maybe his little aggressiveness was brought about by some bad things he was or is going through. Maybe he's gettin' a divorce or something. We don't know, so let's be a little forgiving, everybody—that old boy may end up being one of the best of us, okay?" They clapped and I said, "Now let's get on wit' the show."

To this day I don't why I didn't kick that guy's ass. I would have been within my rights to do so. I now think that this was so close to Donell's illness and death that the pain left me knowing for sure that everyone needs compassion. So on that day I wasn't feeling nobody judging anybody else.

Wasn't havin' it.

Century's End

In early November 1999, as the century was about to end, the wide-body jet touched down in Moscow, Russia. I was here to play some dates for the 10th Efes Pilsen Blues Festival in Moscow. Cold temperatures onstage but loved being over there. They have eight-lane streets. But unfortunately a lot of Moscow reminded me of the slums of Chicago. I saw they had some of the same problems of the American ghetto. A lot of drinking. Some kids were sniffing glue. A lot of children begging on the streets at ten and eleven o'clock at night. Cops chasing them. That told me that certain kinds of problems are universal.

PART 3

PART 3

My People

I look at life as a story. I tell stories in my songs. I'm writing my story with the good Lord. But I ain't special. Everybody writes their own story and sings their own song. Doin' what they gotta do to make life work or to get to where they wanna be. And yet I believe God is the ultimate storyteller, weaving words in and out of our days with his pen. Changing sentences, changing lives.

So much of my story is told in the many faces I've spent so much time with. As 1999 was coming to an end, I realized I had been playing in the same clubs for almost fifty years. Many of the same faces that came to see me in the '60s were the same faces with me in 1999.

Ninety-nine percent of those faces were Black.

I'd see them year after year, some I would call them my fans. I'd call them my friends. For my Black audience bought my house, my land, paid my band, took care of my family, paid for my car, and everything in between. Yes, I give my all to them night after night, no matter what's going on with me. But don't think that I ain't aware that without these folk—I'm cooking barbecue for a living. That audience was and is my rock. I am connected to them in ways I understand and ways I don't. In the 1960s, I can see them sitting at long wood tables covered in white paper tablecloths. Husbands and wives getting some time away from the kids. Also, I remember seeing single men doing the BYOB (bring your own bottle) thing, trying to get some lady to join him at his table. In the '80s I saw a group of women who were out together stand up and wave their hands in the air as I tore into "What's Good for the Goose Is Good for the Gander." They shouted, "That's right!" or "That's my song!" These sisters were feeling a righteous rebellion as I sang about a man gettin' his just desserts. Their joy felt to me like they'd lived some of this, and I loved providing their revenge in song.

What is also true is that unlike my contemporaries, who knew me as the best showman in blues, I was under the radar to the world at large. Some would say I had moved nowhere in fifty years. Not like B.B. King, Buddy Guy, Johnnie Taylor, or even Bobby "Blue" Bland.

I promoted my shows on the Black side of town. In bars and joints that most white folks still didn't go to—even in the year 2000. Even when I had records come out, there wasn't any real press to support me. I didn't get covered much. But I survived for so long as an independent, I wasn't studdin' no one who didn't know about Bobby Rush. And there was an advantage to that.

I made more money than people who've got platinum records all over their house. They got songs everybody knows. People look at them as stars. But lemme tell ya something, I got more money than some of them. Why? Because it cost so much for them to operate. They got bookers, light people, wardrobe people, they fly in high style. They demand top dollar. But top dollar ain't top dollar if you got to take 90 percent of that top dollar and pay it to others. It's like this here, if somebody gets $50,000 a night but they pay big entourage expenses— they may take home $15,000. But if I make $10,000 and take home $6,000, then I ain't too much behind the folks who are high up on the music business food chain. But the food chain I was livin' off, this Southern blues/soul thing, may have been limiting to how high I could go, but ironically there was a certain kind of freedom in it, too.

Also, I've always had the freedom to cut all kinds of deals with small and larger promoters. Throughout the 1980s and '90s, as my reputation rose as someone who could fill up the house, I did more favors for these promoters and small-club owners. And even though many were struggling to keep the doors open, I never lost sight that I work for them. And we both work for the people. If the clubs can't keep the doors open, then that's one less place that I can go. I make money for them, and they, in turn, pay me.

But the Southern blues and soul circuit was home. Where my bread was buttered. When I said earlier that I'm connected to my Black fans in ways I don't know, what I mean is this: my 99 percent Black audience doesn't give a rat's ass about appealing to white folks. While years ago many of my contemporaries gave up on these small dives in the South, there was a group of us who stayed. Me, Denise LaSalle, and Latimore, to name a few. You could say we stayed out of necessity. But there's a whole other side to it. It is like delighting in ourselves. Enjoying our Blackness, our humor in a way that you can't do in any audience of 90 percent white folks. This ain't griping; it's just the facts. Southern blues/soul is an unapologetically Black experience.

Dustin' Off the Harp

As the 2000s approached, I started working with Vasti Jackson again to put together another record on Malaco's Waldoxy label. Vasti knew the upcoming technology—digital home recording. This enabled us to record in my house in Jackson, Mississippi. We also recorded at Malaco Studios and Taylor-Made Studios, both in Jackson. But listening to the recordings in my car, I realized that the quality of sound that we were getting at the house was comparable to that of the higher-priced studios. I called Vasti.

"Hey, buddy, this stuff at my house sounds as good as the stuff we doing at the studio."

"You know, I agree," Vasti said.

Some songs that started off as demos became masters. Vasti knows what the feeling of music is about. That part of music that you almost can't put into words. Those free-flying spirits of music floating 'round in the air. He sees them and can bring them out of the ether into an actual view. He's always a pleasure to work with. The only time we disagreed was over certain takes. For Vasti, it's almost like I fall in love too soon with a take—missing the tiny minor mistakes that, if fixed, could make a more professional record. For me, when it hits me—it hits me and I ain't studdin' about this thing here or that thing there. But we compromise. And it makes our work flow like a river, crashing down a hill after a two-day rain. Some folks call it a process. I just call it the good Lord leading me to a brighter day.

That brighter day was a more rootsy sound. More homegrown to where I came from. Much of my music I had been puttin' out in the last ten years had something of a Malaco sound. Synthesizer punches. Guitar was grittier. It was more modern, less traditional. But one of the biggest shifts is that I started to play more harmonica. When I more or less put down the harp in the mid-seventies, I was just responding to the times. But now the blues—even the crossover blues—was returning to its roots because the fantasy of the blues ever being mainstream again was dead thirty years earlier. The *Hoochie Man* album wasn't any less funky—it's just that the rhythms and rhymes came from more of the original blues setting and feel.

Although it would take me a few albums to get there, *Hoochie Man* would represent the start of a very gradual process that would change the course of my career. In 1998 and 1999, I got nominated as the best Soul Blues Male Artist of the Year by the Blues Foundation. In 2000, I received my first Grammy nomination for *Hoochie Man*.

Much to my flat-out surprise, the Mississippi legislature passed Senate Resolution 43, "A RESOLUTION COMMENDING THE CAREER AND HUMANITARIANISM OF NATIONALLY AND INTER-NATIONALLY KNOWN BLUES SINGER MR. BOBBY RUSH."

Misery and the Miles

There's something about the old juke joints I played in, a certain charm that makes these primitive places feel majestic. One of these majestic places was Dave's CC Club. It sits on many acres in the woods around Tallahassee, Florida. It's been there forever. Got to drive up a long dirt road lined with gigantic trees on one side and cornstalks on the other before you see at the top of a hill this old concrete-block building built on a concrete slab. Somebody was always burning a pit fire out back. Looks like the club is surrounded by those old oak trees that have moss hanging from them. The trees look like they are out of a postcard you would receive in the mail from Florida—without the oranges.

With just a stage in the corner, this juke has a lot of history. B.B., Chuck Berry, Bobby "Blue" Bland, and Little Milton all played here. I was glad to be there in April 2001, as it was not as humid as it would be in the summer. We had a great gig that night. At Dave's, I always just do what I want to do. No typical show. I play different songs. I play some long songs short, and play some short songs long. It's all because I feel at home.

After the gig, we loaded up and I climbed into the second row on the bus. As usual, I was adding up the time. Saying to myself, "Mmm, it's 'round one forty-five a.m., so about three hours to Pensacola and I should be in a warm bed about four-thirty-ish." We couldn't have been more than forty-five minutes west on I-10 when all holy hell broke loose. Our driver had a heart attack. He hit a tree and that enormous bus rolled over three or four times, taking everything in its way with it down a ravine. I was the only one trapped in the bus. I was in a seat wedged tightly in an area between the floor and the crushed metal top of the bus. Once I came to, I could hear everybody talking. "Two are on their way." "You smell diesel?" "Easy!" "They'll be fine." All the while, different siren sounds were coming closer—then going away. All I remember was trying to cooperate with the voices of the police and emergency medical people who were talking to me.

"Are you there?" someone called out.

I weakly said, "Yes."

Every thirty seconds or so they would say the same thing. "Are you there?" I'd say yes.

"Sir, we're going to have to cut you out of there. Okay?"

"Okay."

"Stay with me."

"Okay."

I was just about to lose it when I heard the generator starting up. Sounded like the sweetest lawn mower engine you've ever heard. Soon the hydraulic Jaws of Life were cutting away the silver metal carcass of what was my old Silver Eagle bus. Those strong seats saved me, as they withstood the steel roof being crushed in. Soon I was in a hospital room where a doctor said, "Everyone has injuries, some severe, and I regret to inform you the young lady didn't make it. She was killed instantly."

Latisha Brown and my nephew Andrew Jr.—everybody called him Skip—were thrown from the bus. Skip survived, Latisha didn't. Broken up as I was about Latisha, I thought of her three young children. Such misery. Ain't no comfort for them kids. Your common sense tells you— you are not responsible. But I'd be lying if I said that I didn't think about the roads as I lay there recuperating from my head and neck injuries. Especially those dark, curvy night roads of the South in the wee hours. It ain't the best place for anyone, not to mention a young soul. We were all cut up pretty bad. My pianist, Melvin "House Cat" Hendrex, a Mississippi legend in his own right, spent almost a year in the hospital.

I know putting miles on your body is part of the deal when you play this music that I love. Yes, there are no guarantees in life, but damn— two, three, or four hundred miles to drive at one a.m. is a rough life. But it's my life.

Simple Things

I stayed home recuperating. Since the accident, I have had dreams about it. It has led me to wonderin' about God's grace; after all, I've cheated death more than most. And I know for sure I'm preserved by some kind of mercy. I can't say I had some life-changing sign after the accident, and I didn't even make bargains with God. But I thanked him more—for the simplest of things. The seemingly unimportant wee-little things. Thank you, Lord, for my ability to drive. Thank you for my ability to clean a fish. Thank you for my ability to smile. Thank you for my ability to walk across the room. Thank you for my ability to play a guitar.

So if you wanna say that the Lord turned me 'round, like old folks used to sing, then you can say yes. But all the accident did was make this simple country boy take notice of the simple blessings in the simplest of things.

But I also felt some vulnerability, too. Not to hurt, harm, or danger—but to time. I had a feeling of "shit or get off the pot" kinda thing going. A need to do more, more quickly. And I can also say the accident deepened me. Like they had dredged my riverbed of its mud and the silt. And now a canyon had formed where life's living water could run through me easier.

I got some bad news right near Christmas 2001. My buddy Rufus Thomas, who once met a kid on Beale Street and treated him like a son, died in Memphis. They said of heart failure. But I think it was of a broken heart, as his wife, Lorene, had died just a year earlier—they were inseparable.

Brighter Lights, Same Cities

You don't play the blues as long as I have and not spend a lot of time in Clarksdale, Mississippi. Most consider Clarksdale (and, frankly, a few other places) as the birthplace of the blues. But for all the places that call themselves the home of the blues, places to play that have good sound systems, stages, and lights can sometimes be few and far between. Step in actor Morgan Freeman, attorney Bill Luckett, Memphis entertainment executive Howard Stovall, and Eric Meier. In an awesome labor of love, they resurrected an abandoned building and created the Ground Zero Blues Club. They kept the interior as funky as it could be. But the sound is great. I'm glad to call Bill and Morgan good friends.

It was with that sound and room lighting in mind that I decided to record and film a live album there. I released *Live at Ground Zero*. Love the way it came out.

The spotlight got a lot brighter when I was asked to take part in a ten-episode documentary on the blues. Film icon Martin Scorsese was executive producer. Didn't think too much about it at first, as I've been filmed and interviewed too many times to count. The film crew met me at a gas station in Jackson. They just wanted to talk and hang out on my bus. I had a gig at Larry's Place that night in Nesbit, Mississippi. The drive would take about two and half hours. But Richard Pearce, the filmmaker, had other ideas.

"Mr. Rush."

"Ah, mane, call me Bobby."

"I was wondering if we could take the long way?"

"What'chu mean, Highway 61?"

"Yes, sir."

"Fine by me. Sometimes takin' the long way home is the best way."

"But we don't want to make you late."

"Don't worry 'bout that—the people will wait for me."

Well, it took an extra five or six hours. But I see why Richard wanted to do it that way. I introduced him to the band and sat down and just started tellin' stories as the bus rolled past the wide-open spaces of rural Mississippi. The filmmakers were excited as they got a look right through the front window of a house that most people thought had burned down years ago. And that was the Chitlin Circuit.

This was a universe Richard and his crew had never witnessed before. Down-home folks. Down-home food. Down-home blues. Raunchy and righteous. Pure and dirty. He confessed to me some time later, "Bobby, this is the closest thing that has been filmed where we could see what the world may have been like for Howlin' Wolf, Elmo James, and so many others."

At first, I didn't know if that was a compliment or an insult. But of course I took it as high praise. Because it was true: my life is the current version of what the old cats did.

The documentary also features B.B. King. And it is clear from the film that B.B. had graduated to a much higher level of visibility, money, and fame than I had in 2003. Hell, mostly I'm playing the same joints that B.B. did in the early 1960s.

We arrived at the concert about five minutes before they'd scheduled us to begin. Band got out, unloaded, and set up. They filmed me gettin' ready. I plopped on some hair juice for my Jheri curl, combed it straight back. Clipped my nails, threw some badass shit on, and, although an hour late, I walked to the stage and dove into a raunchier version of "What's Good for the Goose is Good for the Gander."

"Eye for eye.
Tit for tat."

Then gyrating my crotch, I sang:

"If you gonna give away my dog.
I gonna sell some of this cat."

After seeing that, Richard had to have some more of this. This was that uncut funk. That delicious thick slice of bacon. That loose joy that you could only feel in Chitlin Circuit places. They hung on the bus, too. This gave them the grits and gravy of being on the road at the Chitlin level. I was on the phone making unique deals with club owners. I think what impressed Richard and crew was that there was no publicist, manager, wife, girlfriend, or gatekeeper that was trying to control things—in this case, the filmmaker's creativity. I was captain of this here cruise ship. It was me and only me to deal with.

The camera crew was supposed to be with me for one or two days. Richard said, "Bobby, we're getting stories, sights, and sounds that are reminding us why we wanted to make this doc. Could we stay a few days longer?"

Of course I said yes.

Didn't have a clue what a big deal this would be for me. When they first showed the documentary on PBS in early fall of 2003, I got calls from folks I hadn't talked to or seen in years, sometimes decades.

"Boy, you look as good as you did in 1958." It was Dick Gregory. It was a brief conversation, told a few jokes. That was it. Got a lot of them kinda calls. I think people thought I may be dead. When I moved to Jackson twenty years earlier, in 1983, to some I just fell off the map. I was still touring more than ever, even going to new and farther away places. But those weren't known to anybody but the faces in the clubs. The world at large had not heard of me or from me. Life had moved on, and I stayed in my lane doing it my way.

Up until this point, I had largely gotten praise only from my core fans and my peers. Everybody in the business knew me, but nobody really knew me in the world at large. But this film would change that. And they're still showing it today.

The King of the Chitlin Circuit

Daddy used to preach a sermon about the Noah story, that when God gave Noah the power to name all the animals, he gave man (Noah) dominion. The moral is that there is significant power in having the authority to name something. Fifty years ago, I named myself Bobby Rush, changing it from Emmett Ellis Jr. When *Rolling Stone* magazine named me in the documentary's aftermath "The King of the Chitlin Circuit," that name was chosen for me. But in that choice would come a recognition that I had waited for my entire life.

And in *Rolling Stone's* choice would come an acknowledgment that this old Chitlin Circuit where I was planted was connected to the very foundation of American entertainment history. "The King of the Chitlin Circuit" label made me the presiding bishop over these sacred little places where my people, a generation before, self-segregated for our own pleasure and for our release.

And I was king of a long-forgotten kingdom where my peers— many now long gone—learned their craft to entertain.

I was still working hard as ever. But now there was more advance press about my shows. More reviews. More people in the seats.

I ain't no superstar. But I'm a star.

Folk Funk

For a good portion of the mid-'80s and '90s I had chased that gritty, synthesizer-influenced sound. That sound became one and the same with Southern blues. Even though my music was funkier than most, I wanted a change.

The transformation that started in 2000 with my Grammy-nominated album *Hoochie Man* was getting ready to go into high gear. I had a deep-rooted desire to make a record that would conjure up the sounds and feel of the soil of my childhood in the 1940s of Louisiana and Arkansas.

Some folks would call this record traditional blues. I called it what it was: *Folk Funk*. That's right; it's an extension of "Chicken Heads" of 1971. But we would strip this album of the electric stuff of my '80s and '90s sound. This spare sound would just be a simple rhythm section. I recorded at Sonic Temple in Jackson, Mississippi, which added to the vibe. Mane, one of the best decisions I made for this record was to call in Alvin Youngblood Hart. Alvin is a young master of all styles of blues guitar. Alvin put his foot in it. Reminded me of how Little Walter made Muddy's music come alive. His acoustic guitar strokes gave the simplicity of this album the glue that it needed. I had my bass player Steve Johnson with me and Memphis legend Charlie Jenkins on drums.

I was patient when picking the songs for this record. I wanted to capture all the things I felt comin' up through Chicago, but also include all the musical things I had become. A lil' gospel on "Saints Gotta Move." "Ride in My Automobile" is supposed to feel like I'm cruising down Roosevelt Road in Chicago in the late 1950s. I did a Sonny

Boy Williamson–style thing with "Ninety-Nine," and some John Lee Hooker on "Feeling Good—Part One" and "Feeling Good—Part Two." And I got my feet soggy walking through the swamp on "Uncle Esau" and "Voodoo Man."

I was playing harp full-time now, and I will never put it down again. The thin musical setting gave my harp a chance to really breathe. *Folk Funk* was rootsy, funky, and modern. It felt like my past, present, and future were on that record.

Bobby Rush Inc.

As a businessman and entertainer, I sometimes get frustrated with the pace at which others move. I know I move faster than most; I've had to. And throughout much of the '80s, '90s, my operation kept expanding. By the time I started Deep Rush Records in 2003, the mail room in my house had spilled over into another room.

On most days, my phone rings by 8:00 a.m. I spend a lot of time on the wire getting updates on future performances. Talking to nightclub owners, promoters, and festival buyers is all in a day's work. I've been doing this for so long that we often talk about each other's kids, their wives or husbands, or whatever they're going through. That is to say, as much as I've been a persistent businessman, sometimes I've established long-standing bonds.

These business bonds are literally the glue of my career.

Also, since the Southern blues radio stations are a tightly knit group, I spend many hours with them seeing where my current record is on their playlist. In addition, many of the major cities' Black radio stations have blues shows on the weekends. And much of my business always involves some self-promotion to these weekend jocks as their stations' reach is wide. These relationship bonds are now more necessary than ever. Because in the '70s and '80s these radio stations had more of a commitment to what their listeners wanted to hear. And that was good for us Southern blues/soul artists. But it's different now. Younger program directors, some stations are owned by conglomerates, and their playlists are dictated to them from up on high—and not by what the local listeners want. Ironically, public radio has been a blessing for me personally, as they know me as an artist but also a cultural signpost.

So I've had to spend even more time doing the business side of my career.

No one is in front of me in terms of the sheer number of shows I perform each year in the Southern blues/soul market. Now, since I'm on the festivals, too, I've had to even become a more diplomatic businessperson. Walking the tightrope of satisfying my dependable Chitlin Circuit fans and business associates while also satisfying the more crossover fans and business associates of the festivals market.

Southern Energy

One benefit that I didn't consider when I moved to Jackson back in '83 was the incredible amount of talent there. Just because some cats don't take the plunge to move to Los Angeles, Nashville, or New York doesn't mean that the cats down South who play in churches, nightclubs, old folks' homes, schools, or just jam together ain't some of the baddest mofos you'll ever hear.

And you don't do what I do for as long as I've done it without some incredible support behind you. The people you walk to the stage with. The people you glance at out of the corner of your eye and smile to as if to say, "Mane, your ass is cookin' to-nite!" The people who you look at sleeping under their blankets on the moving bus as the sun rises, knowing that they've got families at home, too. So I must, for the record, mention just some of their names. Not taking anything away from all the cats who helped me put the grease in the pan since the early 1950s. But some of these folks still play with me, while some played a spell and moved on.

Current Band:
Bruce Howard (Drums, 38 years)
Kinneth Roy Kights (Guitar, 19 years)
Louis Rodriguez (Guitar, 10 years)
Arthur Cooper (Bass, 14 years)
Joseph Banks (Keys, 20 years)
Loretta "Mizz Lowe" Wilson (Dancer, 18 years)
Erickia Henderson (Dancer, 5 years)

Crew:
Mike McDonald (Driver/Security/PA, 24 years)

Past Musicians:
LaFredrick Taylor (Keyboards, 25 years)
James "Hog Dog" Derrick Lewis (Keyboards, 25 years)
Terry Richardson (Bass, 14 years)
Terrence Grayson (Bass, 7 years)
Jesse Robinson (Guitar, 10 years)
Vasti Jackson (Guitar, 15 years)
Benjamin Wright (Keyboards, 10 years)
Dexter Allen (Guitar, 10 years)

Past Dancers:
Shakila Powell (14 years)
Loretta "Jazzii" Anderson (10 years)
Carolyn Goblet (8 years)
Clorissa Carter (5 years)
Sarah Barnett (7 years)
Georgia Brunt (6 years)
Sharon Spinks (5 years)
Diane Crockett (10 years)

Mizz Lowe, whose actual name is Loretta Wilson, has been a dancer with me since 2002. In many ways, she grew up on the road. When she started out, she would complain after fifty days straight on the road, "When are we going home?" The old-timers in the band would kinda chuckle. But I always said the same thing: "If you wanna be in this business—you got to put in the time." What's beautiful about her is that as country as she is, she loves to engage with all the artists she's met over the years. We were playing at the Lake Tahoe Blues Festival with the Robert Cray Band and Chaka Khan. And she didn't know that Chaka was a fan of mine. And it's a testament to Chaka's down-hominess that she and Lowe hit it off. It was confidence building for her 'cause, woman to woman, Chaka can say some things to her that I can't.

It was the same with Denise LaSalle. As Denise told me later, she reminded Lowe that she was just as much valued as an entertainer as the other musicians were. Denise also told her it was okay to be on the road with men—that she had a rightful place in being there. She didn't let anyone put her down for just being a dancer.

Also, locking down the groove for me for thirty-eight years has been my drummer, Bruce "Hitman" Howard. Bruce can read me almost better than anyone. And that's beyond music. You don't spend almost forty years with a cat where you don't develop a friendship that leaves in the dust the employer-employee relationship. He's been there through ups and downs—which is the place where friendships are tested.

Thirty-eight years is a long time for a cat to be sitting behind you. And Bruce knows what I want and how I want it, and it sets a tone for the rest of the band. Bruce makes sure that the music complements me and yet doesn't overshadow me.

Also very important to me has been my brother Larry Ellis, who for many years was my emcee. Nothing like having a cat around that you trust to the max. That's priceless.

Pride and Joy

If the relationship of father to son could really be reduced to biology, the whole earth would blaze with the glory of fathers and sons.

–JAMES BALDWIN

When Jean and I moved to Jackson, Mississippi, our son Carl was fourteen and in middle school. Jean was more concerned than I was about his adjusting—especially during them teenage years. He adjusted fine. When he graduated from high school, he did not want to go to college. Jean was not happy with that choice. I wasn't either, but let's just say—I was more flexible.

I said earlier that one of my big regrets—maybe in fact my greatest regret—was not finishing my primary education, not graduating from high school. I know I needed that. Especially in expanding my vocabulary. Thanks be to God that Daddy read every day, and that at least gave me an example of how to grow my vocabulary.

As kind of a bypass to Carl not going to college, he went with me on the road, serving as my emcee, road manager, and sound guy. I've never had someone in that position who did it better. Seriously. After some soul searching, Carl went into the police academy and thrived as a police officer. That was his slot 'cause he's good at it. He's a people person. Warm and friendly. He's a noble son and my pride and joy.

Carl ultimately had four children: Carlos, Sherry, Carl Jr., and Marquise. You know what's better than being their grandfather? That's being the great-grandfather of Dylan, Aaliyah, and Carla.

I have been all over the planet, bringing joy through music. At this point in my life there's nothing that brings me more joy than standing at the shore, fishing with my great-grandkids. These little things remind me of the gift of time and love.

Katrina

I remember on one of my first trips to Los Angeles, a long time ago; at the house where I was staying, the host said, "Now if an earthquake hits, stand in the doorway because that's the strongest part of the house." I thought, *Wow, it can hit that suddenly?*

The closer you live to the Gulf of Mexico, the more hurricanes are a part of life. But unlike earthquakes, you know when they are coming. So as Katrina approached the Gulf, it was like just another hurricane. Our attitude wasn't flighty; the Gulf had seen so much of this over the last ten years. Erin and Opal in 1995, Danny in 1997, Georges in 1998, and Lili in 2002.

The thing that made Katrina so deadly was that it was slow moving. This allowed it to pound its force like nobody's business. Of course you know the rest of the story. Katrina turned out to be the worst natural disaster in American history. It wiped part of the Mississippi and Louisiana coast right off the map. Displacing an entire city, some folks never returned to New Orleans. The misery and death of a city 80 percent underwater were just unbelievable.

The storm came right up through central Mississippi. Hit Jackson hard with wind and rain damage. Power was out all around us, but for some blessed reason the power never went out at our house. As for the people that survived, their living situation was no more—there was a mass exodus out of New Orleans. Since we had provisions and power, we let a family of seven live with us for some days before we waved goodbye to them as they headed to South Carolina to build a new life with relatives there. We then had a colorful family from Baton Rouge stay until their lights came on.

Fats Domino's situation broke my heart—lost all his stuff. However, when I saw him, all he said was "Better to be alive."

Honors of the Heart

I've won thirteen Blues Music Awards from the Blues Foundation. And after being nominated fifty-one times, each win is special in its own way. But I would be lying if I didn't say that one stood out more than the others. Being called to the stage in 2006 to be inducted into the Blues Hall of Fame felt unique. Felt personal.

Because I joined men who had molded me: Louis Jordan, Big Joe Turner, Howlin' Wolf, T-Bone Walker, Rufus Thomas, Ray Charles, Sonny Boy Williamson, and others.

I joined men who were dear friends and, like me, were soldiers in the blues army. Buddy Guy, Bobby "Blue" Bland, B.B. King, Fats Domino, Albert King, and others.

There are other reasons this moment was special. One, I've put a lot of sweat, joy, and pain into being an entertainer. My songs, my stage plays, and the musicianship of my band and myself are woven into a fabric called me being a bluesman. The other reason that this May night in Memphis was special is that getting asked to be in the Blues Hall of Fame is like being asked to come into a room of dreamers. In that room they respect you and you respect them. You are members of the same tribe. You had the same dreams, made the same promises to yourself when you were young. So being in this room makes me feel like I kept a promise to myself.

When all is said and done, awards mean different things to different people. Everybody wants to be acknowledged, but some acknowledgments bring with it a power, a strength that is invisible. You can't dust it off and put it on a shelf because the award is on the inside. Getting inducted into the Blues Hall of Fame was a trophy for my heart, mind, and soul.

China

If it's true that good things come to those who wait, then my life has been a Hollywood movie called *If I Knew I Was Waitin', I Woulda Stopped a Long Time Ago*. My career had been on the rise for almost ten years. People started to know who Bobby Rush was. And as much as it gratified my ego, I realized what I had really been seeking all these decades was a kind of independence. But I could only give that to myself.

Having a hit song is great. People know your face and want to come see you perform that song. But there is an ocean of difference between my friends *who wrote their hit song* (and did not get taken) and the ones *who did not write their hit*. The royalties can be tremendous. So glad that I never stopped writing songs. Because as things turned for me in the late '90s, "Chicken Heads" got a second life of its own. Many artists would cover (re-record) it and play the song in their set. In 2007, "Chicken Heads" was used in the Samuel L. Jackson film *Black Snake Moan*. This was an enormous boost for the song. There were other rebirths of songs. "I've Been Watching You" is a song I wrote for the Southside Movement, a band out of Chicago. That song was sampled in "So What'cha Want" by Beastie Boys, "Show Discipline" by Jadakiss, "Woo" by Erykah Badu, "E-Pro" by Beck, and others.

Also in 2007, I got an offer to be the first blues artist to perform in China. After the longest flight of my life, the jumbo jet descended into Beijing.

So many bicycles, mopeds, and people. Futuristic architecture and little places that looked like they hadn't been touched for a hundred years. You could see and feel that there were different classes of people.

Beijing and Shanghai almost smelled like America in that they feel westernized. We sojourned to this extremely rural area where folks followed me around. Wanting to touch me—at first I thought it may be a sign of racism. But I got a feeling that it was just the difference in appearance. Don't think they had ever have seen a Black tall man with my Jheri curl and smile. I looked more than out of place; I probably looked like an alien from another planet. Minus the language barrier, we connected.

Arriving at the Great Wall, I just felt . . . small. Small in size and small in history. I said to myself, "I hope Daddy can see me, 'cause this is something I know he'd be proud of." As humble as my daddy's beginnings were, he knew the globe. He knew there were places on it that were like other planets—planets he would never see. And the Great Wall was another planet.

I crossed a river when I performed in China. Muddy and Bobby Blue didn't get to come here, but this Louisiana boy did. They named me Friendship Ambassador to the Great Wall of China after I performed the largest concert ever held at that site. And I got the title "International Dean of the Blues."

My international life expanded as they asked me to go to Iraq in April 2008 and entertain the troops. After taking a tour where we saw a man-made pond full of goldfish and the spoils of Saddam Hussein's wealth, we had a show to do. But before we started, they had incoming artillery fire, and we had to quickly go underground to the bomb shelter. Scary shit. But when I started the show, I didn't hold back. I laid on them the whole Bobby Rush enchilada. The music, the jokes, the girls, the storytelling, the praise for their effort—and then some. The commanding colonel told me she had not seen the boys have this much fun since she'd been in command. That meant an awful lot to me.

But what meant even more was that after the show, the first people to run up and surround me were all these brothers and sisters from the South: Mississippi, Louisiana, Alabama, Arkansas, the Carolinas. It almost felt like an annual homecoming service at church. I hugged a ton of folk, and they wanted pictures to send back to their people. I felt like I was giving them a little taste of home.

‖‖‖‖‖‖‖

I continued to taste my own home cookin', too. Louisiana style. Still, developing my folk funk kept me enthused. It kept me excited. And, I dare say, it kept me young at heart. Did one of my best albums in 2013 with *Down in Louisiana*. It not only sounded great, but it's super bluesy, super electric, yet super earthy. This album brought me one step closer to where I knew I had to go in my advanced years. Great tunes, if I say so myself.

I got everything on it: shuffles, a little Cajun, a little swampland, and even a number that takes me to church, "Swing Low." Folks have said of this album: "If you want to hear the real Bobby Rush, listen to this record." I can't say they're wrong. Got nominated for my second Grammy for Best Blues Album with *Down in Louisiana*. As I got closer to my roots, I started doing more shows with just me and a guitar. Got invitations to lecture at colleges to just talk about the blues.

Could it be that as I changed my presentations, I was being taken seriously in a fresh way?

Missed Rufus

I love Memphis for many reasons. Barbeque, memories, music (of course), but mostly friends. I can't go to Memphis without saying to myself, "I wish Rufus was still here." But he's not.

Memphis has become a home away from home for a long time. Back in October 2010, the city gave me a high honor, placing my name on the Beale Street Brass Notes Walk of Fame. The brass notes bearing names are inlaid into the sidewalk—not unlike the Hollywood Walk of Fame. So glad that right there on Beale Street where Rufus showed me how to "do that thang," I'm now immortalized in his company. As well as with Elvis, the Staple Singers, Otis Redding, Justin Timberlake, and so many more.

When I come to Memphis I'm treated by fans, city officials, and the media like a cousin coming for Thanksgiving dinner. I can't come here without doing some kind of local TV show, and I'm proud to do it. There is a part of me that was indeed born here.

Once, I was there to record one of Rufus's songs with one of the young lions of hip-hop, Frayser Boy. We were all there to film a documentary called *Take Me to the River*, directed by Martin Shore. The film was produced by my old friend Willie Mitchell's son Lawrence "Boo" Mitchell and the Talking Heads member Jerry Harrison. Mavis Staples, Booker T. Jones, Otis Clay, William Bell, Charlie Musselwhite, and rappers Snoop Dogg, Al Kapone, and Yo Gotti took part, to name a few.

As much as I loved performing with the kid, it did my heart good to see the footage of Bobby Bland. I tried to see him as often as I could in his remaining time on this side of the curtain. And the documentary turned out to be a labor of love 'cause both Hubert Sumlin and my good friend Bobby Blue, who both took part, died before the film debuted in March 2014.

Earlier in the year, as a Grammy nominee for my *Down in Louisiana* album, I was in Los Angeles for Grammy week. All of us who were nominated in the folk, Americana, bluegrass, and blues categories gave a tribute concert at the Troubadour for Phil Everly, who had recently passed.

The Americana Music Association sponsored the night, so they let me and the other performers pick songs that weren't the Everly Brothers' big hits. I did the lesser-known song "Gone, Gone, Gone," as this was one of their most spirited, gutsy songs. Lot of talent in the house on that Saturday night: Rodney Crowell, Ry Cooder, Bonnie Raitt, and T Bone Burnett, to name a few.

It was a grand night of fellowship.

Last Train Home

Just like the old country Black churches have an annual homecoming service, for decades B.B. King had given a homecoming concert in the place of his birth, Indianola, Mississippi.

"Bobby, I need a favor."

"Anything. What'chu need me to do?"

"Need you to play on Sunday, June first."

"Ah, mane, B.B., I'm booked—damn."

"Man, see if you can get out of it—please. I need my people to see me."

"I can't promise you right now, but let me see what I can do."

"Thanks, Bobby—I'm counting on you."

I could hear the love, the weakness, and the urgency in his voice. I loved B.B. King and he loved me. No doubt. But wanting me there was not about me. It was about him—more out of reassuring himself. I knew he wanted me there that night because of his words: "I need my people to see me." He knew he was getting close to being called home. And here's the hard cold fact: since the 1980s less than 10 percent of the people at his Annual B.B. King Homecoming Festival were Black; it was mostly a sea of white folk. He knew it was his last rodeo, and he wanted to see one more time the faces of those that had brung him to the dance.

I had a gig in Memphis. One thing I've benefited from is being decent with these club owners and promoters. I called the promoter Little D and told him my situation. Which he didn't like—but he surely understood. Everybody in blues knew that B.B. was slowing down. He was falling asleep onstage. And he often needed help getting up from his chair.

"Mane, I'm gonna send your five thousand deposit back to you so you can get somebody else," I said.

"Naw, don't do that."

"Why?"

"'Cause you headlining; no one will show up. Just come, and I'll put you on first, giving you enough time to drive to Indianola."

"But won't the peoples that come late be disappointed?"

"Yeah, but I won't have to cancel the whole festival, and if you don't come, I have to. Come on. Do the early set and you can still get to B.B.'s."

"Okay, D, and I damn sure appreciate it."

Did the date in Memphis in the afternoon. And had the band in Indianola in time enough to play for B.B. Lots of Negroes in the house. Mission accomplished.

I performed while B.B. stood in the wings, kinda watching my show; I turned to him and smiled. He smiled back and gave me a thumbs-up. He couldn't have stood there but for a few minutes before they led him back to his dressing room. I passed him in the hall after my set, and he said, "What time are you going on, Bobby?" I said, "B.B., mane, I've already done my show."

I knew B.B. was ailing, but I didn't know to what degree until then.

When he moved on down the road in May 2015, I played on solo harp "When the Saints Go Marching In" in an impromptu concert after his memorial in Memphis. But I'm most proud that I walked beside his hearse through the streets of Memphis when he was laid to rest. He was a gift to this world, and strolling beside his casket was a gift to me.

Jeff

My relationship with Jeff DeLia started like a dandelion seed blowing off its bloom and falling in the right soil—at the right time. The winds blew Jeff to my friend Carl Gustafson, who saw him at a conference for festival promoters. Jeff was there to showcase his artist A.J. Croce. A.J. is the son of Jim Croce, the singer/songwriter who was taken too soon in a tragic plane crash in 1973.

Now, God bless him, but Jeff don't look older than fourteen years old. Yes, baby-faced, but with the hustle of an old soul. Carl immediately recognized him as a go-getter. Carl introduced us and we started talking on the phone, and, in time, a good vibe developed.

Jeff and I started working together in 2013. In 2014, he came aboard officially as my manager. And this decision gained immediate results. He came to me with ideas for this and ideas for that. Sometimes his ideas were things I'd tried before, and sometimes his ideas were things I never even thought of. Despite the age and cultural differences between us, we made an excellent team. He has enhanced my career and therefore my life. Still, many people I have known and I have worked with have not said kind things about Jeff, dismissing him solely because he is white; and too often I have had to defend him, which is exhausting and sad. I've had a manager or two before, but mostly they were involved in getting me gigs—not bringing me deals and being engaged in a way that moved me forward. I never kept those other cats around long. And I was so used to doing things myself, sometimes I had to remember that Jeff was there.

I got even more media: a story in *USA Today*, and my music started to appear on Americana charts. And even the groundwork that I'd laid long before Jeff's arrival bore fruit. Dan Aykroyd and I had become friends and began to play gigs together. In July 2014, months before the James Brown movie *Get on Up* was released, *The Tonight Show Starring Jimmy Fallon* asked Dan to perform; he said he would do it only if he could bring me with him. This would be my first late-night television appearance. We performed James Brown's cult classic "I'll Go Crazy."

They then invited me to South by Southwest (SXSW) that year. The SXSW festival/conference is where the innovators in tech, music, and movies converge. Had a good time performing with Mavis Staples and Booker T. Jones. Still, there's always that ebb and flow of life. 'Cause a bit later, in 2014, my brother Andrew "Bo" Ellis died of cancer. This resurgence or awakening to my career seemed always to be colored with life. I guess that's why I've tried to separate the two—life and career.

This may seem like an oversimplification, but I think that's why I love to work with my hands. It's concrete. It's real in a way the entertainment business is not. I've built extensions on my house. I enjoy repairing my bus and my cars. I do plumbing—not that I need to, but 'cause I want to. For many years it was practical, but now it calms me. Quiets my mind, makes me a little less restless.

In the late fall of 2015, I was home for a rare week off the road. A box arrived at my doorstep. It was my first look at the soon-to-be-released box set of my recording career. *Chicken Heads: A 50-Year History of Bobby Rush*. Released by Omnivore Recordings, it had almost one hundred songs—which still is a small sampling of all the songs I have recorded. I felt really fortunate that I had a team of great co-producers who really made this happen: Jeff DeLia of course, Omnivore head Cheryl Pawelski, and my longtime-devoted publicist Cary Baker.

The box set won the Blues Music Award and *Living Blues* Magazine Award for the Best Historical Release.

Putting on my reading glasses, I thumbed through the thirty-two-page booklet. I read with great affection testimonials by friends Mavis Staples, Benjamin Wright, Keb' Mo', Elvin Bishop, David Porter, Denise LaSalle, Tommy Couch Jr., Leon Huff, and Al Bell. But when I read the list of the songs—with all the different record labels—I hear in my head that Johnny Cash song "I've Been Everywhere."

Blinddog and Dr. John

Carl Gustafson again is my brother from another mother. So it was a no-brainer when he asked me to record some songs with his band Blinddog Smokin'. Some songs quickly turned into an album. The album was called *Decisions* by Bobby Rush with Blinddog Smokin' (and featuring Dr. John). And when I say that Carl's band can play, I ain't bullshittin'. All talented musicians with taste. We cut the record in Los Angeles and New Orleans. Carl said, "Man, you and Mac (Dr. John) gotta do something together on this."

Dr. John has New Orleans in his hands. And New Orleans is a city with a long memory. It's like anybody who's ever made a mark on the piano from N'awlins is right there in Dr. John's fingertips. I have known him for over fifty years. And in all that time we ain't never done anything together. Hadn't seen him in years. People that know him call him Mac.

"Mac, mane, how you been?"

"Not as good as you, mane. Look at your vines!"

It seems for the first thirty minutes we sat down, the conversation went like this:

"Have you seen So and So?"

"Naw, mane, he died."

"When was the last time you talked to So and So?"

"Mane, that boy been dead for twenty years."

After we settled into the fact that most of us were gone, we could relax and tell old tales about Professor Longhair, Freddie King, B.B. We talked about how both chased after Ruth Brown. We reminisced about places we had been and how things had changed. Some for the worse— some for the better. But to the cats who were listening, they just soaked it up like a sponge. Carl said, "Man, hearing you guys talk is like going through an encyclopedia in roots music."

We did a video for our collaboration on "Another Murder in New Orleans," which was the single from the *Decisions* album. The video was produced by Julie Pacino (Al's daughter) and directed by Jennifer DeLia (Jeff DeLia's sister). We shot it on the streets of New Orleans. Had a great time as they put a casting call out and people came from everywhere for a chance to take part with home-towner Dr. John.

Mac was just holding on the day of the video shoot. During breaks in the filming he'd fall asleep, and it was my job to ever so gently wake him up. Softy I whispered, "Mac, Mac." Putting my hand on his back, I said, "Mac, Mac, Mac!" His eyes popped open. He turned his head a lil' to the right, then a lil' to the left and said, "Where in da mutta-fuck am I?" I laughed a little and said, "Hey, mane, we gone take it again—a'ight?"

The *Decisions* album was a critical success and got nominated for a Grammy for Blues Album of 2014.

We finished the shoot, and I walked Mac to his car, where his driver was waiting.

"Now, Mac, let's keep in touch for real this time," I said.

"Bobbyrush, I'm from N'awlins, and you know what they say 'bout us, don't you?"

"Tell me, Mac."

"We don't care what you do; but we want to know what you do!"

I laughed and helped him into the car. Of course we did not keep in touch. And he walked to the other side in 2019.

Haunted

I live on the road.

All of us cats who have chosen or just fell into living out of a suit-case know that life on the road is never ever simple. For almost fifty years I have spent at least two hundred days a year out there.

Giving in to the flesh is one of the occupational hazards of life rolling from city to city. It requires a cat to resist the flesh completely or tame it with a whip like a lion tamer in a three-ring circus. And that's a good comparison, 'cause life on the road often feels like a circus. The circumstances of my slow upward career climb put me so into my music that my flesh didn't have the power over my time like it had for many of my friends. And I wasn't that famous where women were coming on to me without me lifting a finger. B.B. had fifteen kids by fifteen women. Still, I wish I could say that in all of my decades on the road, I have been faithful. I have not. And I'm haunted by it. Haunted by my flesh. I know I'm gonna meet my Maker one day and be held to account for my behavior.

I cry about it. But I ain't telling you to garner sympathy—keep it to yourself. I ain't telling you for you to accept me, either—'cause accepting me would not change a damn thing about the past. I'm tell-ing you because confession is good for the soul, and my soul always could use some mercy.

I cling by the very tip of my fingernails to redemption in Jesus Christ. But don't get it twisted. This ain't me saying I can do anything I want because of my faith in Jesus. I'm a man saying I'm frustrated with myself. I'm frustrated with my flesh. I'm frustrated that my high nature has caused pain.

I believe, as the Apostle Paul said, "My righteousness is filthy rags," and I need the covering of Jesus Christ. Because God knows like many other men and women—I got a few dirty rags in my closet.

It's good for me that Jean isn't intimidated by anything. Because she probably would have killed me long ago. But seriously, in her wisdom she knew she couldn't control anybody. She also knew that if she fell down, a whole lotta other people were gonna fall, too. Probably including me. Jean has been more than a wife. She has been a counselor and friend, and has consistently prayed over my life. And if I believe in prayer—and I do—I can say that her prayers have protected my anointing to sing a joyful blues.

This country boy lives in a world of temptations and joy. I love what I do, even if I have done it with imperfection. A wise old friend of mine said to me a few years back, "There's nothing wrong with accepting responsibility, as long as you don't give yourself a life sentence."

Big-Pond Vision

Even with the award milestone, by the summer of 2015, I was tired. And for me to say I was tired means my workload had exhausted me.

I had been recording, selling, booking, and promoting myself independently for a long time. Since 2003, I had released on my Deep Rush Records label several albums: *Undercover Lover*, *Live at Ground Zero*, *Folk Funk*, *Night Fishin'*, *Raw*, *Look at What You Gettin'*, *Blind Snake*, *Show You a Good Time*, and *Down in Louisiana*. All funded and promoted by me. Not to mention I was booked for over two hundred dates in 2015. So my exhaustion was real.

Rounder Records, a label that has been dedicated to what I would call organic music for fifty years, had tried to sign me in the 1990s. But I said no. Was I stubborn? Yes. Was I crazy? No. I was through with the damn double-dealing of record companies a long time ago. I had had it.

Scott Billington, an executive for Rounder Records, wooed me with more aggression. Scott was a very musical guy I had known since the 1990s when we met at a Recording Academy event. In the mid-2000s he seemed to randomly pop up for my gigs around the South. After a few times of this, he got right to the point.

"Bobby, we have a label dedicated to the blues, and we'd like you to be on it," Scott said.

"Now, Scott, you know I want to remain independent—I'm just happier that way."

"Well, Bobby, just think about it like this: You'd still be independent, but you'd have some help. Maybe it could elevate your career.

So when you go back to being an independent—you'll be that much stronger."

"Well, Scott, I got a new manager, Jeff; maybe you should talk to him."

Jeff and Scott talked. And I must admit I listened to Jeff more and more because he was proving how he helped my career's come-up. But like so many things in my life, my wife Jean said something to me that got me to thinking.

"Bobby, you're an independent and a good one."

"Honey, I know you're gettin' to something—what is it?" I said.

"You need the resources that can take you to another level."

"Jean, I know you right, but giving up my independence—I, I just don't know."

"Bobby, anything that expands your audience is good for your independence."

After talking to Jean, I reckoned I should think about this Rounder Records thing some more. I needed to be by myself and let my mind be free. I drove thirty minutes north on I-55 to Canton, Mississippi, and went fishing. I have a friend who has an enormous property there. The land contains three ponds with one being huge. Many times he doesn't even know I'm there. I do some of my best thinking standing at the shore of the big pond. With the occasional splash of fish jumping up from the water, I only hear the sounds of autumn in Mississippi.

Fishing calmed me—as it always has. I hadn't been out there an hour when things seemed to get even quieter than they naturally were. Now, it was two hours before sunset. The orange sky met the top line of the darkening trees, and below the trees, the pond shimmered. With its dark orange color, the water reflected the sky, just like a perfectly cleaned mirror. Tugging my fishline, I watched the dragonflies spin around the water. Those dragonflies take me back—way back. I thought about Daddy. I remembered that moment almost seventy years ago when his eyes filled up with tears as he looked at that first season of bountiful crops he grew in Sherrill, Arkansas. The rich soil of Arkansas changed his life. I remember when he said, "I'm so sorry I didn't leave Louisiana sooner. I dun worked my chil'ren and myself to the bone."

I wondered about the soil I had planted my career in. Independence was fine and had served me well. But I needed the rich nutrient soil of a recording budget and promotion from a Rounder Records. Or I had to at least try. All the pain of Chess Records, Jerry-O, and all the *almost this* or *I'm sorry that*. It seemed that with recording contracts, life was like a bad recurring dream—that I couldn't control while I slept.

I had been walking a path through the woods for about fifteen years, where it seemed the more I let new stuff in—the newer my life became. I accepted that I can't do all the planting, watering, pruning that a career takes right now. At that moment I felt like Daddy. I had worked myself to the bone. Recording, pressing, and selling my own records was fruitful—but exhausting. Jean was right. I called Scott and said let's do it.

One thing about my album *Porcupine Meat* was that more planning went into it than usual. Jeff and I went to the Rounder Records office in Nashville to meet with what I thought would be Scott and maybe one other person. When we arrived I was a little surprised, as they had every head of every department in the meeting—maybe fifteen people total. Each department told of their plans for the album. This enthused me.

The first thing I did was to let Scott know I wanted Vasti Jackson to work with us. Vasti, who I had been working with a while now, had moved to Hattiesburg, Mississippi, to take care of his ailing mother. I called him.

"I need you to do this record with me."

"Bobby, I'd love to, but you know I got my shows in Europe and of course now I gotta keep my eye on my mother."

"Mane, you're a good son, but I really need you."

"Why?"

"I'm doing this thing with Scott and Rounder Records in New Orleans, and I just don't want the Bobby Rush sound to get lost in the New Orleans sound."

"Okay. I got ya, Bobby. Come on down to Hattiesburg and we'll pull it together."

Magic Bag

The night before I left to drive to Hattiesburg, I stayed up damn near all night. Walked outside a few times. Ate some cold fried chicken. Paced the house some—I was as restless as I could be. Didn't really understand why. Just felt a stirring in my spirit. I've always been able to get along with a little sleep. So I just stayed in my chair till I finally dozed off.

Taking the almost two-hour drive to Vasti's home in Hattiesburg, I felt renewed. Wind in my Jheri curl, I was ready.

I've done a lot of recording. But one reason I continued to work with Vasti was that we didn't need anyone else to put down ideas. I have written a lot of songs, and Vasti feels me and understands my sound. Vasti can take some off-the-wall idea and make it work. Recorded the demos for *Porcupine Meat* in Vasti's home in Hattiesburg. His home became like a comfort zone where I could relax, record, write, and be creative without the constraints of a time clock in a recording studio. We worked out structures and tried song ideas by other writers than me. Scott came up to Hattiesburg a few times, and within a few weeks we had a solid blueprint of what the album would be.

After driving to New Orleans, Scott and I had dinner the day before the sessions were to start. We had a good thirteen or fourteen songs ready to go for the record. But as we sat in my hotel room, I started rubbing my face. Thinking.

"Scott, you sure we don't need one other song?"

"Well, it can't hurt for us to talk about it."

We went through the songs one by one. Discussing what each song brought to the table. We had two ballads that we both liked, but upon us talking about it they just seemed mushy compared with the Bobby Rush style. I thank the good Lord that I have a thousand ideas for songs waiting in the wings. I told Scott to wait a minute—I think he thought I was going to the can, but I went to the door of the room, picked up my suitcase, and produced a plastic grocery bag of cassettes. There were at least fifty in there. It took me some minutes to rummage through them, but I pulled out a tape that said "Porcupine." Scott kind of laughed when I grabbed from my suitcase an old Radio Shack cassette player. Sticking the old cassette in the machine, my demo for the song "Porcupine Meat" came on.

I'm in love with a woman, she don't mean me no good
I would leave that woman if I could
I tried to leave her, many times before
And every time I leave, I walk back for more
I know it ain't right
Oh, it just ain't fair
I want to leave
But I can't go nowhere
It's like porcupine meat, too fat to eat
Too lean to throw away

"Man, you've been holding out on me!" Scott said with laughter.

"Scott, I ain't been holding out on ya—I just thought about it right now as we was talking."

"What else you got in your magic bag?"

Then I played "Me, Myself and I" and "Nighttime Gardener," all old demos of songs I had written over a period of twenty or thirty years but never had put on a record. Scott said, "Bobby, these gotta be on the record."

"Fine by me," I said.

The next day I was sitting in the lounge of the best studio in New Orleans, the Parlor. At my age, I've learned to pray for things that are important to me, but to leave the outcome in God's hands.

So I said, "Lord, just let this record come out the way you want it to. You know I'm going to give it my all. But anoint the hands and minds of every one of us on this project. Amen."

The Parlor Studio is a beautiful and immaculately built recording studio in the guts of an old building. Great wood floors where instruments can resonate, brick and wood walls, and a vocal booth where I could see all the musicians. And most of all, a vintage Neve 8078 console. That console is considered one of the all-time best. Scott had assembled a world-class band. Vasti on guitar of course, two other musicians that I had just worked with on the Blinddog Smokin' record, keyboardist David Torkanowsky, and guitarist Shane Theriot. Drummer Jeffrey "Jellybean" Alexander and bassist Cornell Williams rounded out the rhythm section.

I sang along as the band cut the grooves. I wanted to make sure that the musicians felt the songs and that things didn't get too far away from who I am. Because when you go down to the Big Easy, the cats have a New Orleans flavor. So between me singing along with Vasti and Scott's guidance, we decided how much of that N'awlins Tabasco sauce, cayenne pepper, and roux we're going to put in this album's gumbo. And since the cats had such command of their instruments, they could turn up the funk—instantly. Or turn up the R&B or bluesy elements like flippin' on a light switch.

I'm a bluesman, and one thing about being a true bluesman is he has to feel the moment. Now, the reality is that you rehearse and plan to keep things steady. But the beauty of music and especially the blues is that you have these sparks. Completely unexpected moments that only staying in the moment can give. And that's the spirit of the undefinable, the unstoppable train of creativity.

The *Porcupine Meat* sessions were full of these moments. I was changing a word here and a word there right as I and my producer, Scott Billington, were listening to the playback. I love present-day technology. Where you can take this bit out and put this other bit in and stitch together a performance in the studio. But in my heart, the mic is my stage. I never gave a performance in the studio with the mentality that *Oh, I can do it again*. I walk up to the studio mic like I'm walking up to home plate to bat in the World Series. Every doggone time I'm looking for a home run. I want to knock it outta the park. With only one swing at it. That's how I always stood in front of the microphone.

Champagne

One thing I know for sure is that I'm open. Open to new things, new people, new ideas. I'm not only open, I want to be open. Why? Because I am convinced more than ever that it keeps me young. Keeps my nature high. Keeps me young at heart. However, when Scott said he wanted to bring in a sousaphone (tuba) player, even with my openness I was leery. My looming concern was that I did not want this *Porcupine Meat* album to be too New Orleans-y—and sousaphone is as Bayou City as you get. But I trusted Scott.

And I'm so glad I did. I remember hearing Otis Spann play piano for the first time in the early '50s and saying to myself, "I didn't know the piano could talk like that." Otis had such a gift for bringing out something completely new in an instrument that I had heard a zillion times before. I felt the same way when I heard Kirk Joseph play the sousaphone in the studio. I ain't never ever heard anybody play the sousaphone like that—seriously. He played melodically—just like Motown's bass player James Jamerson. Kirk is a master.

Scott recorded horns, and we sent the songs out for the guest performances of Keb' Mo', Joe Bonamassa, and Dave Alvin to be recorded at their own studios.

When *Porcupine Meat* was released, the response was overwhelming. But not to me. I've been to this rodeo so many times where folks say, "This is the greatest thing you've done." "This takes you to another level." Blah, blah, blah. It's not that I had become cynical, it's just that I had become cautious over the decades about what I got excited about. The first days of recording were exciting. Organizing the songs with

Vasti was exciting. Mixing the record was exciting. But those things are musical. I have some control over that. But all this glorified talk sounds like the bullshit I've been hearing all my life, and I ain't studdin' all of that.

Believe it or not, *Porcupine Meat* was nominated for a Grammy. At that point I had had only two drinks in my life and that was with Muddy Waters in the early 1960s. But on February 12, 2017, I had the third drink of my life, a cold flute of champagne, celebrating my first Grammy win for *Porcupine Meat.*

Denise

2018 began with a call in the middle of the night with the sad news that Denise LaSalle had died. As I sat in front of her casket, I thought how quickly time can flip things. Because this moment was a sad contrast to what I had felt almost a year earlier. 'Cause I truly felt that I had won that Grammy for all my comrades who never got one: like Denise, Tyrone Davis, Little Milton, and others.

I spoke at her eulogy on King Day, January 15. I said, in so many words, that when it came to our friendship Denise and I had no regrets. 'Cause we did for each other everything we could while she was here. In my own way I challenged the attendees not to wait to spend time with those you love 'cause you never know when someone will be called home.

But it was her nephew Morris Allen, a pastor in Denise's birthplace of Belzoni, Mississippi, that told the greatest truth. "Denise LaSalle touched more people and ministered to more lives than most of us preachers do. She was a better psychologist than Dr. Phil ever could be." Sometimes people say something and you just have to snap your fingers and say: "That's it, right there." Because God knows that was the truth about my friend.

As much as people called Denise the Queen of the Blues, she was a queen in so many other ways. Originally wanting to be a writer, she found that she really had a talent for it. Denise was the first to name what so many of us in the South call soul-blues or blues-soul. She gave the best advice and always had a word of encouragement. I miss her.

Home Again

I hadn't seen this much rain in Pine Bluff in a long time; it was coming down in sheets. But inside the Pine Bluff Convention Center, it was a sunny day in my heart. In late November 2018, I was being honored by the Delta Rhythm & Bayous Alliance. A bunch of local bigwigs and some folks I hadn't seen in years showed up. They had an art show that highlighted the bond between the blues and the Black struggle for equality.

There were musical tributes and kind words spoken by folks I knew and folks I didn't. They gave me plaques and proclamations. Pine Bluff, Arkansas, mayor Shirley Washington presented me with a replica of a street sign for what is now Bobby Rush Way in downtown Pine Bluff. A pretty good homecoming for a country boy.

But the highlight for me came when my younger brother Larry presented me with a diddley bow that he made from his own hands. He got the design from his memories as a child when I'd crafted one. I think if this celebration had been held anywhere else but Pine Bluff, it would have not affected me so. But it was in Pine Bluff. The place where I came of age and where my parents died. The Bluff holds a place in my spirit that can't be taken away.

Bobby Rush

Some of us try so hard—to do like others do
What's good for others—sometimes might not be so good for you.
Stick to you own thang—don't worry about anybody else
Just do your thing—whatever it is
And be yourself

"JUST BE YOURSELF"/ *BOBBY RUSH*/1969

Sitting on Top of the Blues

After the tribute in Pine Bluff, I felt honored and sentimental. However, for a man like me, the celebration didn't make me look back; it made me look ahead. And looking ahead in your eighties is like putting on the right turn signal of the big tour bus and exiting off the wide, eight-lane interstate. Because the rest of your journey is a narrow, curvy, two-lane backwoods road. You gotta drive carefully, making adjustments to the bends in the road, watching for deer running in front of you, and the ever-changing weather. In other words, how many years do I have left to do what I do, the way I do it? How many more years can I kick up my leg shoulder-high? How many more years can I jump four feet off the ground?

Strange how we think we are always gonna be able to do what we do, forever. We think our routines will be some kinda four-leaf clover. I think it too. So to break out of my routines for the last few years, musically I kept returning to the dirt of Louisiana. Doing more music that's closer to what I came up with. Rootsier. More organic. Thank God for Vasti Jackson, who knows far more about music than most. I would record an album in 2019 called *Sitting on Top of the Blues*. That title wasn't chosen to puff my chest out. It was simply to say that I'm still excited, still enthusiastic about this music I play. And I'm willing to grow and go where the spirit leads me. That's the whole point of being on top of the blues. I'm not subject to the limitations that once were. I'm still driving my bus, even if it's on a more rural, quiet, and curvy road.

Down-Home Love

When I was a young 'un growing up in rural Louisiana, it took me time to understand how a fig tree or some blackberry vines that you knew for sure were dead could come back to life. Lifeless for two or three years, they would rise up in the Louisiana spring and bear the sweetest fruit. The ebb and flow of life is hard to figure, but restoration seems to be a part of God's plan.

I got to see my career come alive and restored, while others didn't. Or maybe they did. Because that Bible I try to understand more every day tells me life is eternal. So maybe Rudy Ray Moore was sittin' next to me when I saw the final cut of the film about his career, *Dolemite Is My Name*.

You got to greatly appreciate a cat like Eddie Murphy. Because to get *Dolemite Is My Name* made had to be a labor of love. And just like he did thirty years earlier, bringing together the Black royalty of Richard Pryor and Redd Foxx for his film *Harlem Nights*, I thought Eddie showed some down-home love in telling Rudy's story.

The director Craig Brewer and Eddie asked me to take part. Why? 'Cause me and Rudy did countless gigs together. Consequently, it was a natural fit for me to perform in the movie. I played "I Ain't Studdin' Ya" on a movie set made to look like one of them joints Rudy and I used to work in. In that world, there was only one thing you wanted. And that was for the promoter or club owner to beg you to come back.

Like me, Rudy Ray was a Chitlin Circuit regular. With his Dolemite character in the '70s, he established himself as a comedian and emcee. We played in all the spots. The jukes, the bars, old auditoriums,

VFW halls, and dance halls. Most of these joints were small—fifty to hundred folks at best. But when Rudy started selling those albums out of his car, his fortunes changed, and he never looked back. He sold a ton of his crude, shameless, and funny-as-hell albums. Those album covers were priceless: bizarre nude photographs of him and women in off-color positions. You had to ask a record store clerk, "Do you have that Rudy Ray Moore album?" Then, and only then, would he give you the album that was hidden under the counter, wrapped in brown paper. Because of his quick-witted rapping style, he is considered by many the godfather of rap. He made a bunch of money on them vinyl records. That led him to self-financing his Dolemite films.

When you see a Dolemite movie—well, let me just say this: there ain't nothing like a Dolemite movie. Rudy was a funny-looking cat and did all kinds of odd things to get his cult classics to work. He was tryin' to do what today they call a mash-up. Black exploitation meets kung fu meets sexy women meets Chitlin Circuit humor.

But Eddie and Craig's film *Dolemite Is My Name* is really about boldness, backbone, and the power of hope. Rudy had what every great self-made man had: chutzpah. So glad Eddie wanted to tell Rudy's story. 'Cause it wasn't what most people like to think about a cat like Rudy Ray. He wasn't a no-nothing clown. He wasn't a Black buffoon. He was a trailblazer. And just like many Black men and women before him and after, he didn't wait for a ticket of admission to Hollywood— he made his own ticket. He knew he wasn't gonna please everybody. But he knew he could please his own people, and he just leap-frogged over the system to get there. The real lesson of Rudy Ray's life was that in America anything is possible—if you're bold. He was a hell of a business cat who ended up controlling his masters.

Eddie captured the spirit of Rudy Ray. But he also captured the gift of his hustle by simply telling his story.

Last Men Standing

When Buddy Guy came to Chicago in September 1957, we didn't have much contact, but we knew who each other was—and I knew he could burn. I was friends with a cat who had a club on Madison and Holman called Curly's. I knew Curly well, and Buddy played there often.

"Bobbyrush, you and Buddy Guy got sumthin' in common."

"What's that, Curly?"

"Y'all both know how to get people's attention."

People knew of my antics, and Buddy, still new on the scene, had a few of his own. Buddy had seen Memphis Slim down in Louisiana with a one-hundred-foot cord connecting his guitar to his amplifier. When Buddy got to Chicago—he did the same. With his long cord he'd stroll through the audience, wailing on that thing. Wasn't nobody doing that in Chicago. It was great showmanship and audiences loved it.

My close friendship with Buddy took flight late in our lives. We're both from Louisiana, but in the first twenty-five years of knowing each other we didn't even know that. It would take me moving to Mississippi and us doing gigs together, plus our long talks on the phone, before we discovered some of them details.

When we were young, we were both hustling so hard that the kind of friendship we share today we could never have imagined. We have both witnessed the fragile nature of life, having seen so many of our boys, through completely random acts of fate or acts of their own making, not having such a happy ending, and some who shined until they got outta here.

So we take pleasure in being two of the last men standing of a by-gone time. If you heard our late-night conversations, you would hear us cut loose on music, love, days gone by, joy, death, frustration, racism, things lost, and wisdom gained. We can cover the waterfront. And boy does that feel good, hashing it over with someone who saw and heard the same grooves I did in the '50, '60s, and '70s on the streets of Chicago.

Timing is everything, they say. 'Cause you can't spend your life saying woulda, coulda, shoulda. But God knows what the truth is: I wished Buddy and I would have become close decades ago. There is so much familiarity between us. Some things I can only say to him because he's the only guy who'll understand. There is a vibe of comfort and security in that for me, and I guess that's what they call a beautiful friendship.

But I Didn't Cross Out

If you read or listen to my interviews from the last fifteen years or so, you'll hear a repeated sentence pop out of my mouth: "I crossed over but I didn't cross out."

What I mean is that I am, in fact, grateful for finally getting a recognition that makes life easier. Crossover success in my little world of the blues means I'm happy for the things it lets me do with my life. I now play to audiences that most blues artists started playing to sixty years ago—mostly white faces in America and all over the world—especially in Europe. After that bad gig in '96, it now seems I can do no wrong in Europe.

I've won thirteen Blues Music Awards. I've been nominated for Grammys six times and won one. All this praise late in life has given me a better income. Which helps me help my family and others. But along this long, strange trip of finally crossing over bridges to expanded audiences, I am still joined at the hip with the Black folks that come and see me on the Chitlin Circuit. I didn't forget them—I didn't cross them out for so-called greener pastures, and this country boy is a lil' bit proud of that. Gotta tell you also that the Chitlin Circuit isn't as small as you think it is. I headline the Southern Blues Festival in sold-out arenas and amphitheaters where artists like Lionel Richie are performing the following night.

But as they say on late-night TV commercials, "Don't take my word for it—take it from somebody who knows." So listen to what mogul Tyler Perry said about the Chitlin Circuit on the *Arsenio Hall Show* reboot in 2014:

> Man, let me say this about this chitlin circuit. A lot of times we as African American people think that we have evolved so much—that we look down our nose at certain things. But what I found about this circuit. . . . It was so wonderful. You had Josephine Baker and Billie Holiday and all these people—Ella Fitzgerald, who could not perform in white establishments. So they went on the road (and performed) in all these little, small juke joints with chicken, fries, and chitlins. And they traveled the country and they became so famous among their own people that they were able to support themselves and live well. Well, cut to 1998, I'm doing the exact same thing some fifty, sixty years later. Traveling around to African American people that had made me so famous within my own culture that I couldn't walk down the street without being recognized. Get to Hollywood, nobody knows my name—see what I mean. But what I say to people is *Do not despise your beginning—do not despise where you come from.* Because God will plant you somewhere where you can grow so strong and so tall that as long as you don't turn your back on who you are and where you come from—you hold very closely to that—it'll take you all the way to where you want to go.

Damn straight, brother Perry.

Hey, Bobby Rush

Back in the '70s an interviewer asked me, "Why do you talk in the third person so much?" I didn't know what the third person was. But I picked up on what he meant. Yes, I'll often say, "People ask me, 'Bobby Rush, what do you think of this or that?'" I think at least one reason I do sometimes speak that way is that I look at my career as an entertainer as a little separate from who I am.

But in terms of my music, I do call my own name out on records. I can't remember when that started. I know I did on "Sue," but on *Sitting on Top of the Blues* I have songs that have my name in the title, like "Bobby Rush Shuffle" and "Hey Hey Bobby Rush." But to give proper credit, I gotta thank one mane who didn't get all the credit he deserved in his career.

Bo Diddley I knew from Chicago. Didn't know him well then, 'cause unlike a lot of the blues cats, he didn't do small tours. He did extensive tours, so when he was gone, he was gone. But he moved to Washington, DC, around 1960. So I really got to know him from the countless shows we did together in the 1960s and '70s. Bo Diddley was an original. He doesn't often get the credit a Chuck Berry, a Little Richard, or a Fats Domino does 'cause he'd done some things that pissed folk off. He was the first Black cat to pop up on *The Ed Sullivan Show*. But after Ed told him to do a cover tune, and he got up there on national TV and did what he damn well pleased, which was his smash "Bo Diddley," ol' Ed banned him from the show.

But that drum hambone rhythm: he and only he introduced that to rock 'n' roll. He was a musical pioneer. Not a show business pioneer—*but a musical pioneer*. His songwriting. His guitar approach, which had a style that sometimes is hard to put into words. But that pioneering sound is why he stands alone. His first hits, "Bo Diddley" and "Diddley Daddy," both in 1955, put his own name out there—front and center. He told me sometime in the '70s, "Bobbyrush, I did that so there would be no question of who dis is—I wanted *my name* to be the second thing they remembered after that groove of mine."

So that was my second reason for talking the way I do—it just became a habit to say, "Hey, here I am, Bobby Rush."

But Bo Diddley's wisdom seemed to have more weight in the mid-'70s 'cause sometimes DJs would play ten records in a row on the radio without saying who the record was by. And in them days there wasn't any digital radio in your car or home that showed you who was playing. You had to call the radio station and ask, "What's that y'all played twenty minutes ago?" Hell, I did it myself when I wanted to know: *Who was that?* Sometimes they'd tell you and sometimes they wouldn't.

So whenever I could, I'd throw my name in a song—and I have Bo Diddley to thank. Even in my first decade or two in the business I would drop a few bucks on the emcee to say my name several times as I left the stage: "Ladies and gentlemen, you've been entertained by Bobbyrush. Bobbyyyyyyyyyyrush!" For fifty years I pushed, and I pushed and I pushed that name—nonstop. Not Bobby. Not Rush. But *B-o-b-b-y-r-u-s-h!*

My Way and the Way of Patience

I don't think it's too late to say that today I'm more comfortable doing anything I please. Yeah, my name is bigger now than it was twenty years ago. But my comfort ain't based on that. It's because the folks who listen to my music and come see me time and time again know for sure they ain't gonna see nothin' like this funky old man. And maybe—just maybe—others see it that way, too. For it has been in the last ten years or so that festival promoters have been more accepting of me than they were twenty-five years ago. When I performed on NPR's *World Cafe*, there was an approval of me as less of what I am onstage and more of what I express musically. Fewer questions about the girls and my humor—still I ain't gon' never stop being funny. Today there are more questions about my songs and harp playing. Did something in 2019 on *Bluesville* on SiriusXM satellite radio. Way more questions that pertain to who I am as a man and not just as an entertainer.

My comfort also lies in that I didn't die young. Living long enough to see things not only turn around but turn skyward ain't nothing but God's grace in action. That grace has taught me that one of the better qualities to gain in a long life is patience.

Patience means to me to expect the unexpected. Got a call from Jeff about sitting in with my new pal Josh Homme and his rock band Queens of the Stone Age. Of course I agreed. With a sold-out crowd at the Saenger Theatre in New Orleans, he gave me an eloquent introduction that ended with "I'd like to welcome special badass motherfucker, Mr. Bobby Rush!" I played harp and showed that my old legs can jump like a teenager's.

Patience allowed me to see the continued resurrection of songs I recorded decades ago. My first hit, "Chicken Heads," was used in the HBO shows *Ballers* and *The Deuce*. My 1974 classic "Bowlegged Woman, Knock-Kneed Man" has been re-recorded by rockers Widespread Panic, bluesmen Hot Tuna, and the Southern jam band rockers Gov't Mule. I've had songs used in commercials. With my crossover complete, today they include my music with rock and folk artists on formats like Americana and AAA (adult album alternative) radio stations.

Patience has also allowed me to see things come to flower from seeds planted long ago. In 2005, I recorded an album, *Raw*, that is just what it says it is—raw. Simply guitar, my foot stomps, harmonica, and voice. This was maybe one of the most important seeds I planted, because from the sonic turn of *Raw*, people saw me in a different light. When the album blossomed fifteen years ago, I played gigs with just my guitar, harmonica, my voice. I played performing art centers, rock venues, colleges, and folk music settings, and I still do today. Recording *Raw* diversified my career. And I love the fact it's like me ending up where I started, a boy with just a harp, a guitar, and a voice with a burning desire to be heard.

And I did it my way—crossed over without crossing out my Black fans and supporters on the Chitlin Circuit and Southern blues radio.

ıııııııı

In April 2019 I was on a European tour: Finland, Norway, Denmark, France, and Switzerland. But one night I sat in a cafe in London, having a cup of tea, when suddenly yesterday seemed like a lifetime ago. For when I started out as a teenager in the mid-'50s in the juke joints of Arkansas, I was playing cover tunes. And since I didn't have any regional hits till the 1970s, my shows were a mix of my own songs and a good deal of hit songs by my friends, Muddy Waters, B.B. King, Bobby "Blue" Bland, and Ray Charles. But thanks to my rise in media visibility over the last twenty years or so, I've been doing things, as they say, my way. That's why I feel in so many ways that I'm sitting on top of the blues. Because I now do what I want—onstage and in the studio.

Praise be I didn't end up penniless, 'cause I had many peers who did. I also had peers who ended up where I started. They have to play "Mustang Sally" or B.B.'s "The Thrill Is Gone" or "Sweet Home Chicago." I ain't gotta play that stuff (and usually I don't) *unless I choose to* on a given night. That freedom would have never happened if Bobby Rush hadn't developed into the off-the-beaten-track Bobby Rush. People come to see me to hear good music and have a good time, regardless of which songs I play. It's how I became an overnight sensation.

It just took me fifty years to do so.

Junior

In the summer of 2019, I got hoarse. Please believe me when I say that in over sixty-plus years of singing in smoke-filled rooms, I never got hoarse. Never. Doc told me to rest my voice after gigs. No talking. I didn't, but the hoarseness didn't go away. He sent me to the Mayo Clinic at the University of Mississippi Medical Center because throat cancer was in my bloodline.

But I was good.

In 2020, I got COVID-19. The first big American pandemic in over one hundred years. Had a 105°F temperature. Went into the hospital briefly and lay in bed for a couple weeks.

I survived.

June 30, 2020. Glad to be alive. Sitting in my favorite chair—my big feet up, feelin' mighty good. Watching the national news and seeing history roll by me like a fast-moving cloud in the open sky. They took the Mississippi state flag down on that day. The flag with its Confederate emblem in the corner is coming down because of a man no one really knows—but history will know—named George Floyd. His video-taped murder by cops spawned a movement that led to retiring the flag to where it should be. On the trash heap of history. It should have been put there when the South lost the Civil War. But it wasn't. And for an old Black man like me, it makes me damn sad that it would take more fighting, more legislation, more waiting, and ultimately much more dying for time to catch up to what was right.

||||||||||

Since the 2000s, when I go to a music convention and walk into a room, people stand up and applaud. I've got enough good sense to know they are not applauding because I'm a household name. What they're standing for is that I'm still here, doing it my way, and hopefully looking pretty good while I do. I'm honored to have been in the music business as long as I have. And with what I've been through, it's a blessing to get old.

With how my career turned out, if I called a spade a spade, then I might not think much of how my journey went. But that would be some childish, shortsighted thinking. And when you're old, you try to avoid childish thinking.

It's taken me decades to understand this, but my real success came early in my life. I didn't know it then, because my success wasn't conventional. It wasn't the hot lights, gold records, and applause of show business. Only time could make it plain to me that my success was in my friendships. Those cats I met in the mid-'50s and early '60s in Chicago. The easygoing affection between those legends and me was my lifetime achievement award. I've pretty much outlived them all. And it will be those pure moments that we shared—of mutual respect, admiration, and love—that I will carry for the rest of my days. And that recognition was more than enough to keep me going for almost seventy long years.

Sometimes those years were gloomy, sometimes they were golden. But in the days that made up those years, there was always some laughter, some sweet harmony, some bright blues. So I can't complain about the frets and frustrations of my life—everybody's had trials and tribulations.

When I was young and bloomin', I discovered that "Junior" meant that I carried Daddy's name. That intimidated me. The responsibility of being locked to Emmett Ellis Sr.'s name was almost too much to bear. He was idolized by folks all around and, most importantly, idolized by me. When I got bitten by the music bug, I was like a mosquito drawn to the swamps of Mississippi—I couldn't help it. The pull of music made me hang out in places that were not in line with Daddy's name or reputation. I knew I had to change my name. And I became Bobby Rush. That name would never be on the same list as a Prince or

Whitney Houston; as a matter of fact, no blues artist would be. But I would be No. 1 with a bullet on the Bobby Rush list. And now I know that's enough.

My early decades of so-called lack of success was not that at all. It was a stepping-stone that forced me to create a cubbyhole that only I could fit in—and that would be my saving grace.

Because it ain't nuttin' but God's amazing grace that I've played all over the world as a bluesman, singer, musician, stand-up comedian, actor, storyteller, and entertainer—and survived. Folks know my name in places I can't even pronounce. If I wanted to work year-round, my name would afford me the ability to do so. But from a very young age, my given name, Emmett Ellis Jr., would afford me to do some things, too. Hold my head up high, be proud of where I'm from, and never ever think I'm beat.

I still live in Daddy's shadow. Even though he's been gone a long time now, I'm so glad he gave me his name. Because my name is where all my energy was spawned from. It was like by him making me Junior, and not my older brothers, it put me in a rush. To hurry up and make a name for myself. And it took almost seventy years, but I did it. Yet sometimes I can't escape the thought of what could have been.

But in the quiet alone down by the pond, I can close my eyes and hear Maw yell, "Junior!" *And when I feel her voice calling out my name*, I can look back and say for sure that, with all that I have been through, it makes me completely forget about what could have been.

Because I'm oh-so-ever-grateful for what was.

BOBBY RUSH/2021

Acknowledgments

BOBBY RUSH ACKNOWLEDGES:

My wife, Jean, son Carl, and godson Nick Floyd, all of whom surround me with love and support.

My brothers Alvin and Larry and my dear sister Gerdia, who have always been there for me. Also I am grateful for the blessed memory of my siblings who have moved on: Margie May, A. J., Lillie Pearl, Mary Lee, Andrew, and Verdia Mae.

My daughter-in-law Jean and all my grandkids and great-grandkids.

My manager Jeff DeLia, who moves mountains. This book would have not been possible without you.

My musical family, who have kept me in a good groove. Bruce, Kenny, Lou, Arthur, Fred, Joe, my lead dancer MIZZ Lowe, and Erickia, Kila, and Jazzii. And Mike McDonald, my everything man—driver, sound, and security.

My best friend and co-producer, Vasti Jackson—you are a creative firehouse.

Carl Gustafson, my bosom buddy.

Martin Shore, for vision.

Benjamin Wright, Gamble and Huff, and Millie Jackson—you are more than friends, you are blessings.

Rev. Polk, my pastor, for guidance and strength.

Dr. Robert Smith, for healing care and friendship.

Ben Schafer, thank you for believing.

My co-writer Herb Powell, thank you for being you. No way, no how could I have done this without you.

Thanks to my publicist Cary Baker and all the record labels, record stores, newspapers, radio stations, DJs, TV news stations, club promoters, and agents who have supported me for over sixty years.

I have a heart full of gratitude for my fans, who have kept me energized and enthused.

HERB POWELL ACKNOWLEDGES:

Bobby Rush, thank you for a very gratifying collaboration.

My parents, Grady and Bertie Powell, who are my first and greatest blessing.

David Ritz, soulful mentor, unfailing mensch, and great pal. Thanks, Blood!

My family, Saun, Albert, Dot, Harvey, Grady, Danette, Eric, Champ, and Grady III.

Ben Schafer, my wonderful editor, his assistant Carrie Napolitano, and all the great minds at Hachette.

Special thanks to Jeff DeLia, Faith Childs, Herb Jordan, Vivian West, Dave Stein.

Erin Holvey, for your loving light.

Discography,
Awards, and Honors

DISCOGRAPHY

45s

1964   "Someday" / "Let Me Love You" (Jerry-O)

1967   "Sock Boo Ga Loo" / "Much Too Much" (Checker)

1968   "Camel Walk" / "Gotta Have Money" (ABC)

1969   "Wake Up" / "The Things That I Used to Do" (Salem)

1970   "Let It All Hang Out" / "Just Be Yourself/What Now" (Salem)

1971   "Chicken Heads" / "Mary Jane" (Galaxy)

1972   "Niki Hoeky" / "I Don't Know" (Jewel)

1972   "Gotta Be Funky" / "Gotta Find You Girl" (On Top)

1974   "Get It On with Me" / "It's Alright" (Jewel)

1974   "Get Out of Here (Part 1)" / "Get Out of Here (Part 2)" (Warner Bros.)

1976   "I'm Still Waiting" / "She Put the Whammy on Me" (London)

1979   "I Wanna Do the Do" (Philadelphia International)

1979   "Let's Do It Together" (Philadelphia International)

1982   "Talk To Your Daughter" / "Think" (LaJam)

1983   "Sue" (LaJam)

1984　"She Caught Me With My Pants Down" / "Buttermilk Kid" (LaJam)

1984　"Santa Claus Wants Some Too" (LaJam)

1988　"A Man Can Give It (But He Can't Take It)" (LaJam)

1988　"Bad Mother For Ya" / "Nine Below Zero" (LaJam)

1991　"I Ain't Studdin' You" / "Blues Singer" (Urgent)

1992　"I'm Gone" / "Before Sex" (Urgent)

1992　"You, You, You (Know What to Do)" / "Time To Hit The Road Again" (Urgent)

1992　"Handy Man" / "Second Hand Man" (Urgent)

1995　"She's a Good 'Un" / "It's Alright" (Ronn)

1995　"One Monkey Don't Stop No Show" / "Blues With A Felling" (Waldoxy)

1996　"Too Late, I'm Gone" (Waldoxy)

1997　"Booga Bear" / "Feel Like Gettin' It On" (Waldoxy)

2008　"Bobby Rush For President" (Digital Single) (Deep Rush/Thirty Tigers)

2017　"Funk o' de Funk (SMLE Remix)" (Digital Single) (Rounder / Concord Music)

2020　"Dolemite Kid" (Digital Single) (Deep Rush / Thirty Tigers)

LPs

1979　*Rush Hour* (Philadelphia International)

1981　*Sue* (LaJam)

1983　*Wearing It Out* (LaJam)

1984　*Gotta Have Money* (LaJam)

1985　*What's Good for the Goose Is Good for the Gander* (LaJam)

1988　*A Man Can Give It (But He Can't Take It)* (LaJam)

1991　*I Ain't Studdin' You* (Urgent)

CDs

1983　*Making a Decision* (LaJam)

1990　*Man Can Give It but He Can't Take It* (LaJam)

1991　*I Ain't Studdin' You* (Urgent)

1992 *Handy Man* (Urgent)

1995 *She's A Good 'Un (It's Alright)* (Ronn)

1995 *One Monkey Don't Stop No Show* (Waldoxy)

1996 *Wearing It Out* (LaJam)

1997 *It's Alright, Vol. 2*

1997 *Lovin' a Big Fat Woman* (Waldoxy)

1999 *Rush Hour...Plus* (Philadelphia Intl)

1999 *Gotta Have Money* (Reissue—LaJam)

1999 *The Best of Bobby Rush* (LaJam)

2000 *Hoochie Man* (Waldoxy)

2003 *Undercover Lover* (Deep Rush / Thirty Tigers)

2003 *Live at Ground Zero DVD + CD* (Deep Rush / Thirty Tigers)

2004 *Folk Funk* (Deep Rush / Thirty Tigers)

2005 *Hen Pecked* (Malaco)

2005 *Night Fishin'* (Deep Rush / Thirty Tigers)

2006 *Essential Recordings, Volume 1* (Deep Rush / Thirty Tigers)

2006 *Essential Recordings, Volume 2* (Deep Rush / Thirty Tigers)

2007 *Raw* (Deep Rush / Thirty Tigers)

2008 *Look at What You Gettin'* (Deep Rush / Thirty Tigers)

2009 *Blind Snake* (Deep Rush / Thirty Tigers)

2011 *Show You a Good Time* (Deep Rush / Thirty Tigers)

2013 *Down in Louisiana* (Deep Rush / Thirty Tigers)

2014 *Decisions* (Silver Talon Records)

2015 *Chicken Heads: A 50-Year History of Bobby Rush*
       (4-CD Box Set) (Omnivore Recordings)

2016 *Porcupine Meat* (Rounder Records)

2017 "Funk of the Funk—SMLE Remix" (Single)
       (Rounder Records, Concord)

2019 *Sitting on Top of the Blues* (Deep Rush / Thirty Tigers)

2020 *Rawer Than Raw* (Deep Rush / Thirty Tigers)

AWARDS

Blues Music Awards (13)

Sitting on Top of the Blues: Soul Blues Album Award; 2020—
   41st Blues Music Awards

Porcupine Meat: Album Of The Year; 2017—38th Blues Music Awards

Chicken Heads: A 50-Year History of Bobby Rush, Omnivore Recordings; Historical Blues Album; 2017—38th Blues Music Awards

Soul Blues Male Artist; 2015—36th Blues Music Awards

B.B. King Entertainer; 2015—36th Blues Music Awards

Down in Louisiana: Soul Blues Album; 2014—35th Blues Music Awards

Show You A Good Time: Soul Blues Album; 2012— 33rd Blues Music Awards

Soul Blues Male Artist; 2009—30th Blues Music Awards

Soul Blues Male Artist; 2008—29th Blues Music Awards

Acoustic Blues Artist; 2008—29th Blues Music Awards

Raw: Acoustic Blues Album; 2008—29th Blues Music Awards

Soul Blues Male Artist; 2007—28th Blues Music Awards

Soul Blues Male Artist; 2005—26th W.C. Handy Blues Awards

Grammy Award Winner

2017: *Porcupine Meat*: Best Traditional Blues Album

2020: *Rawer Than Raw*: Best Traditional Blues Album

Many Other Awards From:

OffBeat Magazine: Best of the Beat Awards

DownBeat Magazine

Living Blues Magazine

Blues Blast Magazine: Blues Blast Music Awards

NOMINATIONS

Blues Music Awards (51 total nominations)

B.B King Entertainer; 2020—41st Blues Music Awards

B.B King Entertainer; 2019—40th Blues Music Awards

B.B King Entertainer; 2018—39th Blues Music Awards

Porcupine Meat: Soul Blues Album; 2017—38th Blues Music Awards

Bobby Rush with Blinddog Smokin', *Decisions*: Soul Blues Album;
   2015—36th Blues Music Awards

"Another Murder in New Orleans" (Carl Gustafson, Donald
   Markowitz | Bobby Rush with Dr. John): Song of the Year;
   2015—36th Blues Music Awards

B.B. King Entertainer; 2014—35th Blues Music Awards

Soul Blues Male Artist; 2014—35th Blues Music Awards

Soul Blues Male Artist; 2013—34th Blues Music Awards

Soul Blues Male Artist; 2012—33rd Blues Music Awards

Soul Blues Male Artist; 2011—32nd Blues Music Awards

B.B. King Entertainer; 2009—30th Blues Music Awards

B.B. King Entertainer; 2008—29th Blues Music Awards

B.B. King Entertainer; 2007—28th Blues Music Awards

Soul Blues Male Artist; 2006—27th Blues Music Awards

Night Fishin: Soul Blues Album; 2006—27th Blues Music Awards

B.B. King Entertainer; 2006—27th Blues Music Awards

Folk Funk: Soul Blues Album; 2005—26th W.C. Handy Blues Awards

Blues Entertainer of the Year; 2005—26th W.C. Handy Blues Awards

Soul Blues Male Artist; 2004—25th W.C. Handy Blues Awards

Blues Entertainer of the Year; 2004—25th W.C. Handy Blues Awards

Soul Blues Male Artist; 2002—23rd W.C. Handy Blues Awards

Blues Entertainer of the Year; 2002—23rd W.C. Handy Blues Awards

Soul Blues Male Artist; 2001—22nd W.C. Handy Blues Awards

Hoochie Man: Soul Blues Album; 2001—22nd W.C. Handy Blues
   Awards

Blues Entertainer of the Year; 2001—22nd W.C. Handy Blues Awards

Soul Blues Male Artist; 2000—21st W.C. Handy Blues Awards

Blues Entertainer of the Year; 2000—21st W.C. Handy Blues Awards

Soul Blues Male Artist; 1999—20th W.C. Handy Blues Awards

Blues Entertainer of the Year; 1999—20th W.C. Handy Blues Awards

Soul Blues Male Artist; 1998—19th W.C. Handy Blues Awards

Lovin' a Big Fat Woman (Waldoxy): Soul Blues Album; 1998—
19th W.C. Handy Blues Awards

Blues Entertainer of the Year; 1998—19th W.C. Handy Blues Awards

"One Monkey Don't Stop No Show": Song of the Year; 1997—
18th W.C Handy Blues Awards

Blues Entertainer of the Year; 1997—18th W.C. Handy Blues Awards

Grammy Award Nominations

2000: *Hoochie Man*: Best Contemporary Blues Album

2013: *Down in Louisiana*: Best Blues Album

2014: *Decisions*: Best Blues Album

2019: *Sitting on Top of the Blues*: Best Traditional Blues Album

2020: *Rawer Than Raw*: Best Traditional Blues Album

Billboard Charts

Hot R&B/Hip-Hop Songs

"Chicken Heads" peaked at #34 on August 12, 1971

"I Wanna Do The Do" peaked at #75 on August 10, 1979

Top R&B/Hip-Hop Albums

I Ain't Studdin' You peaked at #69 on November 22, 1991

Top R&B Albums

Porcupine Meat peaked at #23 on October 21, 2016

Blues Albums

Down in Louisiana peaked at #15 on March 8, 2013

Upstairs At United, Vol.11 (EP) peaked at #12 on May 2, 2014

Porcupine Meat peaked at #5 on October 21, 2016
Sitting On Top of the Blues peaked at #2 on August 30, 2019
Rawer Than Raw peaked at #7 on September 11, 2020

Independent Albums
Sitting On Top of the Blues peaked at #37 on August 30, 2019

Heatseekers Albums
Sitting On Top of the Blues peaked at #12 on August 30, 2019

Radio Charts

#1 *Living Blues* radio chart
Top 20 Americana radio chart

Received Honorary Keys To The Following Cities

Memphis, Tennessee
Jackson, Tennessee
New Orleans, Louisiana
Jackson, Mississippi
Fayette, Mississippi
Little Rock, Arkansas
Pine Bluff, Arkansas
Baton Rouge, Louisiana
Haynesville, Louisiana
Huntsville, Alabama
Chicago, Illinois
Harvey, Illinois
Detroit, Michigan
Milwaukee, Wisconsin
St. Louis, Missouri

Inductions

Blues Hall of Fame induction in 2006, presented by The Blues Foundation

Mississippi Musicians Hall of Fame induction in 2012

Rhythm and Blues Music Hall of Fame induction in 2015

Other recognitions

Marker on Mississippi Blues Trail, 2008

Cut the ribbon for the Blues Hall of Fame, May 2015

Crossroads of American Music Award given by The Grammy Museum Mississippi, November 2020

Music note on Beale Street in Memphis, Tennessee

Street named after him in Pine Bluff, Arkansas: Bobby Rush Way

Salute from Senate of Mississippi

Salute from Senate of Arkansas

Salute from Senate of Tennessee

Honorary Doctorate Degree from Jackson State University

Honorary Doctorate Degree from Tougaloo College

Honorary Doctorate Degree from Rhodes College

And many more

Index

Index

Index

Index

Index

295

Index

Index

Index

Index

Index

Index